# PRACTICAL
# aCTION
## RESEARCH
SECOND EDITION

*"Study without reflection is a waste of time, reflection without study is dangerous."*

—*Confucius*

# PRACTICAL aCTION RESEARCH

SECOND EDITION

a collection of articles

# RICHARD A. SCHMUCK

EDITOR

CORWIN PRESS
A SAGE Company

*For information:*

Corwin Press
A SAGE Company
2455 Teller Road
Thousand Oaks, California 91320
www.corwinpress.com

SAGE India Pvt. Ltd.
B 1/I 1 Mohan Cooperative
 Industrial Area
Mathura Road, New Delhi 110 044
India

SAGE Ltd.
1 Oliver's Yard
55 City Road
London EC1Y 1SP
United Kingdom

SAGE Asia-Pacific Pte. Ltd.
33 Pekin Street #020-01
Far East Square
Singapore 048763

Printed in the United States of America.

*Library of Congress Cataloging-in-Publication Data*

Practical action research: a collection of articles/editor, Richard A. Schmuck. — 2nd ed.
     p. cm.
Includes bibliographical references and index.
ISBN 978-1-4129-6286-5 (cloth: acid-free paper)
ISBN 978-1-4129-6287-2 (pbk.: acid-free paper)
  1. Action research in education.  2. Action research in education—Case studies.
I. Schmuck, Richard A.  II.  Title.

LB1028.24.P73 2009
370.72—dc22                              2008019171

This book is printed on acid-free paper.

08   09   10   11   12   10  9  8  7  6  5  4  3  2  1

| | |
|---|---|
| *Acquisitions Editor:* | Cathy Hernandez |
| *Associate Editor:* | Megan Bedell |
| *Production Editor:* | Eric Garner |
| *Typesetter:* | C&M Digitals (P) Ltd. |
| *Proofreader:* | Charlotte Waisner |
| *Cover Designer:* | Scott Van Atta |

# Contents

# Preface

Now is the time to bring *Practical Action Research: A Collection of Articles* (2000) up-to-date. In the eight-year interim between that first edition and this revision, I mentored 60 American masters' students in the program on Leadership for Educational Entrepreneurs (LEE) at Arizona State University West over six years as they designed, implemented, and wrote about their action research in public charter schools. I lectured to 50 Canadian masters' students in British Columbia and to 40 American doctoral students in Oregon about educational action research. I witnessed the production of hundreds of publications on action research in 35 education journals worldwide. As I worked closely with the charter-school educators, listened to the many questions and multiple reactions of the graduate students, and reflected on the journal articles I was reading, I decided to revise that first edition with more contemporary contributions on educational action research.

I selected this new collection of articles and case studies (referred to as "Exemplary Projects" throughout the text) to help my students see real action research in action.

I drew 14 articles from refereed educational publications and 13 exemplary projects from unpublished masters' theses approved by higher-education faculty members. These 27 school-based cases and reviews demonstrate that educational action research is participatory, reciprocal, and democratic. They show how teachers enlist students' co-participation to plan and carry out projects, how principals engage faculties and parents, and how superintendents involve staffs, boards, and community networks. We shall see that together, teachers and students, principal and faculty or parents, and superintendents, staff, board, and community implement action research as coequal partners. Indeed, action research invites, as we shall see, democratic participation and egalitarian collaboration among all members of an educational setting.

These articles and exemplary projects also offer living examples of both proactive and responsive action research, the two basic models that differ in when the scientific data are collected and analyzed. We shall see how in the proactive model, action precedes data collection and analysis:

the educator acts first by trying an innovative practice and second, studies the effects of the new actions. Alternatively, we will see how in the responsive model, data are collected and analyzed for diagnosis before new actions are tried: the educator diagnoses the situation and then takes appropriate action based on the diagnostic results. In presenting examples of both models, the articles and exemplary projects show how action and research become alternating parts of the same overall project.

The articles and exemplary projects also demonstrate how action research projects require trustworthy research methods for gathering objective data. They show that the most popular methods for amassing data are questionnaires, interviews, observations, and documents. Through many concrete, real life examples, we shall see that questionnaires are printed lists of interrogative or declarative statements that individuals respond to in writing. For example, academic tests, an aspect of most articles and exemplary projects, are special types of questionnaires. Interviews are conversations in which interviewers pose questions to interviewees. Observations involve attentively watching and systematically recording what is seen and heard. Documents are public records, press clippings, and private journals and diaries.

The First Edition of this "Collection" had 15 articles. This Second Edition has 14 published articles and 13 unpublished case studies. I have chosen seven new articles and have carried over seven; those 14 articles are the best publications on educational action research that I could find in 2007. I believe that the seven new articles, all published within the last six years, will be read and reread by educators worldwide during the next decade. Three were written outside the United States by action researchers in Australia, Canada, and Spain. I believe that the seven articles I chose to carry over from the First Edition are on the way to becoming classics in educational action research.

The 13 unpublished case studies, all of which I edited and rewrote for this book, came from Individual Research Projects of outstanding students I tutored in a charter school–focused graduate program. Those 13 exemplary projects are examples of excellent contemporary action research.

With this new collection of articles and exemplary projects, I hope to illustrate concretely and realistically to educators everywhere what can actually happen when their dedicated colleagues earnestly carry out practical action research for change.

# Acknowledgments

The editor acknowledges the following educators of the program on Leadership for Educational Entrepreneurs (LEE) for their contributions:

Betsy Apolito: Principal at Mound Street Academies, Dayton, Ohio, responsible for special education, technology, and curriculum for alternative high schools serving dropout students. She has also served as an adjunct to the University of Dayton's Education masters' program for eight years. She graduated from the LEE Program in 2006.

Ron Bergez: Headmaster of the Tempe Preparatory Academy, Tempe, Arizona, where he worked previously as a Master Teacher of humanities. He graduated from the LEE program in 2006.

Tatyana Chayka: Principal of the Academy of Math and Science charter school, Tucson, Arizona. Born and raised in Uzbekistan, she has been an educator for 17 years. She graduated from the LEE Program in 2005.

Barbara (Bobbie) Darroch: One of three Directors of the Benchmark School, ranked during the last four years as one of the top 25 elementary schools in Arizona. She graduated from the LEE Program in 2004.

Jill Gaitens: Grant Project Director and Coordinator for No Child Left Behind (NCLB) at Primavera Online High School, an Arizona charter school. She graduated from the LEE Program in 2006.

Lori Grant: Director of Colorado Business and Accountability Services (C-BAS), which consults with schools statewide on financial accountability. She was business manager at Renaissance School for seven years and graduated from the LEE Program in 2004.

Joshua Jordan: Mathematics teacher at Westwind Middle School Academy, Phoenix, Arizona. He graduated from the LEE program in 2005.

Kelli Kreienkamp: Longtime second grade teacher at the Verona area Core Knowledge Charter School (CKCS) in Madison, Wisconsin. She graduated from the LEE Program in 2006.

Verree Laughlin: Executive Director of Provisions for Life, a nonprofit organization dedicated to improving lives of families in poor communities near the United States-Mexican border. She graduated from the LEE Program in 2006.

Heidi Mitchell: Director of Business Administration at Valley Academy, one of Arizona's pioneer charter schools. With 12 years experience in charter schools, she graduated from the LEE Program in 2007.

Margo S. O'Neil: Executive Director and previously, Education Director, of one of the largest charter schools in Phoenix, Arizona. She graduated from the LEE Program in 2004.

Ricci Rodriguez-Elkins: Executive Director of the Center for Charter School Development, Reno, Nevada. She graduated from the LEE Program in 2004.

Lillian Thomas-Wilson: graduated from the University of South Carolina-Aiken in early childhood education (1992) and took leadership in forming the 10th charter school in South Carolina. She graduated from the LEE Program in 2006.

# About the Editor

**Richard A. Schmuck** is Professor Emeritus at the University of Oregon, where he chaired dissertations of 132 doctoral students who are from all parts of the world. He taught thousands of other educators worldwide about action research, group dynamics, and organization development.

He has served on the faculties of the University of Michigan, Temple University, and Leuven University (Belgium), was the first president of the International Association for the Study of Cooperation in Education, and is a visiting Professor at Arizona State University–West.

Richard is the author of 20 books and 190 articles. His best-known book is *Group Processes in the Classroom* (with Patricia Schmuck) in its eighth edition. One article about school development won the Douglas McGregor Award for outstanding applications of behavioral science to practical affairs. One book, published by Corwin Press (*Small Districts, Big Problems*) won the outstanding research award of the National Rural Education Association.

He received The Stevens Award from the Northwest Women in Educational Administration to honor his support of "women in administration," and his "commitment to equity, justice, and democracy," and he received the Campbell Lifetime Achievement Award from the University Council on Educational Administration for "superior scholarship, distinguished service, and recognized international leadership," and "to celebrate an extraordinary and generous career."

At 72 years, Richard teaches, consults, and writes. Along with his spouse of 49 years, he lives at the foot of Mount Hood in Hood River, OR, where he has served for five years on the United Way Board.

# About the Contributors

**Lew Allen** is a faculty member of the Elementary and Social Studies Education Department in the College of Education at the University of Georgia. She is interested in participating in action research projects with teachers to better understand teaching strategies that have the potential to provide students with the skills and dispositions needed for them to become contributing citizens in our democratic society. Since 1990 she has served as co-director of the League of Professional Schools, a university and K–12 public school collaboration focused on improving student learning through democratic school governance and democratic classrooms.

**Douglas E. Arnold,** EdD, is Superintendent of Bristol Virginia Public Schools in Bristol, Virginia. He has been in education for 35 years serving as an English teacher, coach, athletic director, assistant principal, principal, assistant superintendent and superintendent. Dr. Arnold holds a doctorate in Educational Administration from VA Tech. Dr. Arnold has published two articles in NASSP Bulletin. Dr. Arnold was the 1999 and 2005 recipient of the Southwest Virginia Chapter of Phi Delta Kappa Educator of the Year Award.

**Mary Brydon-Miller,** PhD, directs the University of Cincinnati's Action Research Center and is an Associate Professor of Educational Studies and Urban Educational Leadership in the College of Education, Criminal Justice, and Human Services. She is a participatory action researcher who engages in both community-based and educational action research. Her current scholarship focuses on ethics and action research. Other recent publications include work on participatory action research methods, feminist theory and action research, refugee resettlement, literacy, and popular education.

**Emily Calhoun** is the Director of The Phoenix Alliance, which provides long-term support to school districts and state/regional agencies that are committed to improving student achievement through investing in staff learning. Her major work is helping responsible parties study the effects of curriculum and instruction on student learning and strengthen the learning environment for all. Emily's special research interests include literacy development at all levels and the use of action research for individual and organizational development.

**Brenda M. Capobianco** is an Assistant Professor of Science Education in the Departments of Curriculum and Instruction and Engineering Education (courtesy) at Purdue University. Before entering academia, she was an award-winning middle science teacher in Connecticut and an adjunct instructor of university science elementary and secondary methods courses. Her research and publications focus on teachers' development of practice through collaborative action research; teachers' attempts at integrating inclusive pedagogies using action research; and the construction of young women's identity in science and engineering.

**Cathy Caro-Bruce** is currently working as an educational consultant to school districts with the Wisconsin Department of Public Instruction developing their Statewide System of Support (NCLB). For 30 years, she was a Staff and Organization Development Specialist for the Madison Metropolitan School District, and for fifteen years coordinated Classroom Action Research as part of the district professional development program. Cathy was a co-author of *Creating Equitable Classrooms Through Action Research* (along with Mary Klehr), which was published in June, 2007. She also authored a book, *Action Research: Facilitator's Handbook,* published by the National Staff Development Council, to assist educators who want to lead and facilitate action research initiatives. The second edition of the handbook will be published in 2008. She co-authored a chapter in *Educational Action Research: Becoming Practically Critical* (Noffke and Stevenson, Teachers College Press) about implementing action research in a school district. In *Powerful Designs for Professional Learning* (NSDC), she describes the action research design and how it can be implemented in schools. Cathy also works with school districts around the country helping them implement action research based on principles that drive high-quality professional development initiatives.

**Douglas Cheney,** PhD, is Associate Professor of Special Education at the University of Washington, Seattle. He teaches courses on classroom management, school-family collaboration, and functional behavioral assessment; and has been the principal investigator on over ten million dollars of research, demonstration, and personnel preparation grants from the Office of Special Education Programs and the Institute of Educational Sciences. He was President (1998–99) of the International Council for Children with Behavioral Disorders and co-chaired Washington's Statewide Task Force on Behavioral Disorders (1997–99). Dr. Cheney is co-editor of *The Journal of Emotional and Behavioral Disorders,* an Associate Editor for *Intervention in the School and Clinic;* and a Consulting Editor for *Behavioral Disorders.*

**Steve Collins** is a sessional instructor in Curriculum Studies at the University of British Columbia.

**Eva Espido Bello** is an Associate Professor in the department of Pedagogy and Didactics, faculty of science of education, University of Coruna, Spain.

**Allan Feldman** is Professor of Science Education and Teacher Education at the University of Massachusetts Amherst. For the past 20 years his research has focused on science teacher learning and action research. Recently he has begun to study the ways in which people learn to become science researchers in apprenticeship situations. He has been PI and co-PI of numerous NSF projects, most of which have incorporated action research. Before receiving his doctorate at Stanford University he taught middle and high school science for 17 years in public and private schools in New York, New Jersey, and Pennsylvania.

**Kate Ferguson-Patrick** (BEd Hons, MA Children's Literacy and Literature) is Program Convenor BT/BA Primary, a lecturer in Primary education and Assistant Director of Professional Experience Primary at the University of Newcastle, Australia. She has taught for 13 years in primary schools both in Australia and in the United Kingdom. She is presently enrolled in her PhD and is researching early career teachers implementation of cooperative learning using an action research approach. She has been involved in the Australian Government Quality Teaching Project as an academic partner supporting the implementation of Mathematics through Action Learning.

**Bennyce E. Hamilton** is a full-time firefighter/paramedic with the City of Cincinnati and has been for the past 20 years. She is also a certified English and speech teacher. She taught English from 1998 to 2001 with Cincinnati public schools and Princeton city schools in the greater Cincinnati area. Most recently, she completed her doctoral work at the University of Cincinnati in education with an emphasis on literacy. Her dissertation was entitled, "The reflexive journey: One teacher's path to self in the footsteps of her students." She is most interested in teaching pre-service teachers the process of using reflexive culturally relevant pedagogy in the classroom.

**Steve Kroeger** is the Special Education program coordinator at the University of Cincinnati. He taught on the island of St. Lucia in the West Indies, in Peru among the Quechua Indians of the Andean Highlands, as a high school teacher in Detroit, and as an intervention specialist in the middle grades for twelve years. His research focus is student voice and schoolwide systems change. Recent projects include the use of evidence-based instructional practices, and a five-year federal grant aimed at program restructuring to support preservice teachers in their work to become highly qualified teachers.

**Jennifer McCreadie** is currently Director of Assessment and Program Evaluation with the College of Education and Human Development, George Mason University. In addition to providing assessment and program evaluation support to faculty, her interests in action research and portfolio use continue. For the previous twenty years, she did research, evaluation, and assessment with the Madison Metropolitan School District and Indianapolis Public Schools. In Madison, she co-facilitated the classroom action research professional development effort.

**Helen Meyer** is currently an associate professor and the chair of Secondary Education at the University of Cincinnati. She serves as the membership coordinator for the University's Action Research Center.

Helen has worked with several emerging master teachers to conduct action research studies in their own classrooms. Prior to this she worked in Namibia to develop a participatory action research culture as the colleges of education moved from the apartheid-based pre-independence education system to a democratic reform-based education system.

**Mary M. Palombaro** is from the Johnson City Central School District.

**Eleanor Perry** is a tenured Associate Professor Emerita of Educational Leadership at Arizona State University where she founded the nationally acclaimed LEE (Leadership for Educational Entrepreneurs) Masters bridging the MEd and MBA programs. She has published nationally and internationally. Perry is a leading action researcher with higher education, business, and K–12 expertise in district and charter settings as a teacher, school principal, and board member. Most recently, she headed up the National Alliance for Public Charter Schools Leadership Initiative. A graduate of Rutgers University, Perry received her PhD from the University of Oregon in Educational Policy and Management.

**Christine L. Salisbury** is from the Child and Family Studies Program, Allegheny-Singer Research Institute.

**Stephanie Stewart** is near the end of a wonderful career teaching high school English. Stephanie completed her graduate work at the University of Cincinnati, with a master's and an EdD in curriculum and instruction. Following her graduate work she began teaching as an adjunct with the University of Cincinnati, first in education, now in English. She is looking forward to a second career teaching at the college level full time. Stephanie's most recent interest is in the area of postsecondary literacy, working on strategies for struggling readers and writers at the college level.

**Tabetha J. Swartz** is from the Child and Family Studies Program, Allegheny-Singer Research Institute.

**Jami Wassel** is from the Johnson City Central School District.

**Linda L. Wilson** is from the Child and Family Studies Program, Allegheny-Singer Research Institute.

**Ken Zeichner** is a Hoefs-Bascom Professor of Teacher Education and Associate Dean, School of Education, University of Wisconsin–Madison. Zeichner's work focuses on teacher education, teacher professional development, and action research. He has published widely on these topics in North America, Europe, Latin America, and Australia. His books include *Democratic teacher education reform in Africa: The case of Namibia, Reflective teaching, Currents of reform in pre-service teacher education, Creating equitable classrooms through classroom action research, Studying teacher education,* and *Action research and social justice in teacher education.* He is currently an editor of the international journal *Educational Action Research.*

# PART I

## *Defining Action Research*

Educational action research consists of two formal investigations into one's own classroom or school-community setting: professional reflection and research-based practice. It entails planned and continuous observations of one's own professional practice and of one's trials of new practices to enhance outcomes. It unfolds through a spiral of cycles: reflecting, planning, acting, collecting data, and reflecting again. Another spiral could unfold: collecting data, analyzing, reflecting, planning, acting, and collecting data again. Educators use such spirals to find out how they should practice differently to be more effective.

In my efforts to define action research, I have specified four differences between action research and traditional research. The first is *improvement* versus *explanation*. Action research concerns interventions for continuous improvement. Traditional research concerns a search for explanation. Second is *development* versus *knowledge*. Action research seeks to foster development and planned change. Traditional research seeks to build a body of accumulated knowledge. Third is *perspectives* versus *experimentation*. Action research aims to collect trustworthy data on the multiple perspectives of particular individuals and groups. Traditional research aims to obtain objective data from a representative sample of subjects. Fourth is *local* versus *universal*. Action research focuses on local change and improvement. Traditional research focuses on building universal theory and valid generalizations.

In the first article, Kate Ferguson-Patrick, a primary elementary teacher in Newcastle, NSW, Australia, explains in wonderful detail how she engaged in action-research procedures to improve the writing skills of

1

12 six-year-olds. Her article presents a painstakingly beautiful portrait of the four aspects of my definition of action research; improvement, development, perspectives, and local change.

Ferguson-Patrick's astute and concrete observations, focused literature searches, and professional reflections helped her plan for her students to work cooperatively. The students wrote together in helping pairs and as critical friends. Throughout the research period as students changed mates, her continuous observations and reflections lead her to teach them such social skills as active listening and paraphrasing, and such norms of cooperative learning as turn-taking and equal sharing. When she saw the need for individual accountability, she experienced a magical moment as she came up with the simple idea of each student using a different color pencil. Thereafter, whenever students wrote words on paper they used their own special color.

As Ferguson-Patrick's spirals of observing, writing journal entries, reflecting, planning, and acting continued to zero in on the students' microprocesses of cooperative writing, she refined her instructional interventions and learned better how to facilitate development of writing skills in six-year-olds. Her article is a precious specimen of a definition of practical action research.

The second article, Ken Zeichner's rich, scholarly contribution, broadly maps the full terrain of what has become the discipline of educational action research today. In stark contrast to Ferguson-Patrick's novel details of small-scale action research in local context, Zeichner presents the large picture, wide breadth, and contemporary complexity of international educational action research. He examines the intellectual traditions that have been the foundations of its development, especially in English-speaking countries, and discusses how it has been conceptualized, organized, and supported, both as a local improvement activity and as a new form of knowledge production.

# 1

# Writers Develop Skills Through Collaboration

## *An Action Research Approach*

### Kate Ferguson-Patrick

## INTRODUCTION

> The goal of teachers to be professional problem solvers who are committed to improving both their own practice and student outcomes provides a powerful reason to practice action research. (Peterson, 1992 cited in Mills, 2003)

Research points to the fact that quality teachers make a difference both to their students' lives and to their learning (Rowe & Rowe, 2002; NSW Department of Education and Training, 2003). Quality teachers are therefore continually working to improve their teaching and their students' learning. This study arose from my commitment as a practicing teacher to the importance of reflective practice in order to make informed decisions. My understanding of the powerful nature of reflective practice (Dewey, 1933; Schön, 1983; Anderson *et al.*, 1994; Stringer, 2004) was empowering,

SOURCE: "Writers Develop Skills Through Collaboration: An Action Research Approach," by Kate Ferguson-Patrick (2007). *Educational Action Research*, Volume 15, (2), 159–180. Taylor & Francis Ltd., http://www.tandf.co.uk/journals. Reprinted with permission of the publisher.

and therefore my own teaching incorporated aspects of 'active or interactive reflection' (Schön, 1983; Grushka *et al.*, 2005).

The study, prompted by a higher degree dissertation as part of my Master of Arts in Children's Literacy and Literature, focused on a group of 12 children. These children had previously had a year at school so had some writing instruction and were now in their second year (first class, which is generally ages six and seven). They were part of a composite kindergarten/first class that I taught as a full-time teacher while doing my M.A. part time. The school, a large inner-city school (approximately 380 students), is one that has an affiliation with the University of Newcastle.

The study was initiated by the growing interest in cooperative learning. I also had an interest in the development of the beginning writers in my classroom and sought to investigate how the implementation of the instructional strategy of cooperative learning could enhance the literacy learning of the students in my classroom. As part of my reflection into my literacy program for my kindergarten-first class, I decided to focus on the writing taking place within the classroom. The beginning writers study incorporated aspects of action research and was developed by initially planning a change to my practice, acting on and observing the process and any change consequences, reflecting again and replanning (Kemmis & Wilkinson cited in Atweh *et al.*, 1998).

I decided to formulate questions about the ways in which I taught writing in my classroom and endeavoured to systematically investigate how I instigated, monitored and evaluated my writing sessions. My plan was to link the interest I had in cooperative learning, and its highlighted benefits over decades of research, with my interest in beginning writers. With an ongoing interest in cooperative learning I knew that, by taking an action research approach to my investigation, I could focus on a problem or question about the writing that was happening when I asked students to work together for certain writing tasks, act on this, observe any changes, reflect again and continue in this reflective process to improve the student writing outcomes.

I therefore sought to rigorously evaluate my current strategies and practices, plan for and implement some new ones and evaluate such actions, drawing conclusions on the basis of the findings (Macintyre, 1991 cited in Seider & Lemma, 2004). The approach I took is also supported by Peters (2004), who stated: 'Action Research, in particular, is depicted as a means of engaging practitioners in rigorous cycles of planning, observation, action and reflection, which can lead to change in understandings and practice' (Peters, 2004, p. 536). These 'self-reflective spiral of cycles' as first mentioned by Lewin (1952) and supported by Elliott (1991) (both cited in Leitch & Day, 2000) guide this type of practical action research with 'analysis and reflection of the situation, rather than merely fact finding' (cited in Leitch & Day, 2000, p. 184).

This particular research approach also grew from a strong belief that teachers engaging in action research 'grow personally and professionally and . . . this enables . . . them to influence other teachers toward improving curriculum and instruction' (Seider & Lemma, 2004, p. 221). As curriculum leader for English K–6 in a large city primary school in Newcastle, NSW Australia, this was a strong personal mission. As a teacher researcher I wanted to be empowered, increasing my self-confidence in decision-making (Kincheloe, 1991 and Noffke, 1992 both cited in Morton, 2005), and as a result could help to empower other teachers towards improving student outcomes. As a result of such reflection in my action research approach my strong aim was to be more critical 'moving beyond mere interpretation of situations to action resulting in a transformed educational setting' (Carr & Kemmis, 1986 and Morton & Williams, 2002 both cited in Morton, 2005, p. 54).

The learning focus of this study was developed as a result of an interest in increasing the literacy skills in the early years of schooling, as well as an interest in the development of writing skills; the importance of developing regular classroom writing opportunities and the research into the value of collaborative learning in supporting higher achievement, thinking skills and deeper understanding (Hill & Hill, 1990). It seems apparent that writing is crucial to school success and 'is the primary means by which students demonstrate their knowledge in school and the major instrument that teachers use to evaluate academic performance' (Graham & Harris, in press cited in Saddler & Graham, 2005, p. 2). Also, many researchers have suggested that cooperative learning can promote academic achievement and social skills development (Johnson & Johnson, 1975, 1987, 1994; Slavin, 1983, 1987, 1989; Stevens & Slavin, 1995) and this belief led to the change in practice from mainly individual writing activities to paired experiences. It was my intention that this could then lead to larger group experiences if the outcomes of these paired experiences were successful and positive.

## EARLY WRITING DEVELOPMENT AND COLLABORATION—A SELECTIVE REVIEW OF RELATED LITERATURE

The development of strong literacy skills in the early years of schooling is an urgent priority for all Australian State and Federal governments (Department of Education and Science & Committee, 1997) and has resulted in a number of studies: *Mapping Literacy Achievement* (Department of Education and Science & Committee, 1997), *100 children turn 10* (Hill et al., 2002) as well as the recent (2004/05) Australian *National Inquiry into the Teaching of Literacy* (Department Education Science and Training, 2005). Literacy is defined in this most recent inquiry as not 'just a set of cognitive abilities or skills based on an identifiable technology, for example alphabetic script on paper,' but needs to 'be recognised as a social activity embedded within larger social practices and changing technologies' (Department Education Science and Training, 2005, p. 4).

The 1991 Department of Employment Education and Training definition of literacy, which has been widely used in Australia in recent years, is used in the New South Wales Board of Studies English K–6 Syllabus (NSW Board of Studies, 1998):

> Literacy is the ability to read and use written information and to write appropriately in a range of contexts. It is used to develop knowledge and understanding, to achieve personal growth and to function effectively in our society. Literacy involves the integration of speaking, listening and critical thinking with reading and writing. (p. 5)

This definition strongly advocates that the social nature of literacy is of utmost importance. Being literate enables people to function effectively in society. Teachers who recognise this and teach accordingly are preparing students for success in society.

## Literacy

There are many factors that contribute to children's literacy development. Many teachers work with the belief that children do not fit neatly into developmental stages; and in terms of developing skills in literacy, each child has a unique way of making meaning (Clay, 1991). However, the aspect I wanted to concentrate on in this study was the importance of social interaction in literacy development. Vygotsky's (1978) socio-cultural ideas of development assert that the adult, or expert, partners the child and scaffolds the present knowledge to new knowledge. This view would assert that children need social interaction for the scaffolding to take place. Vygotsky's work also indicated the link between children interacting socially with the development of higher order cognitive processes in writing (Vygotsky, 1978). Hill and Hancock support this notion that 'Literacy is a social event: language is learnt in communities' (Hill & Hancock, 1993, p. 9). One technique used to enhance social learning in literacy situations is the use of cooperative/collaborative group work.

## Literacy and cooperative learning

Cooperative learning research demonstrated that when students are organised into small heterogeneous teams (usually two to six students) and where academic tasks are solved with face-to-face interaction, individual accountability, positive interdependence and goal similarity (Hill & Hill, 1990; Hill & Hancock, 1993; Johnson & Johnson, 1994; Slavin, 1995a), then academic abilities are improved. Johnson and Johnson's (1994) model also asserts that there should be some social skills instruction and debriefing (Johnson, 1984) so that, as a result, children's social skills are also improved.

Collaborative and cooperative talk can improve student outcomes. Tasks requiring cooperative talk encourage explanation as well as application of knowledge. Researchers (Hill & Hill, 1990; Johnson & Johnson, 1994; Slavin, 1995b) argue that there is a positive correlation between achievement and giving explanations. They also state that when knowledge is sought and constructed together, it is negotiated. Developing tasks with goal similarity, to ensure positive interdependence, therefore leads to a greater sense of personal responsibility. Hill and Hill (1990) further state that cooperative and collaborative learning supports higher achievement, develops thinking skills and deeper understanding, allows for more enjoyable learning, develops leadership skills, promotes positive views about others and self, helps self-acceptance, builds self-esteem, involves children and provides a sense of belonging. The positive correlation between achievement and giving explanations, when knowledge is sought and constructed together and negotiated, supports the notion of the development of higher order cognitive processes in writing when children work together (Vygotsky, 1978). Children have different strengths and, by working in collaboration, each member of the group is able to develop higher achievements by sharing these different strengths.

In the study the term collaborative is used congruently with peer collaboration, and this is defined as students offering equal amounts of help to each other. This 'symmetric relationship' is based on one child explaining while completing a task but at the same time taking solutions, answers from the other member(s) of the team (De Haan & Elbers, 2005). In comparison, peer tutoring is described as 'one child in a teaching role, offering guidance and assistance to another child' (Morrow, 1993, p. 13), and this definition is supported by De Haan and Elbers (2005, p. 9) who describe the relationship as an 'asymmetric' one. Peer tutoring can also occur under such cooperative conditions as utilised in the study. Therefore the study was developed with the understanding that 'Where there is cooperative learning . . . the quality and quantity of support that each child receives in becoming a successful reader and writer is increased' (Hill & Hancock, 1993, p. 3).

## Writing and links to cooperative writing

From earlier cited definitions about literacy it would seem that to improve writing skills children are required to write effectively for different purposes and different audiences in society and that students should be given plenty of opportunities to write regularly, as 'students' regular classroom writing (which usually includes the processes of drafting, redrafting, and conferencing) reflects higher levels of writing ability than writing completed under more standardised conditions' (Department of Education and Science & Committee, 1997, p. 17). The Mapping Literacy

Achievement Project (Department of Education and Science & Committee, 1997) found that enjoyment of writing was paramount to writing success but that writing enjoyment declined from years three to five so there was thus an imperative for teachers to endeavour to foster enjoyment in writing from the beginning years of school.

Writing appears to be under represented in research and particularly in the early years. The most recent Australian National Inquiry into the teaching of literacy (2004/05) found that often writing is not given the emphasis that is needed and that too often reading instruction is the basis of most inquiries. Writing programmes have developed over the years within Australia from approaches that encourage writing as production or encoding (1960s), to writing as creativity (1970s), to writing as process (1980s), to writing as genre (1990s) (Harris *et al.*, 2003). Many writing programmes within Australia began to draw upon a social model of writing, based on Freebody and Luke's (1992, 1999, 2000 cited in Harris *et al.*, 2003) model of reading. The four sets of writing practices included in this social model are text encoder (written texts that can be read by others and conform to conventions and structures of written language), text participant (composing meaning), text user (writing for social purposes) and text analyst (considering bigger picture consequences of what they write) (Harris *et al.*, 2003).

By allowing children to work collaboratively, they think aloud—and this enables them to think about their thought processes, and hence writing processes, more comprehensively than if they were working alone. When engaged, and with appropriate well-matched scaffolding from the teacher, children are then able to collaborate on writing tasks ensuring they restate, clarify, justify, evaluate as well as reflect throughout the whole writing process (Bruner, 1989 cited in McMahon *et al.*, 1997). Furthermore, when children share the writing they become more likely to take risks and become actively engaged with their writing as well as view errors as learning in progress (Cicalese, 2003).

In summary, it would appear that to become good writers children should be given opportunities to interact regularly with enjoyable writing tasks, and by collaborating with others they are more able to scaffold each other's skills, knowledge and understandings to enable them to achieve higher order cognitive processes in writing. This project therefore was developed with the notion that collaborative writing should support students in their early writing attempts, and in turn this should increase productivity as well as develop and support each other's writing skills.

## CHANGING MY WRITING PROGRAMME

### What was happening before I intervened?

My writing programme prior to the study comprised the students in my class writing individually. Tasks focused on my students planning, reviewing and writing simple literary and factual texts for a variety of purposes, but they were asked to do this alone.

My writing programme, before I decided to introduce collaborative approaches, had begun to draw upon the social model of writing (Harris *et al.*, 2003). For the purpose of the study with my beginning writers I focused mainly on the first three practices of the social model of writing advocated by Harris *et al.*: text encoder, text participant and text user—that is, composing for meaning, conforming to the conventions and structures of written language and considering the social purpose of their writing (Harris *et al.*, 2003). I also engaged my students to reach independent achievement by guiding them through a cycle of modelled, guided and independent writing (derived from the work of Macken *et al.*, 1989, Mooney, 1990 and Painter, 1991 all cited in Harris *et al.*, 2003). As students became independent I concentrated on collaborative approaches to writing.

## Assessing writing abilities

Before the study, the level of the children's writing capabilities had been explored through careful observation. This was done during inter-active, modelled and jointly constructed whole-class writing sessions as well as in individual writing activities. After analysing writing samples, according to NSW Board of Studies (1998) outcomes and indicators, a variety of levels were identified. These were categorised into high-ability, medium-ability or low-ability writers (or working towards, working at or working beyond expected stage levels).

It was at this stage that my programme began to change as I sought to integrate my knowledge of the power of cooperative learning to improve student outcomes (Hill & Hill, 1990; Johnson *et al.*, 1990; Johnson & Johnson, 1994; Slavin, 1995a) with how I felt students best learn to write. I had asked students to write alone at this phase and I felt that many of the group of writers I had were still working at an emer-gent writing stage and were only just beginning to show awareness of sounds in language. The beginning of my first phase of action research thus emerged when I organised these early writers into pairs with all writing times ensuring student interaction and opportunities to practice metacognitive skills (Van Keer & Verhaeghe, 2005). I then began to for-mulate some questions:

- What do children do when they write collaboratively (in pairs)?
- What do both children offer to the writing process?
- What do they talk about?
- Are they on task more than when working individually?
- What kinds of behaviours do they exhibit when working together?
- What about the content of their writing?
- What about the productivity levels when writing with different partnerships?

- Will the type of partnership, that is the mix of ability levels, make a difference to these previous questions of behaviours, talk, content, productivity?
- Could students at such an early stage of literacy achievement help each other write?

The main stages of the changes to my programme were:

- Developing collaborative skills in the students.
- Developing individual accountability procedures to ensure that each child was doing some of the writing.
- Grouping students into pairs and after the first few sessions considering whether the topic should be given or self-chosen and the differences to productivity with this difference.
- Grouping students into pairs and considering whether these should be same-ability or mixed-ability pairs.
- Focusing on listening to and analysing the pre-writing talk.
- Tape-recording sessions in order to analyse the type of talk that was happening during the writing time and whether this talk assisted writing improvement.
- Observing for evidence of *peer collaboration, peer tutoring, co-writing and co-responding* with consideration for their impact on the student's writing.

## RESEARCH DESIGN

### First phase intervention:
### developing collaboration among students

Prior to the writing focus of the study, I saw a need to actively teach basic interpersonal skills in order for collaboration between students to be useful (Johnson & Johnson, 1984). One way this was done was with the use of 'Y' charts (Hill & Hancock, 1993), which promote discussion of a particular social skill. For example, when children are working in a 'think, pair, share' activity, another child is given the responsibility of looking for examples of good eye contact and other non-verbal listening skill cues (e.g. nodding). At the end of the activity they then report back on whom they saw actively listening and how they 'saw' it. The 'Y-chart' is then completed with a class brainstorm (see Figure 1).

These Y-charts were comprehensively developed to practice such skills as turn-taking and positive feedback, which were skills needed in order for students to write together in pairs. Small group games, which developed positive classroom ecology, were also employed in order to create a learning environment that fostered negotiated learning and cooperative skills.

**Figure 1**    Y-chart for teaching social skills

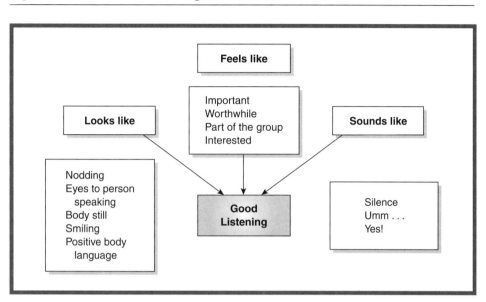

After these whole-class strategic teaching sessions, students were organised into small heterogeneous teams (usually two students) with writing tasks solved with positive interdependence and goal similarity (Slavin, 1995b; Johnson & Johnson, 1994; Hill & Hancock, 1993). By asking students to write in pairs, their knowledge was to be sought and constructed together and therefore was negotiated. The careful setting up of paired writing tasks, by for example ensuring there was some individual accountability, ensured that there was a level of personal responsibility.

**Phase two: considerations of individual accountability**

At the beginning of the study, when analysing samples of writing and when conferencing with children, it was difficult to assess who had completed most of the writing task. Consequently a new aspect of the collaborative writing process was introduced. I asked each child to use a different-coloured pencil. This, I hoped would help ensure individual accountability (positive interdependence) (Johnson & Johnson, 1975; Hill & Hill, 1990; Slavin, 1995a). Each child, through this technique, would become aware of the fact that it was possible to see whether they were on task with the writing process and engaged with the learning, and it would allow them also to self-reflect on their individual efforts even though they were operating in a group situation.

**Phase three intervention: ability level consideration**

The collaborative writing experiences started by students being partnered in heterogeneous (mixed ability) partnerships. It was then decided to mix up the children and ask them to work at times with a teacher-allocated partner. At other times the children could choose their own partners. I wanted to determine whether the changing of high-ability, middle-ability or low-ability writers had an impact on the level of co-writing, co-responding, student engagement and on task behaviours, as well as productivity (amount of words written). True cooperative learning experiences should involve heterogeneous groupings and this change to the study, by ensuring that same-ability partners worked alongside together at times, was an example of how researchers often adapt instructional innovations and models of cooperative learning to fit in with existing prior knowledge of teaching and experience (Cuban, 1996 cited in Siegel, 2005).

### Phase four intervention: considering pre-writing talk

Observing students writing and taking anecdotal notes had been a focus so far in the study. However I sometimes missed the pre-writing talk while setting the students off on their task, and it also appeared that when I was able to listen carefully at the beginning of a writing time, there was little occurring. They appeared to sit down and one partner would take charge of the task and start it without talking about it first. This led me to intervene and start tape-recording one pair's talk during each writing session in order to more easily analyse the type of talk that was happening during the writing time. I hoped that this would help me to hear whether this talk indicated on or off task behaviours and whether this talk assisted writing improvement.

### Phase five intervention: from further reading—recognition and noting of peer collaboration and peer tutoring, co-writing and co-responding

Looking further at the writing process led me to read more about the area of writing in collaboration. I discovered research about peer collaboration and peer tutoring, and my analysis of the transcripts of recorded talk started to determine that at times I could see aspects of both happening. I also then began to look for evidence of co-writing and co-responding. During the analysis of the transcripts I could observe the level of co-writing and co-responding that occurred during different writing approaches (Saunders, 1989 cited in McCarthey & McMahon, 1992). It started to become apparent that some students collaborated on every task including forming of ideas, sentence forming and spelling of individual words within the sentence, whereas others appeared to 'co-respond' and only really interact in the revising (editing) process; that is, when a sentence had been written by one student, another may offer advice about a word that was missed, or misspelt. Saunders' (1989 cited in McCarthey & McMahon, 1992) definition of 'helping,' when writers *voluntarily* help during the writing process, is important when students wrote with others. It was also apparent that students should have the feeling of trustworthiness of their partners when they sought help (Nelson Le-Gall, 1992). If they know they will not be criticised for seeking help, and if the help given is seen as effective, they may seek help again.

## Triangulation

The case study used multiple data collection strategies or triangulation (Stringer, 2004) to increase reliability and validity. During the six-month study, persistent, participant and intensive observation (Stringer, 2004) was used. This improves the internal validity of a study as different methods of data collection allowed for comparison of information and assessed the sufficiency of the data. Many strategies were used to collect evidence. These involved observation, anecdotal note-keeping and reflections in a journal; conferencing with the children as they wrote also ensured the validity of the action research process, establishing credibility and dependability and recording interactions. At the start of the study it was difficult to anticipate how difficult it would be to really listen to the interactions of a pair without being disturbed by assistance being sought from others, or general classroom noise. This is why the tape-recorded sessions were introduced part way through. Verbal interactions were transcribed from the tape recordings. Finally the samples of work were collected and analysed.

# WHAT I LEARNT ABOUT CHILDREN COLLABORATING IN WRITING

## Individual accountability

Dominance of partnerships began to be examined at the beginning of the study. Earlier observed sessions showed the domination of one partner but introducing the coloured pencils ensured both students' accountability, with positive interdependence being made clear and students being made to ' . . . feel a sense of personal responsibility to do their fair share of the work' (Johnson & Johnson, 1994, p. 193). It was obvious, after the introduction of the coloured pencils, how the task was shared. Students shared tasks in different ways. These included sharing the writing one letter at a time (Ross and Aaron, Appendix 1), one word at a time (Cassie and Casey, Appendix 2) or two words, or a mixture of turn-taking, at a time (Hayley and Victoria, Appendix 3). The use of different-coloured pencils was still used after the study finished as it was a way of students realising that visually I was aware of their contribution.

## Pre-writing talk

Analysis of the first few observations suggested an absence of pre-writing talk. The dominant personality or higher ability writer tended to instigate the start of the writing process by either writing a title and/or the lines (which represent the words to be written in that sentence).

There was also no pre-writing talk at any of the seven tape-recorded sessions. The introduction of the tape-recorder was to try and improve my ability to really listen to the interactions of a pair, without being disturbed by assistance being sought from others, and to alleviate problems of general classroom noise. However, as the study progressed it became obvious that, even when not being closely observed with me sitting on the same table as the students, they were still not involved in pre-writing talk. Maybe the tape-recorder restricted this as they felt that they were being 'watched' and should therefore start to write immediately. Perhaps the students felt there was the pressure of individual accountability and I would be checking that they had started their task immediately as it was being taped. The absence of pre-writing talk suggests that whoever has the next turn to write decides on how the writing will continue. I reminded children to talk and think before writing after noticing this absence of planning prior to writing. However this did not appear to happen at subsequent sessions. It was disappointing that collaborative learning did not improve pre-writing skills.

## Re-reading for meaning

The use of the tape-recorder also highlighted another skill that beginning writers use constantly. Observations and transcription of tape-recorded sessions revealed that students used the re-reading strategy constantly to determine meaning of their written texts. This strategy is possibly relied on more when students wrote collaboratively in pairs than during individual writing sessions, as the two students had to determine the sense of the partner's writing before continuing on. Although the communication suggests a slowing down of the writing process, a suggestion that this could decrease productivity, the results conclude that productivity increased dramatically over the course of the study with the average number of words increasing from almost eight in April to 21 in September.

## Cooperative behaviours/skills analysis

As the study continued I was able to analyse, again mainly through the use of transcribed tape-recorded sessions, some cooperative behaviours. Turn-taking was the most common cooperative skill used in the study and this skill was developed from the beginning to end. Due to the individual accountability built into the task, individuals were more likely to encourage each other's efforts to achieve (Johnson & Johnson, 1994). Some of the statements made by the children support this notion of turn-taking and peer tutoring or peer collaboration.

> We'll write about yours Ross! (His news)
>
> How about we make it Marvella and the star? (Suggest alternative, creative story line/title)
>
> You write dress—make a space there! (Help with writing conventions)
>
> Come on we have to think of some more ideas! (The joint goal acknowledged)
>
> Do you know how to spell 'our'? (Child sought assistance and acknowledged partner's strength)

## Ability level of child and its impact on the study

I found that the numbers of words increased if they were given a partner (by me or through random allocation) rather than self-selecting one (Table 1).

**Table 1**      Writing production

|  | Mean (average number of words written) |
| --- | --- |
| **First phase (seven sessions)** | |
| Given partner | 11.28 |
| Own partner | 9.6 |
| **Second phase (seven sessions)** | |
| Given partner | 20.55 |
| Own partner | 13.95 |

When self-selecting a partner, most students chose different students each time and so developing a writing relationship was difficult. On the other hand, Casey and Tayler selected each other three times during the study. They were both high-ability writers and often felt frustrated in the peer teaching role. They enjoyed the fluency of writing with each other.

## Peer tutoring

The strategy of constantly re-reading in order to ensure the writing made sense needed to be constantly encouraged and modelled during shared/modelled writing sessions with these beginning writers. The strategy of re-reading for sense-making worked well with beginning writing demonstrations. When two high-ability children worked together there was an absence of talk or interaction. This could be because their knowledge of high-frequency words was good, because they recorded these silently and could also be because their more advanced reading skills enabled them to reread quickly and silently. In session 14 a child was taught this re-reading strategy by another and then went on to use it in a different partnership (session 15) (see Figure 2).

Various observations supported the notion of children working in collaboration and using their own strengths, with the 'zone of proximal development' shifting depending on what was being discussed or attempted. In session 14 a child shares his knowledge of the length of words (see Figure 3).

Another child in a session remembers a teaching tip about not using too many 'ands', and she reminds her partner (see Figure 4).

Two other students help each other with spellings and reinforce the alphabet by singing it together (see Figure 5).

These transcripts thus highlight peer tutoring as a powerful collaborative teaching strategy. When engaged, and with appropriate well-matched scaffolding from the teacher, children are able to collaborate on writing tasks by ensuring they restate, clarify, justify, evaluate as well as reflect throughout the whole writing process (Bruner, 1989 cited in McMahon *et al.*, 1997).

**Figure 2**    Teaching each other

| | |
|---|---|
| **Daniel** "We." | *Daniel starts the interaction but it is obviously Mitchell's turn to write the letters.* |
| **Mitchell** "e, we, e, e." | |
| **Mitchell** "e, we, e, e." | *Mitchell attempts to sound it out and Daniel gets annoyed that he doesn't know how to write it.* |
| **Daniel** *rereading* "On Wednesday we . . . went!" | *Daniel is using the strategy that Tayler has demonstrated last week - rereading to find out what word should be written next! Peer teaching has worked!! Mitchell seeking help/clarification. Daniel sounding out unknown words.* |
| **Mitchell** "This one?" *(pointing at alphabet card?)* | |
| **Daniel** "We nt 't' 'nt.'" *sounding out.* | |

**Figure 3**    Sharing knowledge

| | |
|---|---|
| **Together** "'N', 'i', 'n', 'n'" *Sounding out together.* | *Tayler is excited when he knows how to spell a word.* |
| **Tayler** "I think I know how to spell that!" | *Tayler obviously knows the word Daniel is attempting is a longer one than Daniel has drawn the line for.* |
| **Daniel** "plna" | |
| **Tayler** "Make your line bigger!" | *Helping each other.* |
| Together "t', 's'." | *Tayler uses this strategy to work out the next word he is to write.* |
| **Tayler** *Rereading* | |
| **Daniel** "I know how to spell 'we'". | *Daniel excited about knowing how to spell a word.* |
| **Tayler** "Hang on, it might not be 'we'." | *Tayler wants Daniel to be sure this is the right word to write next - maybe he is encouraging him to use the previous strategy?* |
| *They continued writing and then proceeded to argue about what comes next. Rereading and pointing at words to justify.* | *Arguing about ideas / meaning?* |

**Figure 4**     Teaching tips from students

Hayley kept on task and Victoria went on and off task.

**Hayley** *kept repeating* "**I'll tell the teacher. . .**"

**Hayley** *tried to continue but found it hard to re-read Victoria's writing attempts.* "What does this say?"

**Victoria** "Remember, Miss Ferguson said to not write too many 'ands."

*Hayley didn't comment and didn't alter writing (maybe did not understand?).*

*Hayley continuing to be frustrated by Victoria.*

*This shows the problem of two children working together and not really sharing the task - Hayley is finding it hard to reread Victoria's attempts.*

*Victoria remembers my advice / teaching about 'ands'*

*but Hayley obviously hadn't remembered / understood or seen the importance.*

**Figure 5**     Helping each other

**12 August**
**Ross and Aaron**
**Information Report - "All we know about Space"**

*Aaron and Ross taking it in turns to write lines to represent words, but not conferring before they do this. No pre-writing planning occurring.*

*Ross said the word they were attempting to write and Aaron saying the sound(s) he could hear. Ross said the letter name and wrote it.*

**Ross** "This is how you write an 'I', 'p'"!

**Aaron** "'p' for Peter!" (*saying the alphabet aloud and looking at the alphabet card for the 'p'.*)

**Ross** "O"

**Aaron** "I'll draw the 'o'." (*Re-reading and heard a 't' that Ross had obviously previously missed.*) "How do you draw a 'b'?"

**Ross** "Easy!" (*Showing Aaron the alphabet card and singing the alphabet to get to the letter.*) "We're helping each other, aren't we?"

*This is a very common occurrence to have no pre-writing talk and planning.*

*Sharing the load and their knowledge of different letter/sound correspondences. "Zone of proximal development' shifting continuously.*

*Peer teaching.*

*Using the alphabet card to find out how to write letters.*

*Aaron wants to write the letters he knows how to write - 'o' is in his name. Rereading is a strategy they don't use enough.*

*Ross also using the alphabet card to locate a letter for Aaron. Co-operative behaviour, acknowledging that they both have knowledge to share.*

## Peer collaboration

There were two instances noted from the tape-recorded sessions where I could claim interactions of peer collaboration. Casey and Cassie gave each other equal help in one session: 'How about I do the letters and then you do the letters?'; and Ross and Matthew did so in another: 'I learnt to write "o" and "t"!,' 'That's an "h", this is an "n".' Interestingly both pairs of students were similar-ability whereas clear examples of peer tutoring (locating letters, telling what letters represented different sounds, sounding out for spelling, re-reading work) resulted when students were paired with a different-ability partner. By allowing children to work collaboratively they think aloud, and this enables them to think about their thought processes, and hence writing processes, more comprehensively than if they were working alone.

I began to note that at times the higher ability partner became frustrated and hindered in this peer-tutoring role so it was important for these students to be given opportunities to not always work in such partnerships. I began to recognise that they needed opportunities at times to work beyond their own individual capabilities by working with others of the same ability level as well as other times when they could be in this peer-teaching role.

'Helping' occurred numerous times in the study, when students peer tutored and peer collaborated with letter names, sounds, locating letters on an alphabet strip, showing where spaces need to go between words, trying to get their partner back on task, reminding their partner about turn-taking, encouraging re-reading for meaning and demonstrating one-to-one correspondence. These helping behaviours were more apparent when listening to and transcribing the tape-recorded sessions. This suggests that teachers' focused observations are very necessary in order to examine and understand what is occurring in the classroom.

Some students were identified by their peers, when interviewed at the end of the study, as 'good helpers'; interestingly, more girls than boys were identified. Good helpers were perceived as caring and cooperative members of the class, both being supporting and accepting. The study suggests that 'good helping' skills need to be made explicit; that is, the question needs to be constantly explored with the students: *What does it mean to be caring and cooperative?*

I had a strong belief that collaborative learning supports higher achievement, develops thinking skills and deeper understanding, allows for more enjoyable learning, develops leadership skills, promotes positive views about others and self, helps self-acceptance, and builds self-esteem whether this be with a similar-ability or a mixed-ability partner. As a result it was a realisation that I would continue to change these partnerships in my writing programme and at times have students write with an opportunity to be a helper and provide scaffolding of others' learning, and other times give higher ability students an opportunity to bounce ideas, develop thinking skills and enjoy learning with a similar-ability partner. As well as the value of students assisting in skills development, the 'helping' aspect of providing social support in a learning task was also obviously of assistance when encouraging quantity of writing.

This increased productivity (quantity) is shown in Appendix 1, which shows an increase in productivity over the 14 sessions of collaborative writing. High, middle, low refers to the ability of the partner. Collaborative writing sessions were approximately 20–45 minutes. This increased quantity may not have been as a direct result of the study and of the placing of students in pairs to write; however, it depended significantly on the partner they were working with. Lower ability students reduce fluency due to their inability to write high-frequency words quickly, but also higher ability students tended to strive for perfection, both factors slowing down the amount written. Tayler (high ability) worked with four lower ability, three middle ability and three higher ability partners during the study. He demonstrated in a number of sessions that he did not want to progress to writing the next word until he was sure the previous one was worked out correctly. This slowed down the process of writing for both him and his partner. Hayley (middle ability), however, was a great risk-taker and this speeded up the process of her writing, increasing productivity.

## IMPLICATIONS FOR MY TEACHING

The study has supported the findings of others who have researched collaboration and literacy. These studies show how children share strengths (Vygotsky, 1978) as well as the positive outcomes of students working together (Johnson & Johnson, 1975, 1987, 1994; Slavin, 1983, 1987, 1989; Stevens & Slavin, 1995).

My action research approach has enabled me to closely observe, analyse, change, reflect and re-plan my writing programme, allowing me to make teaching decisions based on action research. The study found various types of interaction and involvement depending on a number of variables. Mixed-ability grouping results suggest that teachers should vary their partnerships. When children work with a higher ability partner, peer tutoring is likely to occur in various ways. Although most enjoy the tutoring role, some students get frustrated. This suggests teachers should vary their partnerships and allow students at times to work with similar abilities in order to share strengths and jointly help (peer collaborate). At times, 'issues relating to peer acceptance and reading competence' can 'complicate children's interactions during literacy events' (Matthews & Kesner, 2003, p. 208).

Children shared the writing tasks in different ways, but after the different coloured pencils were introduced to encourage individual accountability (Johnson & Johnson, 1994) the children were most likely to write a word in turn and this then improved both children's writing production. This individual accountability is of crucial importance when working with cooperative activities, and the careful division of the task in order to achieve *task interdependence* as well as resources to achieve *resource interdependence* are two of the crucial elements suggested by

Johnson and Johnson (1994). It is this cooperative incentive structure that is distinctive to cooperative learning (Killen, 2003). At the start of the study I had not really considered these crucial elements and therefore the sharing of the tasks was sometimes not apparent with the higher ability student taking over the majority or all of the writing.

Some of the cooperative behaviours displayed included turn-taking, helping and supporting. Social skills development is also crucial to cooperative activities and the study highlighted the need to be constantly explicit about 'good helping' skills.

Productivity was also examined and the study found a positive correlation between being given a topic to write about with explicit teaching input and scaffolding, as well as when children were given a partner to write with, rather than self-selecting their own partner. Off-task behaviours were more common when working with a friend. Peer collaboration occurred between similar-ability partners, and this was a common choice for children to make.

These conclusions explain some of the benefits of children writing together. This small sample of students benefited from working in collaboration with others and enhanced my understanding about children's collaborative writing processes and behaviours by my continual reassessing of my teaching process. The study certainly demonstrated the complexity involved in collaborative writing sessions and demonstrated how teachers can learn from listening to their students' conversations. It helped to impact on my professional practice by enabling informed choices about teaching/learning in the context of literacy and collaboration.

Somekh (2003) cites Elliott (1994) who stated 'Through action research the ideas of theorists are problematised.' She goes on to say:

> By this I think he means that through action research all practitioners, across professions and sectors, problematise their own and other people's theories as an integral part of their day-to-day experience. Other people's theories become personally owned, as we engage with them experientially, once action research becomes a way of life. (Somekh, 2003, p. 260)

My intention is to further 'problematise' my own and other's theories on collaborative and cooperative learning and engage with them experientially with other teachers as action research becomes a way of life in their classrooms.

## REFERENCES

Anderson, G. L., Herr, K. & Nihlen, A. S. (1994) *Studying your own school: an educator's guide to qualitative practitioner research* (Thousand Oaks, CA, Corwin).

Atweh, B., Kemmis, S. & Weeks, P. (Eds) (1998) *Action research in practice; partnership for social justice* (New York, Routledge).

Cicalese, C. (2003) *Children's perspectives on interactive writing versus independent writing in primary grades.* Unpublished M.A. dissertation, Kean University, NJ.

Clay, M. (1991) *Becoming literate: the construction of inner control* (Portsmouth, NH, Heinemann).

De Haan, M. & Elbers, E. (2005) Peer tutoring in a multiethnic classroom in the Netherlands: a multiperspective analysis of diversity, *Comparative Education Review,* 49(3), 365–388.

Department of Education and Science, & Committee (1997) *Mapping literacy achievement: results of the 1996 National School English Literacy Survey* (Camberwell, Vic., Dept. of Employment, Education, Training and Youth Affairs).

Department Education Science and Training (2005) *National inquiry into the teaching of literacy* (Commonwealth of Australia, ACT).

Dewey, J. (1933) *How we think: a restatement of the relation of reflective thinking to the educative process* (Boston, D.C. Heath).

Grushka, K., Hinde McLeod, J. & Reynolds, R. (2005) Reflective thinking, *Reflective Practice,* 6(5), 239–246.

Harris, P., McKenzie, B., Fitzsimmons, P. & Turbill, J. (2003) *Writing in the primary school years* (Tuggerah, NSW, Social Science Press).

Hill, S. & Hancock, J. (1993) *Reading and writing communities: cooperative literacy learning in the classroom* (Armadale, Eleanor Curtain).

Hill, S. & Hill, T. (1990) *The collaborative classroom: a guide to cooperative learning* (South Yarra, Eleanor Curtain).

Hill, S., Comber, B., Louden, W., Reid, J. & Rivalland, J. (2002) *100 children turn 10: a longitudinal study of literacy development from the year prior to school to the first four years of school, a two volume report* (Canberra, Department for Education, Science and Training).

Johnson, D. (1984) *Circles of learning: cooperation in the classroom* (Alexandria, VA, Association for Supervision and Curriculum Development).

Johnson, D. & Johnson, F. (1987) *Joining together: group theory and group skills* (Englewood Cliffs, NJ, Prentice-Hall).

Johnson, D. & Johnson, R. (1975) *Learning together and alone: cooperation, competition, and individualization* (Englewood Cliffs, NJ, Prentice-Hall).

Johnson, D. & Johnson, R. (1994) *Learning together and alone: cooperative, competitive and individualistic learning* (Boston, MA, Allyn and Bacon).

Johnson, D., Johnson, R. & Johnson Holubec, E. (1990) *Circles of learning: cooperation in the classroom* (Alexandria, VA, Association for Supervision and Curriculum Development).

Killen, R. (2003) *Effective teaching strategies: lessons from research and practice* (3rd edn) (Tuggerah, NSW, Social Science Press).

Leitch, R. & Day, C. (2000) Action research and reflective practice: towards a holistic view, *Educational Action Research,* 8(1), 179–193.

Matthews, M. & Kesner, J. (2003) Children learning with peers: the confluence of peer status and literacy competence within small-group literacy events, *Reading Research Quarterly,* 38(2), 208.

McCarthey, S. & McMahon, S. (1992) Peer interaction during writing, in: R. Lazarowitz & N. Miller (Eds) *Interaction in cooperative groups: the theoretical anatomy of group learning* (New York, Cambridge University Press).

McMahon, S., Raphael, T., Goatley, V. & Pardo, L. (Eds) (1997) *The book club connection: literacy learning and classroom talk* (New York, International Reading Association).

Mills, G. E. (2003) *Action research: a guide for the teacher researcher* (2nd edn) (Columbus, OH, Merrill Prentice Hall).

Morrow, L. (1993) *Promoting independent reading and writing through self-directed literacy activities in a collaborative setting* (Athens, National Reading Research Center).

Morton, M. L. (2005) Practicing praxis: mentoring teachers in a low income school through collaborative action research and transformative pedagogy, *Mentoring and Tutoring*, 13(1), 53–72.

Nelson Le-Gall, S. (1992) Childrens instrumental help-seeking: it's role in the social acquisition and construction of knowledge, in: R. Lazarowitz & N. Miller (Eds) *Interaction in cooperative groups: the theoretical anatomy of group learning* (New York, Cambridge University Press).

NSW Board of Studies (1998) *English K-6 syllabus* (Sydney, Board of Studies).

NSW Department of Education and Training (2003) *Quality teaching in NSW public schools: an annotated bibliography* (Sydney, Professional Support and Curriculum Directorate).

Peters, J. (2004) Teachers engaging in action research: challenging some assumptions, *Educational Action Research*, 12(4), 535–555.

Rowe, K. J. & Rowe, K. S. (2002) *What matters most: evidence-based findings of the key factors affecting the educational experiences and outcomes for girls and boys throughout their primary and secondary schooling* (Melbourne, ACER).

Saddler, B. & Graham, S. (2005) The effects of peer-assisted sentence combining instruction on the writing performance of more and less skilled young writers, *Journal of educational Psychology*, 97(1), 433–54.

Schön, D. (1983) *The reflective practitioner: how professionals think in action* (New York, Basic Books).

Seider, S. & Lemma, P. (2004) Perceived effects of action research on teachers' professional efficacy, inquiry mindsets and the support they received while conduction projects to intervene into student learning, *Educational Action Research*, 12(2), 219–238.

Siegel, C. (2005) Implementing a research based model of cooperative learning, *Journal of Educational Research*, 98(6), 339–351.

Slavin, R. E. (1983) Effects of cooperative learning on the social acceptance of mainstreamed academically handicapped students, *Journal of Special Education*, 7(2), 171–182.

Slavin, R. E. (1987) Cooperative learning and the cooperative school, *Educational Leadership*, 45(3), 7–13.

Slavin, R. E. (1989) *School and classroom organization* (Hillsdale, NJ, Erlbaum Associates).

Slavin, R. E. (1995a) The cooperative elementary school: effects on students' achievement, attitudes, and social relations, *American Educational Research Journal*, 32(1), 321–351.

Slavin, R. E. (1995b) *Cooperative learning: theory, research, and practice* (2nd edn) (Boston, MA, Allyn and Bacon).

Somekh, B. (2003) Theory and passion in action research, *Educational Action Research*, 11, 247–264.

Stevens, R. & Slavin, R. E. (1995) Effects of a cooperative learning approach in reading and writing on academically handicapped and non-handicapped students, *The Elementary School Journal*, 95(3), 241–263.

Stringer, E. (2004) *Action research in education* (NJ, Pearson Education).

Van Keer, H. & Verhaeghe, J. (2005) Effects of explicit reading strategies instruction and peer tutoring on second and fifth graders' reading comprehension and self-efficacy perceptions, *Journal of Experimental Education*, 73(4), 291–329.

Vygotsky, L. S. (1978) *Mind in society: the development of higher psychological processes* (Cambridge, MA, Harvard University Press).

**Appendix 1**

*Date/number of words written*

| Name: | 24/4 | 29/4 | 6/5 | 22/5 | 17/6 | 24/6 | 15/7 | 22/7 | 29/7 | 5/8 | 12/8 | 19/8 | 2/9 | 24/9 |
|---|---|---|---|---|---|---|---|---|---|---|---|---|---|---|
| Hayley (H) | 9 | 12 | 15 | 11 | 12 | 13 | 17 | abs | 24 | 31 | 19 | 17 | 45 | 19 |
| | M | L | H | L | L | M/H | M | | M | M | M | M | M | M |
| Jami (M) | 10 | 6 | 6 | 17 | 16 | 13 | 11 | 12 | 13 | 19 | 22 | 13 | 8 | 55 |
| | M | M | L | M | M | M | M | M | L | M | H | H | M | H |
| Victoria (M) | 10 | 7 | abs | 15 | 5 | abs | 9 | 5 | 12 | 31 | abs | 17 | 23 | 22 |
| | M | L | | M | M | | M | L | M | M | | H | M | M |
| Cassie (M) | 5 | 7 | 10 | 15M | 5 | 13 | 16 | 6 | 32 | abs | 16 | 13 | 18 | 41 |
| | L | M/L | M/L | | M | M/M | L | M | L | | L | L | L | L |
| Casey (H) | 8 | 19 | 10 | 33 | 10 | 11 | 8 | 10 | 32 | abs | 22 | 19 | 45 | 44 |
| | M | H | M | M | M | M | H | H | H | | M | M | M | M |
| Larrissa (M) | 8 | 8 | 10 | abs | 5 | 10 | 6 | 12 | 21 | abs | 8 | 19 | 23 | 31 |
| | H | M | H | | H | M | L | M | M/H | | M | H | M | M |
| Daniel (M) | 4 | 6 | 7 | abs | 10 | 10 | 11 | 7 | 21 | abs | 19 | 23 | 15 | 22 |
| | M | M | M/L | | H | M | M | M | M/H | | M | H | L | M |
| Tayler(H) | 10L | 19 | 15 | abs | 11 | abs | 8 | 10 | 21 | 8 | 16 | 23 | abs | 28 |
| | H | M | M | | L | | H | H | M/M | L | H | M | | L |
| Mitchell (L) | 10 | 7 | 6 | 11 | 12 | 7 | 16H | abs | abs | 8 | abs | 5 | 15 | 19 |
| | H | M | M | M | M | L/M | | | | M | | L | M | M |
| Aaron (L) | 5 | 12 | abs | abs | 11 | 7 | 6 | 5 | 13 | 8 | 12 | 5 | 18 | 28 |
| | H | M | | | H | L/M | M | M | M | H | M | L | H | H |
| Matthew (M) | 9 | 7 | 10 | 17 | 16 | 7 | 17 | 7 | 12 | 19 | 8 | 9 | 8 | 44 |
| | M | M | H/L | M | M | L/L | M | M | M | M | M | M | M/M | H |
| Ross (L) | 4 | 8 | 7 | 33 | 5 | 11 | 9 | 6 | 24 | 8 | 12 | 9 | 8 | 31 |
| | L | H/L | M | H | L | H | M | H | M | M | L | M | M/M | H |
| | M | 8 | M/L | H | M | H | M | H | M | H | L | M | M/M | M |
| Average no. of words written | 7.67 | 9.83 | 9.6 | 19 | 9.83 | 10.2 | 11.17 | 8 | 20.46 | 16.5 | 15.4 | 14.33 | 20.55 | 32 |

Underlined dates = children have self selected topic
Shaded columns = children have self selected partner
H,M,L next to the child's name in first column refers to their ability
H,M,L (High, middle, low) within the table refers to the ability of the partner they worked with

# 2

---

# Educational Action Research

## Ken Zeichner

The difficult thing about doing action research is that you have to override most of what you've learned about research as an activity. In a traditional research culture you begin by framing a question, setting up a situation which might provide some information, collecting data which bears on the question, then writing up the results. Action research isn't like that at all. The research activity begins in the middle of whatever it is you're doing—something happens you didn't expect . . . and you begin wondering what's going on . . . The hardest part of beginning an action research project is developing the discipline to keep a written account of what's happening, particularly when you have no idea of what you're looking for. For unlike traditional research, action research begins not with a research question but with the muddle of daily work, with the moments that stand out from the general flow . . . (Newman, 1998: 2–3)

Last year I noticed that the children in my class were creating groups segregated by gender, and I wrote about it in my journal as I wrote about other issues and events. What I did not do last year was to start out by saying, 'I'm going to study gender issues in my classroom,' and to limit my observations and notes to that. (Streib, in Threatt et al., 1994: 237)

---

SOURCE: "Educational Action Research", by Ken Zeichner (2001) in Reason, Peter and Bradbury, Hilary (eds.) *Handbook of Action Research*, Chapter 25, pp. 273–283. SAGE, Ltd. Printed with permission.

My question emerged out of what I understood to be problematic classroom dynamics that surfaced immediately at the beginning of the year. For one thing, eight boys . . . dominated the classroom especially during all class discussions. A second interesting pattern emerged. Whenever I asked the class to voluntarily form groups, line up, or make a circle, they did so in exactly the same fashion—sorting themselves neatly first by gender, then by ethnic and racial affiliation. My questions were: How can I increase participation in all class discussions by those less willing or able to share? How can I help the students in my classroom feel comfortable working with diverse groupings of classmates and ultimately overcome, at least part of the time, their desire to always be with their friends? (Coccari, 1998: 2–3)

These excerpts from the action research reports of teachers in the USA illustrate some of the variety that exists in the ways that teachers[1] have conducted action research. In the first two cases, the teachers began by keeping journals on many aspects of their practice and eventually, for the second teacher, the issue of gender segregation in small-group work emerged for further study. This teacher's documentation was broad-ranging, focusing on many issues simultaneously and the inquiry did not necessarily follow the action research spiral of plan, act, observe and reflect (Kemmis and McTaggart, 1988). In the third case, the teacher began with a specific focus on two questions and the research proceeded, as do most studies in this school district-based programme, according to the action research spiral.

This chapter will examine some of the variety that has come to exist in educational action research in English-speaking countries. We will begin with an examination of the different traditions of action research that have exerted much influence on the emergence of educational action research in many different countries. Then, after a discussion of the different ways in which educational action research is conceptualized, organized, and supported in North America, we will examine educational action research both as a professional development activity and as a form of knowledge production.

## TRADITIONS OF ACTION RESEARCH IN EDUCATION

There are five major traditions of educational action research in English-speaking countries that have exerted influence, in conjunction with local factors, on the development of action research in the educational systems of many countries. First, there is the action research tradition in the USA that developed directly out of the work of Kurt Lewin and was brought into US schools by Stephen Corey and others at the Horace Mann-Lincoln Institute at Columbia University. Secondly, there is the British teacher-as-researcher movement that evolved in the 1960s and 1970s out of the curriculum reform work of British teachers and the support provided by several academics like Lawrence Stenhouse and John Elliott. Thirdly, there is the Australian participatory action research movement, supported by the work of Stephen Kemmis and Robin McTaggart at Deakin University and other Australian academics, that was greatly influenced by educational action research in the UK but that also developed in response to indigenous factors within Australia. Fourthly, there is the contemporary teacher researcher movement in North America that has been developed since the 1980s primarily by teachers, often with the support of their university colleagues and subject matter associations. Finally, there is the recent growth of self-study research by college and university educators who inquire into their own practice as teachers and teacher educators. Educational action research has also been influenced by the tradition of participatory research which developed in Africa, Latin America and Asia with oppressed groups and later was adapted to community-wide research in North America. This explicitly political form of action research (see Fals Borda, Chapter 2 and Hall, Chapter 15) often includes attention to the education sphere, but usually goes beyond it.

### The action research tradition in the USA

In the 1940s and 1950s Stephen Corey, head of the Horace Mann-Lincoln Institute for School Experimentation at Columbia University, and his colleagues drew directly upon the work of social psychologist Kurt Lewin and brought action research into education. The Institute was formed in 1943 to improve the rate of curriculum change in schools and to reduce the gap between research knowledge and practice in classrooms (Olson, 1990). Corey (1953) believed that teachers would make better decisions in the classroom if they conducted research to determine the basis for their decisions.

Corey and his associates at the Institute worked cooperatively with teachers, principals and supervisors in school districts across the USA in the late 1940s and 1950s on a variety of group research efforts in what was referred to as the 'cooperative action research movement' (e.g., Cunningham and Miel, 1947; Foshay, Wann and Associates, 1954).

Like Lewin, Corey saw action research as a cyclical process with each cycle of research affecting subsequent ones. Corey (1953) outlined several distinct phases of the action research process: (1) the identification of a problem area; (2) the selection of a specific problem and formulation of a hypothesis or prediction that implies a specific goal and a procedure for reaching it; (3) the careful recording of actions and accumulation of evidence to determine if the goal has been achieved; (4) the inference from this evidence of generalizations regarding the relation between actions and the desired goal; and (5) the continuous retesting of these generalizations in action (pp. 40–1).

Corey's understanding of the action research process was generally similar to Lewin's in terms of the focus on the research being conducted in a group and the emphasis on the recursive nature of the action research process where researchers need to allow their initial understandings of a problem to shift to remain relevant to changing situations. Corey's view of the action research process differed from Lewin's, however, because of his emphasis on hypothesis formulation and testing. For Corey's students and those who followed him on the faculty at the Institute, action research increasingly became a linear problem-solving process as opposed to the recursive cyclical process that it had been for Lewin and Corey (e.g., Taba and Noel, 1957). It also increasingly became identified as a form of inservice teacher education as opposed to a methodology for knowledge production in education (e.g., Shumsky, 1958).

Corey spent much effort in defending action research as a legitimate form of educational inquiry (e.g., Corey, 1949) against attacks from the mainstream academic research community, but he was largely unsuccessful in doing so. Action research was severely attacked by academic researchers (e.g., Hodgkinson, 1957) and largely disappeared from the USA education literature until the 1980s when a new North American teacher research movement appeared.

### The teacher-as-researcher movement in the UK

Following the decline of action research in the USA by the early 1960s, the idea of action research in the field of education emerged in the UK in the context of school-based curriculum development in the 1960s. According to John Elliott (1991, 1997) who was one of the central players in this movement, both as a secondary school teacher and university academic, this teacher-led movement arose in response to large-scale student disaffection in British secondary schools. In Elliott's view, it was from the attempts by teachers in some innovative secondary modern schools to restructure and reconceptualize the humanities curriculum that the ideas of teacher-as-researcher, teaching as a reflexive practice, and teaching as a form of inquiry emerged.

Another influence on the development of educational action research in Britain during this period was the Tavistock Institute of Human Relations which had been set up in 1947 to develop further practices that psychologists had used during the Second World War to train officers and resettle prisoners. There were strong parallels between the work of this institute and the Research Center for Group Dynamics that Lewin had set up in the USA (Wallace, 1987). According to Bridget Somekh (February 1998, personal communication), two other influences on the development of the teacher-as-researcher movement in Britain were the Educational Priority Area Programme that involved teachers and academics in collaborative research and the US social studies curriculum, 'Man: a Course of Study'.

The bottom-up curriculum reform work initiated by British teachers and later conceptualized and documented by academics like Lawrence Stenhouse, John Elliott, Jean Ruddick and others involved many different initiatives designed to make the curriculum more relevant to the lives of students, such as restructuring the content of the curriculum around life themes, transforming the instructional process from a transmission mode to a more interactive and discussion-based mode, using multiage grouping patterns, etc.

A number of major curriculum reform projects were initiated in the 1960s and 1970s by Stenhouse, Elliott and others, which employed and further developed the idea of action research as curriculum development. These included the 'Humanities Curriculum Project', which dealt with the teaching of controversial issues (Stenhouse, 1968), the 'Ford Teaching Project', which dealt with implementing an inquiry/discovery approach to teaching (Elliott, 1976/77) and the 'Teacher-Student Interaction and Quality of Learning Project' which focused on the problems of teaching for understanding within the context of a system of public examinations (Elliott and Ebutt, 1986).

All of these projects involved university academics working with teachers and represented a rejection of a standards or objectives-based approach to curriculum development in favour of one that is based on a pedagogically driven conception of curriculum change as a process dependent on teachers' capacities for reflection. According to this view, the act of curriculum theorizing is not so much the application in the classroom of theory learned in the university as it is the generation of theory from attempts to change curriculum practice in schools (Elliott, 1991; Stenhouse, 1976).

The efforts of John Elliott, Peter Holly, Bridget Somekh and many others in the UK led to the establishment of the Collaborative Action Research Network (CARN), an international network that has sponsored conferences, published action research studies and discussions of action research methodology. This network was instrumental in establishing the journal *Educational Action Research* which is the major international journal for action research in education today.

## Participatory action research in Australia

Grundy (1997) describes a number of political, social and economic conditions that fostered a receptivity within Australia to the idea of teachers as producers of educational knowledge. Among these were three projects in the 1970s funded by the Commonwealth Schools Commission, 'The Innovative Grants Project', 'The Language and Learning Project' and the 'Curriculum Development Centre'. These projects, as well as changing conceptions of inservice teacher education at the state level, and the growth of action research in the education units of tertiary institutions, stimulated a lot of school-based curriculum development and evaluation, and teachers studying their own practices in Australian schools.

Australian educational action research developed with close ties to the British teacher-as-researcher movement because Stephen Kemmis, one of the leading proponents of educational action research in Australia, as well as other Australian academics, had spent time working with Elliott and his colleagues at the University of East Anglia. Grundy (1997) argues, though, that despite this link, the Australian movement developed its own practices and epistemology that distinguished it from the British movement.

Kemmis and his colleagues at Deakin University built on a strong movement among teachers for school-based curriculum development and for grassroots involvement in policy-making (Grundy and Kemmis, 1988) and developed a view of 'emancipatory action research' based in critical theory (Carr and Kemmis, 1986) that challenged other models of action research as conservative and positivistic. The 'Deakin group,' as well as other university academics across Australia (e.g., Tripp, 1990), articulated a methodology for educational action research in the form of an action research spiral (plan, act, observe and reflect) that was linked with an intent to promote greater equity and social justice in schools and the society (Kemmis and McTaggart, 1988). Although a number of projects of the critical emancipatory type are described in various publications (e.g., Kemmis and Grundy, 1997), there is some question as to the degree to which teachers throughout Australia who became engaged in action research took on the critical emancipatory purposes advocated by university academics (Grundy, 1982).

### The North American teacher research movement

In the 1980s a new teacher research movement emerged in North America that was not derivative of the British teacher-as-researcher movement or a re-emergence of the co-operative action research movement of the 1950s. Anderson, Herr and Nihlen (1994) identify a number of influences on the development of this new emphasis on educational action research: (1) the growing acceptance of qualitative and case study research in education which more closely resembles the narrative forms of inquiry used by practitioners to communicate their knowledge; (2) the highly visible work of a number of teachers of writing like Nancy Atwell (1987), who conducted case studies of the teaching of writing; (3) the increased emphasis on action research in university teacher education programmes (e.g., Cochran-Smith and Lytle, 1993); and (4) the reflective practitioner movement in teaching and teacher education that recognized and valued the practical knowledge of teachers (e.g., Zeichner, 1994).

Cochran-Smith and Lytle (1999) also discuss other influences on teacher research in North America such as the National Writing Project, Breadloaf School of English, the National Council of Teachers of English, the Prospect School in Bennington Vermont and the North Dakota Study Group (e.g., Carini, 1975; Goswami and Stillman, 1987; Mohr and Maclean, 1987; Perrone, 1989).

This emerging teacher research movement followed a number of years of 'interactive research and development' and other forms of collaborative research in education involving university academics and teachers (e.g., Oja and Smulyan, 1989). These collaborative projects involved teachers in some aspects of the research process but were not owned and controlled by teachers. Currently, although some teachers engage in action research in the context of university courses, projects and degree programmes (e.g., Freedman et al., 1999; Gitlin et al., 1992) many others have formed teacher research communities that, although they may involve collaboration with academics, are controlled by teachers (e.g., Gallas, 1998a).

### The tradition of self-study research

Although most of the action research conducted within all of the traditions discussed so far has involved elementary and secondary school staff in studying their practice, there has also been a growing tradition in which college and university faculty have conducted research on their own teaching within the academy. In the 1990s there has been a growing acceptance of action research as a method for self-study within colleges and universities, especially among teacher educators.

Recently there has been a tremendous growth in the publication of self-study research by teacher educators (e.g., Hamilton, 1998; Loughran and Russell, 1997; Russell and Korthagen, 1995) and calls for the academy to recognize the legitimacy of high-quality self-study research in tenure and promotion decisions (Adler, 1993). In 1992 a special interest group 'Self-Study of Teacher Education Practices' was formed in the American Educational Research Association and it has become one of the largest interest groups in the association.

The self-study research of college and university faculty has employed a variety of qualitative methodologies and has focused on a wide range of substantive issues. For example, some studies in this genre have employed narrative life history methods and describe the connections between teacher educators' life experiences and their current teaching practices (e.g., Cole and Knowles, 1995; Zeichner, 1995). Some self-study research has involved inquiries about the use of particular strategies (e.g., Grimmett, 1997; Richert, 1991) or of the implementation of particular educational philosophies in teacher education programmes (e.g., Ahlquist, 1991; Macgillivray, 1997). Many recent studies focus on the struggles of teacher educators with issues of race, class, and gender (e.g., Ahlquist, 1991; Cochran-Smith, 1995; Martin, 1995).

## DIMENSIONS OF VARIATION IN EDUCATIONAL ACTION RESEARCH

Currently, there is a wide variety of approaches to conceptualizing, organizing and supporting educational action research. The dimensions along which action research in education have varied include the purposes and motivations of those who engage in the research, the conceptions of the action research process and the form and content of action research studies, the ways in which the findings of the research are represented by researchers to others, the relation of action research to externally produced research, the sponsorship and organizational location of the research, the structures in place to support the research, and the assumptions about knowledge and teacher learning that are reflected in particular research programmes. The following framework, based largely on educational action research as it exists today in North America, is presented as a starting-point for better understanding the varieties of educational action research throughout the world.

Noffke (1997) has outlined three different motivations that have existed for teachers who have conducted research about their own practices. First, there is the motivation to understand better and improve one's own teaching and/or the contexts in which that teaching is embedded. Here the main interest is in how the research can contribute to the betterment of one's own individual situation as a teacher and life in a classroom, school and community. Secondly, there is the motivation to produce knowledge that will be useful to others, either in the same setting or other settings. Here action researchers are interested in sharing their research with others through seminars, conference presentations and publications. Finally, consistent with the 'democratic impulse' that was originally associated with the emergence of action research in the US in the 1940s (Foshay, 1994), there is the motivation to contribute to greater equity and social justice in schooling and society. Here there is an explicit agenda by educational action researchers to work for social change by working on issues of equity within the classroom and beyond (Anderson, Herr and Nihlen, 1994).

A second dimension along which educational action research has varied is in terms of the sponsorship of the research. Here there have been many different sponsors of research, including teachers themselves (e.g., Gallas, 1998a, 1998b), school districts and local professional development centres (e.g., Caro-Bruce and McReadie, 1995; Richert, 1999), teacher unions (e.g., The British Columbia Teachers' Federation), colleges and universities, school/university partnerships (e.g., Troen, Kamii and Boles, 1999), professional subject matter associations (e.g., The National Council of Teachers of English), and local and national governments. Among the colleges and universities that have been involved in sponsoring educational action research are those that offer specific courses on action research, support action research masters theses and doctoral dissertations, and those like the University of California-Davis, that support educational action research on a broad scale for teachers in area school districts (Wagner, 1995).

Educational action researchers have conducted their inquiries under a variety of contextual arrangements. For example, they have conducted research alone, as part of small collaborative groups composed of peers, or in school faculty groups that involve everyone in a particular school (Calhoun, 1993). Most of the time educators voluntarily participate in conducting research, but in the case of some schoolwide action research programmes, participation by all staff members is compulsory. When the research has been done in connection with a group, the groups have varied according to their size, the basis for their formation, and whether there is an external facilitator and/or university involvement. Some action research groups involve educators from the same team, department or school, and others mix together people from different schools. There have been a variety of external incentives provided to educators for participating in action research, including time away from their schools to think together with their colleagues, money, and university and professional advancement credits. Some action research programmes involve teachers for a year or less and others enable them to continue working on their research for several years.

Within the research programmes themselves, there is much variation in the form and content of action research studies. For example, Cochran-Smith and Lytle (1993) have described four different forms of systematic and intentional inquiry by teachers in North America: (1) journals which provide analyses of classroom life over time; (2) oral inquiries which consist of teachers' oral examinations of their practice in a group setting; (3) studies which represent teachers' explorations of their work using data based on observations, interviews and document analysis; and (4) essays which represent extended interpretations and analyses of various aspects of schooling. Cochran-Smith and Lytle (1993) argue that this broad view of practitioner inquiry in education accounts for some of the ways that educators inquire about their practice that do not fit with university models for doing research or with standard conceptions of action research.

As was indicated by the three brief vignettes at the beginning of this chapter, some educational action research involves the investigation of specific research questions and follows some variation of the well-known action research spiral: plan, act, observe and reflect (e.g., Elliott, 1991; Kemmis and McTaggart, 1988; McNiff, 1997). This is what Cochran-Smith and Lytle (1993) refer to as 'studies.' Other educational action research is more holistic and focuses simultaneously on a variety of questions (e.g., Gallas, 1998b).

Educational action researchers have investigated a variety of questions and issues in their inquiries. The following framework generated from an analysis of action research studies in the Madison, Wisconsin school district, is illustrative of the nature and scope of the questions that are addressed in educational action research studies (Zeichner, 1999a). This framework shows that the action research of educational practitioners include studies that focus within the educators' immediate domain of the classroom, beyond the classroom but within the school, and on issues that extend beyond the school. In the Madison school district's classroom action research programme over 400 studies have been done by educators since 1990. These studies have investigated a variety of questions and issues designed to:

1. Improve practice - e.g., How can I hold better discussions in my classroom and have a more learner-centred class?

2. Better understand a particular aspect of practice - e.g., Do I conduct my classes in a manner where students feel free to express different

opinions and even to disagree with me? How does my school's behaviour management system affect students from different ethnic groups?

3. Better understand one's practice in general - e.g., What is going on in my third period biology class?

4. Promote greater equity - e.g., How can I help the girls in my mathematics class feel more confident about their abilities in maths and to participate more in classroom activities?

5. Influence the social conditions of practice - e.g., How can I get the school district to reallocate funding to support teacher-initiated professional development work?

In addition to the different kinds of questions and issues investigated by educational action researchers, their studies also vary in the ways that they relate to externally generated knowledge, including academic educational research and studies done by other practitioners. Troen, Kamii and Boles (1997) describe three patterns that emerged when they examined teachers' research studies in their Brookline, Massachusetts teacher inquiry community. Some teachers used concepts, questions and ideas from external research as the starting-point for their research. An example here would be a teacher who studies the ways in which multiple intelligence theory helps explain student learning within her classroom. Others consulted external research later on in the research process, but did not do so at the onset of the research. Finally, some researchers deliberately did not consult external research because they felt that it would not be helpful to do so.

Educational action research programmes also differ in terms of the structural conditions that are set up to support the work of researchers. These differences include the rituals and routines that are established in action research groups (e.g., what group facilitators do to help researchers think more deeply about their practice), the resources that are provided to researchers (e.g., materials to read, literature searches, publication support), the opportunities that are provided for researchers to interact with others about their work (e.g., local action research conferences), and the ways in which researchers are encouraged, supported or required to represent their research to others (e.g., as papers, on videos, through conference presentations).

Finally, one of the most significant dimensions along which educational action research varies is in terms of the philosophical orientations towards knowledge, teachers and their learning that are embedded in the structures, human interactions and organization of action research programmes. Some action research efforts, despite a rhetoric of teacher empowerment, replicate the hierarchical patterns of authority and dim view of teachers' capabilities that is characteristic of dominant forms of teacher professional development, while others display a deep respect for teachers and their knowledge and seek to break down authority patterns which limit teacher autonomy and control (Zeichner, 1999a).

# EDUCATIONAL ACTION RESEARCH
# AS PROFESSIONAL DEVELOPMENT

Many educators who have engaged in action research have done so for reasons of professional development rather than out of a desire to publish or in other ways disseminate their findings to others. Over the years, many claims have been made about the benefits of teachers engaging in research about their own practices. For example, it has been asserted that doing self-study research helps teachers to become more flexible and open to new ideas (Oja and Smulyan, 1989), makes them more proactive in relation to external authority (Holly, 1990), boosts teachers' self-esteem and confidence levels (Dadds, 1995), narrows the gap between teachers' aspirations and realizations (Elliott, 1980), helps develop an attitude and skills of self-analysis which are applied to other situations (Day, 1984), changes patterns of interaction among teachers to more collegial interactions (Selener, 1997), alters teacher talk about students from a focus on student problems to an emphasis on student resources and accomplishments, and leads to more learner-centred classrooms (Cochran-Smith and Lytle, 1992).

Despite the growing testimony in the literature about the positive outcomes associated with teachers doing action research, there are a number of problems with drawing conclusions from these statements alone about the value of action research as a professional development activity. First, many of the references in the literature to the value of action research are anecdotal in nature and are not the result of systematic and intentional explorations of educators' research experiences. Secondly, even if we accept the accuracy of the claims that have been made about the value of action research, we are often provided with little or no information about the specific characteristics of the research experience and/or research context that would enable us to explain the particular conditions responsible for the positive impact. Given the tremendous variety in the conceptionalizations and arrangements for organizing and supporting educational action research described above, it is important to begin to identify the particular conditions of the action research experience that are associated with the kind of positive outcomes for teachers and their students that are so frequently cited in the literature.

There have been relatively few cases where the professional development process associated with educational action research has been systematically studied. In the few cases that do exist (Allen and Calhoun, 1998; Burgess-Macey and Rose, 1997; Calhoun and Allen, 1996; Dadds, 1995; Gallas, 1998a; Joyce et al., 1996; Richert, 1996, 1999; Troen, Kamii and Boles, 1997, 1999; Zeichner, Caro-Bruce and Marion, 1998), researchers, often in collaboration with those doing the action research, collected data over time to examine the conditions under which the action research was organized and supported, and its impact on teachers, pupils and schools. In addition to analyses by others of teachers' action research experiences, some work has been done by Kemmler-Ernst in examining a wide variety of cases of teachers' self-reports of the learning that occurs while doing action research. Drawing on the published personal narratives of teacher researchers and their contributions to electronic mailing lists, Kemmler-Ernst (1998) discusses the ways in which action research may contribute to changes in teachers' thinking, practice and collegial relationships by examining the reports of teachers who participated in research through graduate university classes or organized teacher collaboratives and networks.

In an analysis of both systematic studies of the nature and impact of educational action research and Kemmler-Ernst's investigation of teachers' self-reports, Zeichner (1999a) concluded that under certain conditions, action research seems to promote particular kinds of teacher and student learning that teachers find very valuable and transformative. Specifically, there seems to be evidence that under particular conditions, the experience of engaging in self-study research helps teachers to become more self-confident about their ability to promote student learning, to become more proactive in dealing with difficult issues that arise in their teaching, and to acquire habits and skills of inquiry that they use beyond the research experience. Zeichner (1999a) also cites evidence of links between conducting action research under these conditions and a movement towards more learner-centred instruction and improvements in student learning.

The particular conditions that appear to be related to these positive outcomes for teachers and students are:

1. The creation of a culture of inquiry that respects the voices of teachers and the knowledge that they bring to the research experience. This does not mean a romantization of teachers' voices and an uncritical acceptance of everything that emerges from their research because it is asserted by a teacher. It does mean, though, that teacher knowledge is taken as seriously as other forms of knowledge and is evaluated according to both moral and educational criteria (Zeichner and Noffke, in press). A balance is achieved between honouring teachers' voices and expertise and asking them to critique what they know (Gallas, 1998b).

2. There is an investment in the intellectual capital of teachers which results in teachers having control over most aspects of the research process, including whether to participate or not, the research focus and the methods of data collection and analysis.

3. There is intellectual challenge and stimulation in the work and teachers are helped to think more deeply about their practice rather than given 'solutions' for their problems.

4. The research takes place over a substantial period of time (at least a year) in a safe and supportive environment. Predictable rituals and routines are established in groups of teacher researchers that help build community.

5. Participation in the research is voluntary.

There are other aspects of the action research process (e.g., whether or not teachers are required to write a research report at the end of the experience) where the connection to the kind of teacher and student learning described above is less clear. At this point in time, given the limited study of educational action research as professional development, the conditions identified above represent only a place from which to begin more in-depth investigations.

## EDUCATIONAL ACTION RESEARCH AS KNOWLEDGE PRODUCTION

Although most teachers who have done action research have been uninterested in sharing their inquiries with others beyond their local research communities, an increasing number of teachers have published their work and/or presented it at local, regional and national conferences. Also, as academics have become involved in doing self-study research, increased acceptance of this work has developed as part of the tenure and promotion process. Generally, there has been increased citation of action research studies in educational research publications and an explosion of courses in colleges and universities that deal with action research as a legitimate form of educational inquiry (see Cochran-Smith and Lytle, 1999; Zeichner and Noffke, in press). There has also been an increased presence of educational action research and writing about educational action research at academic professional conferences such as the annual meetings of the American Educational Research Association (Zeichner, 1999b).

This increased acceptance of action research as a legitimate form of inquiry that can potentially inform practitioners, policy-makers, researchers and teacher educators has not been without controversy. For example, Cochran-Smith and Lytle (1999) discuss two critiques of educational action research that question its existence as a legitimate form of educational inquiry and the value of the knowledge that it produces. Huberman (1996) has questioned the claim that action research is a distinctive form of educational inquiry that provides unique insights into schooling and has argued that it needs to be judged according to standards applied to traditional academic interpretative inquiry. Fenstermacher (1994) has questioned the idea that teachers can generate knowledge valuable to others through their self-study research and also argues that action research needs to be governed by epistemological standards that are applied to academic research. On the other hand, many have argued that educational action research is a distinctive form of educational inquiry that should be judged by its own set of standards (e.g., Anderson, Herr and Nihlen, 1994). A literature has emerged in recent years that examines various aspects of the question of whether educational action research is a legitimate form of educational inquiry and if so, by which standards it should be judged (see Anderson and Herr, 1999; Whitehead, 1989;

Zeichner and Noffke, in press). In many ways, these issues are just beginning to be debated and discussed in both academic and practitioner research communities.

# CONCLUSION

Most of the literature discussed in this chapter has been written in English and was generated by academics in the USA, Canada, the UK and Australia. The discussion of educational action research traditions, dimensions of variation in conceptualizations and patterns for organizing action research programmes, and of literature on action research as professional development and knowledge production, has not included the growing literature on educational action research in other languages and in other parts of the world (e.g., Barabtarlo y Zedansky and Poschner, 1998; Hollingsworth, 1997; McTaggart, 1997; Walker, 1995). This chapter also has not included more than a few voices of teachers about the methodology of educational action research. Despite recent progress in the accessibility of educational action research studies, it still remains very difficult to access this work beyond, and even at the local level, and teachers have not been active participants in the public dialogue about action research as a research methodology in education. Ways must be found to make educational action research studies more easily available to others and to involve teachers actively in the important discussions about the role of action research in educational research, policy-making and teacher education. The conceptual frameworks and analyses presented in this chapter need to be examined and critiqued from a broader perspective that takes into account the work on action research that has been done in other parts of the world not included within the scope of this review.

Some of the most ambitious work in educational action research today is being done in developing countries in Latin America and Africa. For example, in Namibia, action research has been used since independence in 1990 as a major strategy in a comprehensive educational reform programme that has sought to transform teaching and teacher education from autocratic to more learner-centred fortes (Dahlstrom, Swarts and Zeichner, 1999). Throughout Namibia, student teachers, teachers and teacher educators have been conducting action research that has focused on such things as increasing the participation of learners in the classroom, promoting greater understanding of content through more interactive teaching approaches, etc.

As action research has come to be used in education within developing countries, concern has arisen about the colonialist implications in the importation of action research models developed in the USA, the UK and Australia to the developing world, and arguments have been made about the importance of adapting external models and developing indigenous forms of educational action research that take into account the particular cultures and traditions in the contexts in which it is used (Zeichner and

Dahlstrom, 1999). Although educational action research can potentially be a liberating and emancipatory force, there is also the danger that it can slip into becoming another form of oppression in the developing world.

## NOTE

1. The term 'teacher' will be used to refer to secondary educators (e.g., classroom teachers, principals, counsellors) and the term 'academic' will be used to refer to faculty and staff in colleges and universities. The term 'educator' will be used to refer to both teachers and academics.

## REFERENCES

Adler, S. (1993) 'Teacher education: research or reflective practice,' *Teaching and Teacher Education*, 9 (20): 159–67.

Ahlquist, R. (1991) 'Position and imposition: power relations in a multicultural foundations class,' *Journal of Negro Education*, 60 (2): 158–69.

Allen, L. and Calhoun, E. (1998) 'Schoolwide action research: findings from six years of study,' *Kappan*, 79 (9): 706–10.

Anderson, G. and Herr, K. (1999) 'The new paradigm wars: is there room for rigorous practitioner knowledge in schools and universities?' *Educational Researcher*, 28 (5): 12–21.

Anderson, G., Herr, K. and Nihlen, A. (1994) *Studying Your Own School: an Educator's Guide to Qualitative Practitioner Research*. Thousand Oaks, CA: Corwin Press.

Atwell, N. (1987) *In the Middle: Writing, Reading, and Learning with Adolescents*. Portsmouth, NH: Boyton Cook/Heinemann.

Barabtarlo y Zedansky, A. and Poschner, T. (1998) 'Participatory action research in teacher education: a methodology for studying the everyday reality of teaching in Latin America,' in G. Anderson and M. Montero-Sieburth (eds), *Educational Qualitative Research in Latin America*. New York: Garland.

Burgess-Macey, C. and Rose, J. (1997) 'Breaking through the barriers: professional development, action research, and the early years,' *Educational Action Research*, 5 (1): 55–70.

Calhoun, E. (1993) 'Action research: three approaches,' *Educational Leadership*, 52 (2): 62–5.

Calhoun, E. and Allen, L. (1996) 'The action research network: action research on action research,' in B. Joyce and E. Calhoun (eds), *Learning Experiences in School Renewal: an Exploration of Five Successful Programs*. Eugene, OR: ERIC Center on Educational Management, University of Oregon. pp. 136–74.

Carini, P. (1975) *Observation and Description: an Alternative Methodology for the Investigation of Human Phenomena*. Grand Forks, ND: University of North Dakota Press.

Caro-Bruce, C. and McReadie, J. (1995) 'What happens when a school district supports action research?' in S. Noffke and R. Stevenson (eds), *Educational Action Research*. New York: Teachers College Press. pp. 154–64.

Carr, W. and Kemmis, S. (1986) *Becoming Critical: Education, Knowledge, and Action Research.* London: Falmer Press.

Coccari, D. (1998) 'We want to work with our friends,' in C. Caro-Bruce (ed.), *Assessment and Health and Wellness Classroom Action Research.* Madison, WI: Madison Metropolitan School District.

Cochran-Smith, M. (1995) 'Uncertain allies: understanding the boundaries of race and teaching,' *Harvard Educational Review*, 65 (41): 541–70.

Cochran-Smith, M. and Lytle, S. (1992) 'Communities for teacher research: fringe or forefront, '*American Journal of Education*, 100 (3): 298–324.

Cochran-Smith, M. and Lytle, S. (1993) *Inside-Outside: Teacher Research and Knowledge.* New York: Teachers College Press.

Cochran-Smith, M. and Lytle, S. (1999) 'The teacher research movement: a decade later,' *Educational Researcher*, 28 (7): 15–25.

Cole, A. and Knowles, G. (1995) 'Methods and issues in a life history approach to self-study,' in T. Russell and F. Korthagen (eds), *Teachers Who Teach Teachers.* London: Falmer Press. pp. 130–51.

Corey, S. (1949) 'Action research, fundamental research, and educational practices,' *Teachers College Record*, 50: 509–14.

Corey, S. (1953) *Action Research to Improve School Practices.* New York: Teachers College Press.

Cunningham, R. and Miel, A. (1947) 'Frontiers of educational research in elementary school curriculum development,' *Journal of Educational Research*, 40 (5): 365–72.

Dadds, M. (1995) *Passionate Inquiry and School Development.* London: Falmer Press.

Dahlstrom, L., Swarts, P. and Zeichner, K. (1999) 'Reconstructive education and the road to social justice: the case of post-colonial teacher education in Namibia,' *International Journal of Leadership in Education*, 2(3): 149–64.

Day, C. (1984) 'Professional learning and researcher intervention: an action research perspective,' in R. Halkes and J. Olson (eds), *Teacher Thinking.* Lisse: Swets & Zwertlinger.

Elliott, J. (1976/77) 'Developing hypotheses about classrooms from teachers' practical constructs: an account of the Ford teaching project,' *Interchange,* 7(2): 2–22.

Elliott, J. (1980) 'Implications of classroom research for professional development,' in E. Hoyle and J. Megarry (eds), *Professional Development of Teachers.* London: Kogan Page.

Elliott, J. (1991) *Action Research for Educational Change.* Milton Keynes: Open University Press.

Elliott, J. (1997) 'School-based curriculum development and action research in the UK,' in S. Hollingsworth (ed.), *International Action Research: a Casebook for Educational Reform.* London: Falmer Press. pp. 17–28.

Elliott, J. and Ebutt, D. (eds) (1986) *Case Studies in Teaching for Understanding.* Cambridge: Cambridge Institute of Education.

Fenstermacher, G. (1994) 'The knower and the known: the nature of knowledge in research on teaching,' in L. Darling-Hammond (ed.), *Review of Research in Education* (vol. 20). Washington, DC: American Educational Research Association. pp. 3–56.

Foshay, A. W. (1994) 'Action research: an early history in the US.' *Journal of Curriculum and Supervision*, 9: 317–25.

Foshay, A. W., Wann, K. D. and Associates (1954) *Children's Social Values: an Action Research Study.* New York: Teachers College Press.

Freedman, S., Simons, E., Kalnin, J., Casareno, A. and the M-class teams (1999) *Inside City Schools: Investigating Literacy in Multicultural Classrooms*. New York: Teachers College Press.

Gallas, K. (1998a) *Teacher Initiated Professional Development: the Lawrence School Teacher Study Groups*. Chicago, IL: The Spencer and MacArthur Foundations.

Gallas, K. (1998b) *Sometimes I Can Be Anything: Power, Gender, and Identity in a Primary Classroom*. New York: Teachers College Press.

Gitlin, A., Bringhurst, K., Burns, M., Cooley, V., Myers, B., Price, K., Russell, R. and Tiess, P. (1992) *Teachers' Voices for School Change*. New York: Teachers College Press.

Goswami, D. and Stillman, P. (eds) (1987) *Reclaiming the Classroom: Teacher Research as an Agency for Change*. Portsmouth, NH: Boyton Cook/Heinemann.

Grimmett, P. (1997) 'Breaking the mold: transforming a didactic professor into a learner-focused teacher educator,' in T. Carson and D. Sumara (eds), *Action Research as a Living Practice*. New York: Peter Lang. pp. 121–36.

Grundy, S. (1982) 'Three modes of action research,' *Curriculum Perspectives*, 2(3): 23–34.

Grundy, S. (1997) 'Participatory action research in Australia: the first wave, 1976–1986,' in R. McTaggart (ed.), *Participatory Action Research: International Contexts and Consequences*. Albany, NY: State University of New York Press. pp. 125–49.

Grundy, S. and Kemmis, S. (1988) 'Educational action research in Australia: the state of the art,' in S. Kemmis and R. McTaggart (eds), *The Action Research Reader* (third edition). Geelong, Vic: Deakin University Press. pp. 321–35.

Hamilton, M. L. (ed.) (1998) *Reconceptualizing Teaching Practice: Self-study in Teacher Education*. London: Falmer Press.

Hodgkinson, H. (1957) 'Action research: a critique,' *Journal of Educational Sociology*, 31 (4): 137–53.

Hollingsworth, S. (ed.) (1997) *International Action Research: a Casebook for Educational Reform*. London: Falmer Press.

Holly, M. L. (April, 1990) 'Teachers' theorizing: research and professional growth.' Paper presented at the annual meeting of the American Educational Research Association. Boston. MA.

Huberman, M. (1996) 'Moving mainstream: taking a closer look at teacher research,' *Language Arts*, 73: 124–40.

Joyce, B., Calhoun, E., Carran, N., Simser, J., Rust, D. and Halliburton, C. (1996) 'The university town program: exploring governance structures,' in B. Joyce and E. Calhoun (eds), *Learning Experiences in School Renewal: an Exploration of Five Successful Programs*. Eugene, OR: ERIC Clearinghouse on Educational Management, University of Oregon. pp. 52–93.

Kemmis, S. and Grundy, S. (1997) 'Educational action research in Australia: organizations and practice,' in S. Hollingsworth (ed.), *International Action Research: a Casebook for Educational Reform*. London: Falmer Press. pp. 40–8.

Kemmis, S. and McTaggart, R. (1988) *The Action Research Planner* (third edition). Geelong, Vic: Deakin University Press.

Kemmler-Ernst, A. (April, 1998) 'Collaborative inquiry as a catalyst for change.' Unpublished paper, Harvard University Graduate School of Education.

Loughran, J. and Russell, T. (ed.) (1997) *Teaching about Teaching: Purpose, Passion, and Pedagogy in Teacher Education*. London: Falmer Press.

Macgillivray, L. (1997) 'Do what I say, not what I do: an instructor rethinks her own teaching and research,' *Curriculum Inquiry*. 27 (4): 469–88.

Martin, R. (ed.) (1995) *Practicing What We Preach: Confronting Diversity in Teacher Education.* Albany, NY: State University of New York Press.

McNiff, J. (1997) *Action Research: Principles and Practice.* London: Routledge.

McTaggart, R. (ed.) (1997) *Participatory Action Research: International Contexts and Consequences.* Albany, NY: State University of New York Press.

Mohr, M. and Maclean, M. (ed.) (1987) *Working Together: a Guide for Teacher Researchers.* Urbana, IL: National Council of Teachers of English.

Newman, J. (1998) *Tensions of Teaching.* New York: Teachers College Press.

Noffke, S. E. (1997) 'Professional, personal and political dimensions of action research,' in M. Apple (ed.), *Review of Research in Education,* 22: 305–43.

Oja, S. and Smulyan, L. (1989) *Collaborative Action Research: a Developmental Approach.* London: Falmer Press.

Olson, M. W. (1990) 'The teacher as researcher: a historical perspective,' in M. W. Olson (ed.), *Opening the Door to Classroom Research.* Newark, DE: International Reading Association. pp. 1–20.

Perrone, V. (1989) *Working Papers: Reflections on Teachers, Schools, and Communities.* New York: Teachers College Press.

Richert, A. (1991) 'Case methods in teacher education: using cases to teach reflection,' in B. R. Tabachnick and K. Zeichner (eds), *Issues and Practices in Inquiry-oriented Teacher Education.* London: Falmer Press. pp. 130–50.

Richert, A. (1996) 'Teacher research on school change: what teachers learn and why that matters,' in K. Kent (ed.), *Breaking New Ground: Teacher Action Research, a Wealth of New Learning.* Redwood City, CA: Bay Area IV Professional Development Consortium.

Richert, A. (April, 1999) 'The learning teacher for the changing school: teacher research as a methodology of change.' Paper presented at the annual meeting of the American Educational Research Association, Montreal.

Russell, T. and Korthagen, F. (ed.) (1995) *Teachers Who Teach Teachers: Reflections on Teacher Education.* London: Falmer Press.

Selener, D. (1997) *Participatory Action Research and Social Change.* Quito, Ecuador: Global Action Publications.

Shumsky, A. (1958) *The Action Research Way of Learning: an Approach to Inservice Education.* New York: Teachers College Press.

Stenhouse, L. (1968) 'The humanities curriculum project,' *Journal of Curriculum Studies.* 23(1): 26–33.

Stenhouse, L. (1976) *An Introduction to Curriculum Research and Development.* London: Heinemann.

Taba, H. and Noel, E. (1957) *Action Research: a Case Study.* Washington, DC: Association for Curriculum and Supervision.

Threatt, S., Buchanan, J., Morgan, B., Streib, L., Sugarman, J., Swenson, J., Teel, K. and Tomlinson, J. (1994) 'Teachers' voices in the conversation about teacher research,' in S. Hollingsworth and H. Sockett (eds), *Teacher Research and Educational Reform.* Chicago, IL: University of Chicago Press. pp. 223–33.

Tripp, D. (1990) 'Socially critical action research,' *Theory into Practice,* 29 (3): 158–66.

Troen, V., Kamii, M. and Boles, K. (April, 1997) 'From carriers of culture to agents of change: teacher-initiated professional development in the learning/teaching collaborative inquiry seminars.' Paper presented at the annual meeting of the American Educational Research Association, Chicago, IL.

Troen, V., Kamii, M. and Boles, K. (April, 1999) 'Transformative professional development: teacher research, inquiry, and the culture of schools.' Paper presented at the annual meeting of the American Educational Research Association, Montreal.

Wagner, J. (1995) 'Research universities, schools of education, and the schools: a case of implementing cooperative research and extension in education,' *Educational Policy*, 9(1): 24–53.

Walker, M. (1995) 'Context, critique, and change: doing action research in South Africa,' *Educational Action Research*, 3(1): 9–27.

Wallace, M. (1987) 'A historical review of action research: some implications for the education of teachers in their managerial role,' *Journal of Education for Teaching*, 13 (2): 97–115.

Whitehead, J. (1989) 'Creating a living educational theory from questions of the kind: how do I improve my practice?' *Cambridge Journal of Education*, 19 (1): 41–52.

Zeichner, K. (1994) 'Conceptions of reflective practice in teaching and teacher education,' in G. Harvard and P. Hodkinson (eds), *Action and Reflection in Teacher Education*. Norwood, NJ: Ablex.

Zeichner, K. (1995) 'Reflections of a teacher educator working for social change,' in T. Russell and F. Korthagen (eds), *Teachers Who Teach Teachers: Reflections on Teacher Education*. London: Falmer Press. pp. 11–24.

Zeichner, K. (1999a) *Action Research as Professional Development for K–12 Educators*. Washington, DC: US Department of Education.

Zeichner, K. (1999b) 'The new scholarship in teacher education,' *Educational Researcher* 28 (9): 4–15.

Zeichner, K., Caro-Bruce, C. and Marion, R. (1998) *The Nature and Impact of Action Research in One Urban School District*. Chicago, IL: Spencer & McArthur Foundations.

Zeichner, K. and Dahlstrom, L. (eds) (1999) *Democratic Teacher Education Reform: the Case of Namibia*. Boulder, CO: Westview Press.

Zeichner, K. and Noffke, S. (in press) 'Practitioner research,' in V. Richardson (ed.), *Handbook of Research on Teaching* (fourth edition). Washington, DC: American Educational Research Association.

# PART II

## *Understanding Action Research*

Ken Zeichner clearly explained, in his comprehensive analysis, that to understand the nature and significance of contemporary action research, we need to recognize and appreciate the variety of forms it can take in a school community. This section includes two articles and three exemplary projects. Each illustrates alternative ways of understanding how action research can be designed.

In the first article, a professor-student team at the University of Cincinnati describes its stimulating "journeys of discovery and renewal" in a nine-month seminar on action research. Meyer and Brydon-Miller co-taught the course. Hamilton, Kroeger, and Stewart, each a secondary teacher, were three of their graduate students doing their own action research projects.

Hamilton describes how she drew upon personal narratives from African American literature in doing action research with an 11th grade English class. Kroeger explains how he used the process of Photovoice (photographs and narratives) in collaborative action research with a team of middle-school teachers and its 12–14-year-old students. Stewart asked 17–18-year-old students to write introspective journals while they prepared required Senior Exit Projects in her action research. Since the seminar was new territory for both Meyer and Brydon-Miller, they did their own action research on it. Overall, the Cincinnati team's written reflections on its four projects help us understand how diverse action research can be.

In the second article, Emily Calhoun, a frequent contributor to the literature on educational action research, describes three types of action research that differ in purpose, emphasis, and results. After offering a brief overview of the benefits of action research, Calhoun writes a detailed analysis of the three types: individual teacher research, collaborative action research, and schoolwide action research. We have examples of individual teacher research in Ferguson-Patrick's writing project with 12 six-year-olds, Hamilton's use of narrative with an 11th grade class, and Stewart's use of journal writing with 12th graders. Collaborative action research is carried out by a research team and can focus on problems and changes in a single class or in several classes. An example is Kroeger's Photovoice project with middle school teachers and students. A whole faculty carries out schoolwide action research on issues of common interest.

I selected the three exemplary projects that are here in order to present additional examples of the multiple forms of educational action research. O'Neill uses the proactive model to track the effectiveness of Spalding instruction with a team of five primary teachers in a combination of individual teacher research and collaborative action research. Grant's project is also a sort of collaborative action research, but she demonstrates that action research can contribute to educational institutions external to school faculties, such as in her case a Colorado network of school business managers. Mitchell uses the responsive model as she fashions a school Web site while doing schoolwide action research.

These two articles and three exemplary projects offer multiple ways of understanding how action research can contribute to educational improvement.

# 3

# The Unexpected Journey

*Renewing Our Commitment to Students*
*Through Educational Action Research*

Helen Meyer, Bennyce Hamilton, Steve Kroeger,
Stephanie Stewart, and Mary Brydon-Miller

## INTRODUCTION

There are no roadmaps to guide the classroom teacher interested in conducting action research. That is not to say that there are not some excellent guidebooks (e.g. Kincheloe, 1995; McNiff et al, 1996; Zuber- Skerritt, 1996a; Mills, 2003; Stringer, 2004), and accounts by fellow travelers (Cochran-Smith & Lytle, 1993; Anderson et al, 1994; Noffke & Stevenson, 1995), but by its very nature action research is an exploration of new territory frequently with a defined starting point, but an unknown destination. We embark on the journey with questions, with concerns, with some still-developing ideas for the ways in which we might change our practice as teachers. We often take a wrong turn along the way, at times we feel completely lost and we're never sure exactly where the process will take us. However, as with the life of an explorer, the rewards can be great. Whether

SOURCE: "The Unexpected Journey: Renewing Our Commitment to Students Through Educational Action Research", by Helen Meyer, Bennyce Hamilton, Steve Kroeger, Stephanie Stewart, and Mary Brydon-Miller (2004) *Educational Action Research*, Volume 12, (4), 557–574. Taylor & Francis Ltd., http://www.tandf.co.uk/journals. Reprinted with permission of the publisher.

it's a new way of presenting an idea, a shift in our understanding of our students or a renewed commitment to our role as change agents, action research provides a means for teachers to rediscover what may unknowingly have become lost in the structure of schools and the tumult of the lives traveling within them.

The year-long seminar upon which the journey was based was established as a research induction experience, designed to mentor students engaged in a complete cycle of action research from the conceptualization of a research question through the preparation of a final publishable paper. This was the first year in which the seminar had been offered and the students in the course were drawn from either a newly established doctoral program in urban educational leadership or, as in the case of these student authors, from the existing program in curriculum and instruction.

In the initial quarter of the action research seminar students were introduced to the various theoretical frameworks that inform action research. Through readings and discussions, we focused on the non-positivistic frameworks, such as critical theories (Freire, 1970/1993; Kemmis, 2001; Giroux, 2003), post-colonial theories (Spivak, 1988; Pratt, 1991), feminist theories (Morawski, 2001; Maguire, 2001), and critical race theories (Ladson-Billings, 1999; Delgado, 2000).

As we discussed the different theoretical frameworks and the practice of action research, we also introduced the students to a selection of qualitative and quantitative research methods they could employ in their own studies. Steve, for example, became intrigued with Photovoice, a research strategy in which members of a community use photographs, and individual and collaborative interpretations of these images to generate a shared understanding of critical issues (Wang & Burris, 1994, 1997; Wang, 1999; McIntyre & Lykes, 2004). He used this as a research and learning tool for a group of middle-school students identified by their teachers as being at-risk. Before embarking on the Photovoice process, he and his teaching and research team engaged in a process of sharing life histories, and went on to discuss the cultural influences and values embedded within these experiences (Wallerstein, 1987).

In studying the impact of senior exit projects, Stephanie selected a range of qualitative methods typically used by teachers in classroom action research. In addition to keeping her own journal on her research, she asked the students to keep journals, write reflective essays and engage in class discussions about their projects. In addition, she conducted small group and individual interviews, and used an anonymous survey to gain a deeper understanding of how the students viewed these projects.

Bennyce's action research methods evolved as her journey hit various roadblocks, but all along she had the sense that developing a better understanding of her own experience might lead her to new insights into the lives of her students. In the end, Bennyce employed personal narrative as suggested by Black feminist scholars (Collins, 1991; hooks, 1994; Mullings, 1994) and critical race theorists (Ladson-Billings, 1999; Delgado, 2000) to explore stories of her experiences as a school child and as a teacher, using her own life stories and reflections as a window to understanding the values and cultural influences embedded in her classroom pedagogy.

As the following descriptions make clear, by drawing on different theoretical frameworks and different methods, each of these three student authors found that action research provided a new understanding of and commitment to the students in their own classrooms.

# STEVE'S CASE: PHOTOVOICE— TRANSFORMING TEACHING PRACTICE

My study took place in a middle school, grades 6–8, in a socio-economically diverse suburb of a large, midwestern city. The middle school, designed in line with the National Middle School Standards, incorporated a team approach. In this paper I describe the transforming role of my educational action research project on my team of middle school teachers' practice. In addition to the changes we saw occurring in our students, the research process itself was an empowering force for renewed hope and perseverance among team members.

The teachers on my team included Christine[1] in reading, Beth in mathematics, Cathy in science, Randy in social studies, Andrea in language arts, Cari, a student teacher, and me, a special educator. As a team, we brought diverse experiences and interests to the process, but we also shared a desire to improve our practice. Early in the 2002 school year, I asked my teaching team if they would consider collaborating in an educational action research project (Zuber-Skerritt, 1996b). Christine suggested that we use this opportunity to assist the students on our team who were failing all academic subjects, but did not qualify for special education services. As a team, we determined that this would be an excellent use of our time. We identified the students with the most significant risk factors; they complained of significant home problems, encountered extremely negative peer interactions or were socially isolated in school.

The action research project took place during and became part of our school day. Over the course of the project, we covered each other's duties and regularly negotiated extra time for short meetings with the students. We did this in such a way as to not interrupt academic time. We also met as a team outside of the school building once a month until the end of the school year.

As teachers we knew that when faced with a student who is failing we could revert to a dangerous assumption that says that the student does not want to do the work and does not care. Until the student wants to do something about the problem, the reasoning goes, teachers are powerless to help. No matter how much truth may be embedded in this thinking, it remains only a partial truth. We were concerned that when we had previously found ourselves in such situations we might have relayed this message to the students. Would the action research process help move us from that negative self-fulfilling prophecy?

As a first step, we decided to change what we had power to change, ourselves. According to Connelly and Clandinin (1988), through narrative we study humans' experience in the world and the construction and reconstruction of personal and social stories. Storytellers are characters in their own and others' stories. Life narratives provide a context for making meaning of school situations. By listening we enter into another person's thinking or perceiving making narrative inquiry a process of collaboration, involving mutual storytelling, and re-storying as the research proceeds. Our personal narratives and student Photovoice seemed like a perfect fit for our action research inquiry.

Therefore, as a team we investigated our own value system as a starting point. The decision to explore our biographies flowed from our belief that in order to understand the students on our team, we first needed an explicit understanding of our own values and cultural influences (Harry, 1999). We scheduled monthly after-school meetings outside the school building. Meetings usually lasted 2 hours and began with questions that we created ourselves. At the first meeting, with a tape recorder running, we asked ourselves, 'Why do I continue to teach?' and 'What are the core values that drive my practice?' Later in the year, after we began meeting with students during the school day, student narrative influenced our after school agenda. As the lead investigator, I helped set the agenda, scheduled meetings and transcribed all recordings. As a team member, I was also a full participant in all discussions.

From the moment of our first meeting, something good was happening to us. In spite of our schedules, we had carved out time to reflect on our practice and our students. While the simple act of reflection does not guarantee improved practice, we agreed it was the place to begin. As we rediscoverd our own cultural values, we began to change the ways we understood our students. As we learned about our students, we questioned ourselves about our school experiences and how they led us into teaching.

Randy recalled this classroom experience, 'I had an instructor who quickly realized I was bored to tears and he set up an independent study for me. I loved it and learned so much. He was a teacher who saw a need and responded to it in a way that just fit.' Andrea described it this way:

I was the kid who just sat in the classroom and wanted to disappear. I hated school, could not stand it, except for language arts classes. My teachers [language arts] were so different from the adults in my life. They were so creative, they took risks, and nothing embarrassed them.

Experiences of poor teaching were also significant. 'Mostly they assumed that I would never go anywhere,' Cathy explained. 'I remember in junior high, sitting on the half of the class with those that were going nowhere in their [the teachers'] opinion. Clearly, nobody knew me. They made this judgment based on my background. Because of that I wanted to do something in spite of them.' I described my own experiences of rejection: 'I was rejected by a peer group that I wanted to be a part of. The rejection seemed irrational and yet it had such a negative impact on me as a student.'

Our growing understanding of one another helped us to see the significance of our students' experience when we entered into dialogue with them. We could see commonalities and connections with our students that would otherwise have remained hidden. As we recalled our experiences as students—the times of recognition, alienation and isolation—we began to see our struggling students in a new light and developed an empathy leading to advocacy for our students.

At the same time that we were discussing our life narratives, the students engaged in the process of Photovoice. The photographs provided a forum for them to construct their narratives. Wang (1999) described Photovoice development as a three-stage process: selecting, contextualizing and codifying. In the first stage, selecting, participants choose the photographs they want to share from all the pictures they have taken. The second stage uses the photographs in a process of contextualizing through storytelling. For example, one student discussed a photograph of his dog. He talked about how the animal changed by gradually becoming calmer as it grew older. During codifying, the third stage, participants in a group process create shared meanings for the images. So, when pictures and discussion of pets occurred week after week, it was important to look for the meaning the pets represented.

As I listened to the students, both in Photovoice sessions and after as I transcribed the audiotapes, it became clear that the primary concerns of our students had little to do with our content areas or to our own sense of priorities. During one Photovoice session, I had to step out twice, but the tape recorder kept rolling. During the transcribing I could hear the knock on the door and me stepping out. Back in the room, students shifted the discussion to their pets' pictures. They told stories of the various antics the animals performed. I re-entered the room and the conversation returned to more school-focused discussions. Another knock, I stepped out, the students immediately returned to the discussion of their animals. On other occasions, students had used meeting times to introduce their pets. They explained their pets' personalities and habits to one another. Initially, as teachers, we viewed this talk of a non-school-related topic as a distraction.

However, over time the discussion of pets led to new meanings as the students began to discuss trust, trusting the humans in their lives, humans in general and the process of building community in our culture.

After hearing students describe their photographs, Beth reported, 'I really liked getting a better picture from the students, to know where they are coming from, to know more of the whole person. It is eye opening. It reminds you to be very accepting and understanding of where that person is coming from.' Connection to our own vulnerabilities was a key theme in our discussions. As Randy so eloquently put it, 'I think that our vulnerability is related to how we relate to certain children on the team who have those same vulnerability issues. I want to do something. How can I get involved outside of stopping people from running him into his locker, taking his books, and throwing them all over the room?' Understanding ourselves was part of understanding our students and became increasingly important to us.

After we finished the research, Beth wrote a note saying:

> This was a powerful study that made us stronger educators. Through our reflections and listening to the children's narratives and voices, we explored new and different approaches to take with each individual child. Without listening to their stories, we would never have thought of or considered these new strategies. Learning in the classroom became true differentiation. As a teacher, I felt empowered to know the children on such a different level.

Noddings (1999) contends that children need more than a caring decision, children need the continuing attention of adults who listen, invite, guide and support them. Caring favors a differentiated curriculum because, when teachers work closely with students, teachers will be moved by their clearly different needs. One of the greatest gains of our research was not the change we were making in our classrooms or even the gradual improvement of scores, but the deepening of our bonds with students who were at risk.

In our team, there was agreement that the project was worth our time and we began to make plans to use Photovoice the following year. We continued to make connections with students, and think of creative ways to tap student interest and motivation. Understanding the settings and cultural values of the students added a rich layer of insight in daily lesson planning.

Teachers can reach a point where they feel they have done everything they know to help a student. Regardless of behaviors, such as apathy or disruption, when students are not doing well, teachers must do what they can to help. This educational action research study allowed us to deepen our commitments to and become advocates of these students.

## STEPHANIE'S CASE: EVALUATING THE SENIOR EXIT PROJECT

Perhaps it was fate. There I was, a high school English teacher struggling to spark the interest of 17–18-year-olds held captive in my classroom several times a day. I also happened to be a doctoral student in Curriculum and Instruction enrolled in an action research course. I had very little idea what action research was, but when I learned that I must find a researchable topic of interest and value to me, the choice was easy. It sat right in front of me everyday.

I was teaching at a predominantly White, middle class suburban high school with about 1400 students located 20 miles east of the city. Few of my seniors would be listed as underprivileged and, other than a few notable exceptions, most were typical 12th graders, poised on the brink of the rest of their lives, possessing more potential than anything else. Sadly, as I saw it, these students had fallen victim to a common malady that results in glazed eyes, lethargy and semi-consciousness.

I'm talking about 'Senioritis,' all too familiar to high school teachers. Senioritis is not just an inconvenience; it's a condition that has ramifications beyond high school (Education Trust, 1999). Three years prior to this action research project, a colleague and I had developed what we hoped would re-invigorate our seniors' interest, the Senior Exit Project (SEP). The SEP, a year-long project, had four major components: research paper, portfolio, original product and presentation. It was a project-based learning experience based on the assumption that if students were afforded the right circumstances, all of them could become enthusiastic about learning.

When I began my action research project I had no real concept of how to go about research, but I knew what I wanted to find out by doing it. It takes courage to inquire into one's professional practice; you may discover what you are not comfortable knowing. Nonetheless, I commenced by looking at the goals of action research, one of which was improving my practice. In order to improve my practice around the senior research project I wanted to learn about its effects. I knew that my research was grounded in the assumption that all students can achieve success (albeit different for every student) and that I needed to listen to as many voices of senior students as possible.

My research question evolved into three ideas I needed to understand from my students' point of view: Is the senior project (1) challenging, (2) meaningful, and (3) valuable for all students? I had never conducted a research project before, but based on my new-found knowledge gained in the action research course, it seemed like a qualitative study using a variety of methods was the best plan. I began my data gathering with a research journal almost immediately and later added student journals and reflections, class discussions, small and large group interviews, and finally an anonymous student survey. With an overall research goal, research questions and research methods in hand, I began the process of getting to know my senior students' values about learning and my students, as people, in a new way.

This is what some of my students had to say about learning and the SEP, and this is who a few of my students are. The results of my research showed that the SEP was a challenging project, but the challenge was different for each student. For the general 12th grade English students, including special education students, it was a great challenge. It was a year filled with many firsts for these students—a first time conducting independent and personal research, and a first time documenting their learning. It was their first experience with a formal presentation, and many said that they had to read and write more this year than in all other high school years combined. For example Ben,[2] a low-achieving student, had somehow managed to get to his senior year without ever writing a research paper and he had not the slightest idea what a bibliography was. It was exciting for me to watch his satisfaction when it all came together. He handed it in accompanied with a high-five and an 'I did it!' His presentation was very well done, since talking came more easily than writing. However, presenting new material that he had uncovered was a different kind of talking and he seemed to enjoy it.

For the advanced students, the challenge varied as well. For example, Lindsay had numerous starts and stops in selecting a topic, finally settling on researching the emotional drawbacks to being a nurse in the delivery room. In order to do this she needed to gain permission to shadow a nurse in the hospital. She sought and received permission to videotape a delivery, although she was only allowed to video the staff, and then designed a video- documentary for her final presentation. Lindsay faced many institutional and technical challenges as she prepared a comprehensive project. Setting their sights high, these high-achieving students faced many challenges rarely arising in classrooms, requiring persistence and problem solving typically not taught in high school.

Did the students find SEP to be a meaningful experience? This proved to be highly dependent on the topic selected and their reasons for making this choice. Students who chose topics based on a current or passing interest later regretted it. For example, Roger selected 'The History of Muscle Cars' as his topic and at the end he commented, 'I learned a bunch of stuff and had some fun, but I wish I could go back and choose something more serious.' Another regrettable tactic was the choice of a topic about which the student already knew a good deal, looking for an easy way out. Burt insisted on doing Coaching Techniques in Baseball, which in his final word 'was dumb, I just picked it 'cause it was easy, but when my friends were learning new stuff related to their topics I regretted it.' Although the topic choices seem less than significant, the students'reflections on their own learning was meaningful.

Students who chose topics of interest, subjects that were true passions, had experiences that were markedly more positive. Rachel selected astronomy because it truly interested her. She had a marvelous experience, incorporating both myth and science into her research. The most meaningful experiences though were with students who chose topics that related to the future, either college or career plans, or ones that provided them with a new look at what the future could be like if the proper investment was made now. As one student put it, future seniors should 'pick something that goes with your future and have fun with it.' Kevin provided a particularly insightful example of this.

Kevin whose high school career had been troubled and who many teachers thought would never graduate, did his SEP on Police Officers because, as he said in the beginning, 'I want to find out why cops are out to get kids in trouble.' As he progressed through his project, he grew to know himself and understand his future potential as his final journal reflection demonstrates:

> Now that I have finished my research paper, my binder and my original product, I realize that I have learned more from this project than any other report or project I have ever had. Being

a teenager with a cocky attitude and a bad reputation like myself I always figured that me and a police officer would butt heads. Without having to do this SEP I probably never would have spoken to a cop if I didn't have to. Now, I know I want to be one and I know the steps I have to take to do that. I'm already enrolled and ready to go in the fall. Someday maybe I'll get to talk to some cocky senior and set him straight.

Finally, in terms of value, student remarks and survey comments indicated the students felt extremely proud of their work and/or felt that it would benefit them next year in college or technical school. Some reported that the SEP was valuable because it taught them not to procrastinate or, as one student stated on the survey, 'this project may seem demanding, pointless, and time consuming, until you're done. But it is worth the lessons you learn from it.' Another student wrote, 'I feel that the SEP was very valuable to me.

I know I complained a lot, but that is mainly because I complain if I have to do any work.' Others said it was important because it made them feel special when younger students, parents or staff asked about the project. They liked feeling smart enough to pull something like this together. 'Now that I have about completed the entire thing it feels good to look back at my creation of work from my senior year.'

The challenge, meaning and value of SEP came together in very personal ways. This was demonstrated in Linda's project based on her experience of losing a friend in a drunk driving accident. She chose to use her sad experience in a positive way. After researching several aspects of the problem, she gave an inspiring presentation to the junior and senior classes before prom. Enlisting the aid of volunteers, she called the names of 22 victims (she learned through her research that everyday 22 teenagers are killed due to drinking and driving). With the lights dimmed in the auditorium, the volunteers, wearing banners with names of victims, silently walked and stood on the stage while the screen behind them flashed actual photos of victims. It was an emotional experience for all, one that deeply touched other students who learned from her personal experience.

Despite these transformative experiences and the positive remarks at the conclusion of the project, during this action research project I sometimes became discouraged when my efforts seemed only to produce negative responses from students. The process was difficult for my students and myself; however, one of the unexpected outcomes of this cure for Senioritis was what I learned about my students. The students accepted not only the challenges of the SEP, but also let me in so that I could learn about them. They took risks in topic selections and presentations that exposed their interests, passions, hopes and fears. As a teacher, researching with my students, I gained new insight into those sleepy seniors waiting to get out of the door that left me hopeful about the students we are sending forth. This action research helped me to learn not only about my teaching and the effectiveness of the senior exit project, but to also learn about the challenges that face today's students, the ideas and passions they hold, and the meaning and the value they place in the future.

## BENNYCE'S CASE: RACE IS SO PERSONAL

I am an African American, female and a teacher, and because of this I bring into the classroom experiences accompanying each of these. I never really paid much attention to how each of these parts intermingle and play out in the classroom until I began this reflection. Each of these separate parts makes up the whole me, and each of these parts determines what I bring. I cannot change them nor would I want to, but I choose to be conscious of them, because they determine what I bring into the classroom.

Teaching students of color presents a unique dynamic in the classroom. A number of researchers have offered explanations for this (see, for example, Ladson-Billings, 1999; Nieto, 1999; Smitherman, 2000). Moreover, teachers play a critical role in how children see schooling—whether it's viewed as a place of revolution and growth, or a place that tends to diminish the fire from within.

As an African American teacher of predominantly African American students, I have a firm belief that my lived experiences are the greatest research tool that I possess for understanding what and how I choose to teach the children in my classes. Unlike the posture advocated by traditional research—unbiased and objective—'lived-experiences' requires one to view oneself as 'situated in the action of research' (Rapp, 1982).

According to hooks (1989), subjective experience and theory from personal experience are important because each acknowledges the need to examine self from a critical standpoint.

This narrative presents a critical look at how a few of my lived experiences have shaped my identity as a classroom teacher. Black feminist thought frames this research and requires me to look at past events from my standpoint as a Black woman. By doing so, a consciousness develops that promotes change (Collins, 1991; hooks, 1994). Mullings (1994) holds that women of color engender a 'unique consciousness' informed by the triple consciousness of being at the forefront of race, class and gender conflict.

I chose this project for a number of reasons. First, there was a great deal of soul-searching and questioning about my own pedagogical practices.

For years I questioned why I chose to teach and what I could do to help my students learn. In this context of continual questioning, I became more cognizant of my motives and intent in the classroom. Teachers' views are often overlooked in discussions about education. To avoid being marginalized, I must find my voice as an African American female teacher. I must seek answers. I must speak out.

Narration allows me to take you on this journey to finding my voice. We start back in my own childhood and connect it to my present. Ladson-Billings (1994) and hooks (1994) used narration in research as a way to understand the present as connected to our past experiences. They also discuss 'connectedness,' as described by the strong kinship bonds that exist in Black communities and the tendency of non-kin to take on social roles. Studies have shown that extensive kin networks existing in Black communities contribute significantly both to the material and non-material well-being of children (Hill, 1972; Stack, 1974). Collins (1991) extended the concept to individuals occupying institutional roles, like teachers. In developing a Black feminist epistemology, she explored the influence of non- kin women on the social and intellectual development of Black children. She concluded that this influence is embodied in the phenomenon called 'community othermothers' and Black women teachers share in this role.

Two Black female teachers had a profound impact on my social and intellectual development. They were Mrs Backs[3] and Mrs Ellis—my first and seventh grade teachers, respectively. Mrs Backs taught me how to read and encouraged me to do so as often as possible. She introduced me to the school library. I often checked out four or five library books at a time. It was my belief that the more I read the more I would learn, and that the more I learned, the smarter I would become. Mrs Backs continually praised me for my diligence.

By the time I got to seventh grade, desegregation was a way of life in Kentucky, but Mrs Ellis continued to foster my intellect. She was my last African American teacher prior to college. In her class I completed more writing assignments than reading. Mrs Ellis encouraged me to write about my experiences—those things that were important to me. I wrote about my dreams, my family, my friends and my desires. I wrote short stories, poetry and plays. In her classroom I discovered that I could write my ticket to freedom—freedom that came from knowing that I could achieve anything I set out to accomplish.

Mrs Backs instilled in me a love of reading and the power of knowledge through reading. Mrs Ellis set my knowledge free as she empowered me to write in my own voice. She instilled in me a critical consciousness that was inspirational and empowering. Their encouragement, inspiration and praise set a standard for me to reach that connected me to them and to the world in my future.

When I entered the fourth grade, everything changed. During the second week of school the teacher passed out a letter for my parents indicating that I could attend Pleasant Ridge, a predominantly White school in a neighboring community. Bus transportation would be provided from Fallsway, the school I was currently attending. My mother and the mother of my best friend decided that this would be a 'good opportunity' for us. My best friend had two siblings so the four of us made the daily trek to catch the bus to 'the White school.'

At Pleasant Ridge, none of the teachers looked like me. There were only four other Black students in a school of about 350. The stories and books I read had no Black characters nor was any other minority represented. No pictures of Black people lined the room nor was any reference made that would lead me to believe that Blacks existed outside the classroom.

Pleasant Ridge was a place to learn and prepare for my future. It was also a place where physical and mental competition were encouraged. I remember feeling so alone (even though my best friend was there). Looking back, I also remember feeling like I was under a microscope. My every move was on display.

The connection that I felt to myself, my community and my own learning were gone. I was left to stoke the fire within. As I look at my role as a teacher now, I reflect on these different experiences with the White and Black teachers in my past, and I better understand how connectedness or lack thereof leads to issues of power and control.

Power and control are two factors that impact students and must be considered when teaching students of color. Janice Hale (1986) stated that students should view teachers and principals as significant adults in the community. Too often, however the relationship between students of color and teachers is not a relationship conducive to learning. It is a relationship of oppression, lack of respect and failure. Teachers' fear of losing classroom control often causes a destructive use of power and, for African American high school students, the need for power is immense. They are at an age where they recognize the fact that society views them negatively and that perception plays out in classrooms where they see themselves as powerless. Finding this delicate balance of significant adult authority, while acknowledging my students' place in society, was essential for me.

I now see Dillard's (1995) concept of 'authentication' as helping me to create this balance. Authentication is enacting confirmation and feedback from a place of authority. Lorde (1984) believes the notion of authentication for African American women comes from the African tradition of using and sharing power. This example from my teaching demonstrates how community, connection, power and authentication became part of my pedagogy.

In my third year of teaching, I was teaching eleventh grade, non- honors English and the majority of my students were African American. There were 15 in this particular class—one male and 14 females. Absenteeism was high and the students' attitudes about learning were not good. I had several incidents where students were disruptive in the classroom.

I found an article in the newspaper that discussed how Black students were failing in schools and listed the reasons why. I wanted my students to see what other Black people were saying about them. I copied the article for each of them thinking that perhaps this would get their attention. As I passed it out, one of my Black female students yelled, 'What is this (expletive)?' I explained to her that it was an article expressing the author's opinion, and that we would read and discuss it in class. As we read it, she continued to make comments about how it wasn't right and that it did not apply to her.

As we began to discuss it, I became overwhelmed with emotions. I told her that this was an article written by an African American man and that he was not the only one to feel that way. Finally, with tears streaming down my face, I asked her, 'Don't you get it? What you do in here is exactly what he is talking about. What he is saying is that many of you, both Black and White, don't get it. Either you don't come to school or if you do, you spend half your time giving your teachers grief because they are trying to teach you something that you don't know!' Other students voiced their opinions about being in school to learn and boasted about their low rate of absenteeism. We were a tearful mess. In the midst of our tears, my students were beginning to think critically about their lives.

Black feminist consciousness that promotes change involves engaging students to think critically. hooks (1994) insists that Black students, regardless of class, gender or social standing, must have the capacity to think critically about themselves and their lives. She concludes that engaged pedagogy between herself and her students is crucial to her development as a professional. In order for students to feel that school is revolutionary, they have to feel some responsibility for their learning. They have to experience some freedom, like I did as a schoolchild, to find and explore knowledge with personal meaning that connects them to their community.

Writing this narrative has been a struggle that reflects the need for this kind of work to be conducted. It is a difficult chore to be on the front lines of justice. Here, I have attempted to examine how my experiences as a student influence my practice as a teacher. I am an African American female, teacher and student. Each of these roles has some impact on my classroom pedagogical practice. I value my own experiences as a student and use them to teach my students who are oppressed.

To some, this may seem no more than self-reflection. I strongly disagree. My contention is that this piece is the revelation that I have been searching for since I began my teaching career. It is the foundation or springboard that was absent from my university classroom discussions of teaching. It is my personal epistemology and the creation of a new critical voice born from the experience of my own point of view.

## HELEN AND MARY'S CASE: SHARING THE STRUGGLES AND THE SUCCESS

This year-long action research sequence was also new territory for us. Just as our student co-authors found through their projects, we discovered that in researching our teaching we also learned about our own students and in compiling this manuscript we have re-engaged with them and continued the process. The passion they bring to their teaching activities and the concerns and interests they take in their students' lives are a model of what excellence in teaching looks like.

In reflecting on these descriptions from our students as they engaged in action research we are struck by the fact that such seemingly different paths all led to a common experience of forming deeper connections with their students as individual learners who bring distinct challenges and contributions to the classroom.

Critical race theorist Richard Delgado has described what he calls counter storytelling, the use of narratives to, on the one hand create 'bonds, represent cohesion, shared understandings, and meanings' among members of oppressed communities while simultaneously being able to 'shatter complacency and challenge the status quo' (2000, p. 61) by representing experience from the point of view of those silenced within the dominant discourse. In a similar vein, post-colonial theorist Gayatri Spivak (1988) has raised the issues of subalternity and representation calling upon academics to question this dominant discourse by actively engaging the experience of the oppressed.

Drawing on photographs, journals and personal narrative, our co-authors have provided their students with just such opportunities to reveal their own lives and experiences, and in doing so have allowed us to hear their unique voices. As Delgado suggests, this process shatters the complacency of both researcher and reader alike. No longer can we see the at-risk student as 'the student does not want to do the work and does not care.' Instead, as Steve's project shows us, these are students with important insights to share with us, students deserving of our support and commitment. Nor can we continue to be complicit in allowing students to disengage from education during their final year of high school when we can now see how transformative an experience like Stephanie's senior exit project can be. Finally, in reading Bennyce's experiences and those of her students we are called upon to take a more active role in challenging continuing educational inequalities that rob young poor and minority students of the opportunity to succeed.

Educational action research is a process of exploration—of ourselves as educators, of the lives and unique perspectives of our students, of the structures and practices of the educational system. The lesson we take from this shared journey then is a revitalization of our commitment to teaching, a deepened respect for the knowledge and skills of the students with whom we are privileged to work and a renewed dedication to working together to bring about positive change in our schools and communities.

*Correspondence*

Helen Meyer, College of Education, University of Cincinnati,
PO Box 210002, Cincinnati, OH 45221-0002, USA (helen.meyer@uc.edu).

## NOTES

1. The names of the students in this section are all pseudonyms; however, all teachers on the team worked collaboratively and are presented with their actual first names.

2. All student names in this section are pseudonyms.

3. All teacher and school names are pseudonyms.

# REFERENCES

Anderson, G., Herr, K. & Nihlen, A. (Eds) (1994) *Studying Your Own School: an educator's guide to qualitative practitioner research.* Thousand Oaks: Corwin Press.

Cochran-Smith, M. & Lytle, S. (Eds) (1993) *Inside/Outside: teacher research and knowledge.* New York: Teachers College Press.

Collins, P.H. (1991) *Black Feminist Thought: knowledge, consciousness, and the politics of empowerment.* Boston: Unwin Hyman.

Connelly, M. & Clandinin, D. J. (1988) *Teachers as Curriculum Planners: narratives of experience.* New York: Teachers College Press.

Delgado, R. (2000) Storytelling for Oppositionists and Other: a plea for narrative, in R. Delgado & J. Stefancic (Eds) *Critical Race Theory: the cutting edge.* Philadelphia: Temple University Press.

Dillard, C. B. (1995) Leading with Her Life: an African American feminist (re)interpretation of leadership for an urban high school principal, *Education Administration Quarterly*, 31, pp. 539–563.

Education Trust (1999) Ticket to Nowhere: the gap between leaving high school and entering college and high-performance jobs, *Thinking K–16,* 3, pp. 1–32.

Freire, P. (1970/1993) Pedagogy of the Oppressed. New York: Continuum.

Giroux, H. (2003) Critical Theory and Educational Practice, in A. Darder, M. Baltodano & R.D. Torres (Eds) *The Critical Pedagogy Reader.* New York: Routledge.

Hale, J. (1986) *Black Children: their roots, culture, and learning styles.* Baltimore: Johns Hopkins University Press.

Harry, B. (1999) Cultural Reciprocity in Sociocultural Perspective: adapting the normalization principle for family collaboration, *Exceptional Children,* 66, pp. 123–136.

Hill, R. (1972) *The Strengths of Black Families.* New York: Emerson Hall.

hooks, B. (1989) *Talking Back: thinking feminist, thinking Black.* Boston: South End Press.

hooks, B. (1994) *Teaching to Transgress: education as the practice of freedom.* New York: Routledge.

Kemmis, S. (2001) Exploring the Relevance of Critical Theory for Action Research: emancipatory action research in the footsteps of Jurgen Habermas, in P. Reason & H. Bradbury (Eds) *Handbook of Action Research: participative inquiry and practice.* London: Sage.

Kincheloe, J. (1995) Meet Me Behind the Iron Curtain: the struggle for a critical postmodern action research, in P. McLaren & J. Giarelli (Eds) *Critical Theory and Educational Research.* Albany: SUNY Press.

Ladson-Billings, G. (1994) *Dreamkeepers: successful teachers of African American children.* San Francisco: Jossey-Bass.

Ladson-Billings, G. (1999) Just What Is Critical Race Theory and What's It Doing in a Nice Field Like Education? in L. Parker, D. Deyhle & S. Villenas (Eds) *Race is . . . Race Isn't: critical race theory and qualitative studies in education.* Boulder: Westview Press.

Lorde, A. (1984) *Sister Outsider.* Trumansburg: Crossing Press.

Maguire, P. (2001) Uneven Ground: feminisms and action research, in P. Reason & H. Bradbury (Eds) *Handbook of Action Research: participative inquiry and practice.* London: Sage.

McIntyre, A. & Lykes, B. (2004) Weaving Words and Pictures In/Through Feminist Participatory Action Research, in M. Byrdon-Miller, P. Maguire & A. McIntyre (Eds) *Traveling Companions: Feminism, Teaching and Action Research.* Westport: Praeger.

McNiff, J., Lomax, P. & Whitehead, J. (1996) *You and Your Action Research Project.* New York: Routledge.

Mills, G. (2003) *Action Research: a guide for the teacher researcher.* Upper Saddle River: Merrill Prentice Hall.

Morawski, J. (2001) Feminist Research Methods: bringing culture to science, in D. Tolman & M. Brydon-Miller (Eds) From *Subjects to Subjectivities: a handbook of interpretive and participatory methods.* New York: New York University Press.

Mullings, L. (1994) Images, Ideology, and Women of Color, in M. Zinn & B. Dill (Eds) *Women of Color in U.S. Society.* Philadelphia: Temple University Press.

Nieto, S. (1999) *The Light in their Eyes: creating multicultural learning communities.* New York: Teachers College Press.

Noddings, N. (1999) Care, Justice and Equity, in M.S. Katz, N. Noddings & K. A. Strike (Eds) *Justice and Caring: the search for common ground in education,* vol. 1. New York: Teachers College Press.

Noffke, S. & Stevenson, R. (1995) *Educational Action Research: becoming practically critical.* New York: Teachers College Press.

Pratt, M. L. (1991) Arts of the Contact Zone, *Profession,* 91, pp. 33–40.

Rapp, R. (1982) Family and Class in Contemporary America: notes toward an understanding of ideology, in B. Thorne & M. Yalom (Eds) *Rethinking the Family: some feminist questions.* New York: Longman.

Smitherman, G. (2000) *Talkin that Talk: language, culture and education in African America.* London: Routledge.

Spivak, G. C. (1988) Can the Subaltern Speak? in C. Nelson & L. Grossberg (Eds) *Marxism and the Interpretation of Culture.* Basingstoke: Macmillan.

Stack, C. (1974) *All Our Kin: strategies for survival in a Black community.* New York: Harper & Row.

Stringer, E. (2004) *Action Research in Education.* Upper Saddle River: Pearson/Merrill.

Wallerstein, N. (1987) Empowerment Education: Friere's ideas applied to youth, *Youth Policy,* 9, pp. 11–15.

Wang, C. (1999) Photovoice: a participatory action research strategy applied to women's health, *Journal of Women's Health,* 8, pp. 185–192.

Wang, C. & Burris, M.A. (1994) Empowerment through Photo Novella: portraits of participation, *Health Education Quarterly,* 21, pp. 171–186.

Wang, C. & Burris, M.A. (1997) Photovoice: concept, methodology and use for participatory needs assessment, *Health Education & Behavior,* 24, pp. 369–387.

Zuber-Skerritt, O. (Ed.) (1996a) *New Directions in Action Research.* Washington DC: Falmer Press.

Zuber-Skerritt, O. (1996b) Emancipatory Action Research for Organizational Change and Management Development, in O. Zuber-Skerritt (Ed.) *New Directions in Action Research.* Washington DC: Falmer Press.

# 4

# Action Research

## *Three Approaches*

### Emily F. Calhoun

Differing in purpose, emphasis, and results, three types of action research allow educators to investigate areas of concern and meet the challenges within their classrooms and schools.

Anita Simmons records her 1st graders' responses to questions about simple fractions after using different displays and activities with them. She wants to determine which presentations are more effective than others.

Four middle school teachers—Elitrus and Paula from Rogers School, and Angie and Robert from Wilshire School—experiment with mnemonic key words in their science classes. They want to help students better retain and understand key science concepts and terms. They consult frequently with a member of the county intermediate agency and a professor from the nearby state university, both of whom are experimenting with the same method.

The faculty at Thomas High School wants to increase student achievement. To obtain this goal, all faculty members add a new instructional strategy, such as the inquiry approach or inductive thinking strategies. They observe and record student responses to the change in instruction and discuss their findings. A leadership team meets bimonthly for technical assistance with the Consortium for Action Research, a regional group sponsored by the state department of education.

SOURCE: "Action Research: Three Approaches", by Emily F. Calhoun. In the October, 1993, issue of *Educational Leadership, 51 (2)*, p. 62–65. © 1993 ASCD. Used with Permission. Learn more about ASCD at www.ascd.org.

These three scenarios all describe action research. The first, carried out by a single teacher, is individual teacher research. The second, conducted by a volunteer group working with a university professor and staff development officer, is collaborative action research. The third, involving an entire faculty in conjunction with a school consortium, is schoolwide action research. True to earlier concepts of action research, the work centers on the practitioner; this is research done by teachers and administrators.

> *Action research remains a powerful tool for . . . improving the practice and the health of an organization.*

Action research was here before, in the 1940s and '50s, developed by Kurt Lewin and his colleagues as a collective problem-solving cycle for improving organizations (Lewin 1947, 1948; Corey 1953). The term action research captured the notion of disciplined inquiry (research) in the context of focused efforts to improve the quality of an organization and its performance (action). Today, action research remains a powerful tool for simultaneously improving the practice and the health of an organization.

## BENEFITS OF ACTION RESEARCH

For teachers, principals, and district office personnel, action research promises progress in professionalization. The process allows them to experience problem solving and to model it for their students. They carefully collect data to diagnose problems, search for solutions, take action on promising possibilities, and monitor whether and how well the action worked. The cycle can repeat itself many times, focusing on the same problem or on another. The process can help develop a professional problem-solving ethos (Corey 1953, Joyce 1991, Schaefer 1967, Sirotnik 1987).

Action research can revitalize the entire learning community, as well as aid teachers in changing or reflecting on their classroom practices. It can support initiatives by individual teachers, schools, schools working with communities, and districts. In addition, more than one type of action research can be used in a given setting at the same time.

Selecting one type of action research over another has important implications for the school renewal process. From my work with action research as a consultant, coordinator, and researcher, I have gathered data on action research from 76 schools in three states. These data indicate that besides the obvious distinctions about how many people are involved, the three types of action research vary in their emphasis on achieving equity for students, improving the organization as a problem-solving unit, and developing collegial relations among teachers. Further, each type has different long-term objectives, purposes, and results. The key to selection is the purpose of the inquiry.

Faculties and individuals choosing the type of action research that will best serve their needs should consider five elements: (1) purpose and process; (2) support provided by outside agencies such as universities, intermediate service agencies (for example, the Regional Service Educational Agency in Georgia), consortiums, and central office personnel; (3) the kind of data utilized; (4) the audience for the research; and (5) the expected side effects.

## INDIVIDUAL TEACHER RESEARCH

**Purpose and process.** Individual teacher research usually focuses on changes in a single classroom. A teacher defines an area or problem of interest in classroom management, instructional strategies or materials, or students' cognitive or social behavior. The teacher then seeks solutions to the problem. Students may or may not be directly involved in helping to generate alternatives and determining effects. If parents are involved, they are usually consulted as sources of information.

**Outside support.** Individual teacher research is frequently inspired by university courses, a descriptive article about action research, or an encouraging supervisor, principal, staff development coordinator, or professor (see Oja and Smulyan 1989, Rogers et al. 1990, and Strickland 1988). Because support by administrators varies by site and by their personal interest in the area being explored, external agencies often provide teachers with the needed support. Sometimes the external agent acts as a mentor to the teacher.

**Data utilized.** Some individual teacher researchers use quantitative data, developing measures and forming and testing hypotheses. They experiment with different actions fashioned to address the problem, study and record the effects of those actions, and keep, modify, or discard ways of acting based on their findings. Some teachers use qualitative data in similar processes. A few teachers, operating more like phenomenologists, prefer to let the hypotheses emerge from the process (Carr and Kemmis 1983).

**Audience.** The primary audience for the results of individual teacher research is the teacher conducting the research. If students have participated directly in the investigation, then they, too, form part of the primary audience. Whether the results are shared with secondary audiences through staff development presentations, professional conferences, school district newsletters, or articles in professional journals is at the discretion of the individual teacher.

**Side effects.** The effects of individual teacher research may or may not reach outside the classroom. Several teachers within the same school may be conducting action research on a similar topic, but they may or may not discuss their experiences and results. The amount of sharing depends on the collegiality of the individuals. Where such sharing occurs, collegiality at the school may be enhanced.

## COLLABORATIVE ACTION RESEARCH

**Purpose and process.** Depending on the numbers of teachers involved, collaborative action research can focus on problems and changes in a single classroom or on a problem occurring in several classrooms. A research team might even take on a districtwide problem, but focus its inquiry on classrooms. The research team may include as few as two persons, or it may include several teachers and administrators working with staff from a university or other external agency. The team follows the same investigative and reflective cycle as the individual teacher-researcher.

**Outside support.** Teachers and administrators often work with university staff, intermediate service agency personnel, or members of an educational consortium when doing collaborative action research (Holly 1991, Sagor 1991, Whitford et al. 1987). Collaborative action research frequently involves school-university partnerships and mutual support from each participating organization (see Allen et al. 1988). The relationship is similar to the interactive research and development framework of the late 1970s (Tikunoff and Mergendoller 1983).

Teachers engaged in collaborative action research generally volunteer to participate or seek out affiliation with local university personnel who have expertise in particular curriculum areas. Professors, district office personnel, or principals may recruit teachers to explore an area in need of improvement or to field-test promising approaches. Recruiting teachers for field-testing is especially prevalent when agency personnel initiate the study.

**Data utilized.** As in individual teacher research, the data utilized by collaborative action researchers may be qualitative or quantitative. Data are more likely to be quantitative if the central office or intermediate service agency defines the study area. The larger collaborative research team might also use a greater variety of methods than the individual teacher-researcher and divide the labor, focusing on different dimensions of a problem. For example, in a study of disciplinary action, one member might survey parents, a second member might interview teachers, and a third might count referrals and organize them by cause and consequences.

**Audience.** The members of the research team are the primary audience for results from collaborative action research. Depending on their involvement in formulating and shaping the investigation, students and parents may form part of the primary audience. If the school administration, the district office, or a university sponsored the research, then these groups also form part of the primary audience.

*Collaborative action researchers appear to share results with secondary audiences.*

Collaborative action researchers appear to share results with secondary audiences more frequently than do individual teacher-researchers and participants in schoolwide action research. This may result from the involvement of university personnel in the process, who, besides providing support to teachers, are exploring their own areas of professional interest. Because their university positions require them to generate and share knowledge, university personnel often have more time to write about the action research experience and more opportunities to present the results. This writing and presentation is often done in collaboration with one or more of the participating practitioners.

**Side effects.** While the work between school or district practitioners and university personnel is collaborative and mutually beneficial, a major benefit to practitioners is the almost tutorial role university personnel play in helping them develop the tools of social science inquiry. Some groups stay together for several years, conducting several studies in areas of common interest, while their technical skills and expertise in inquiry continue to grow. Such collaboration also generally improves collegiality.

## SCHOOLWIDE ACTION RESEARCH

**Purpose and process.** In schoolwide action research, a school faculty selects an area or problem of collective interest, then collects, organizes, and interprets on-site data. Data from other schools, districts, or the professional literature are funneled into the collective decision-making process of the faculty, who then determines the actions to be taken. The process is cyclic and can serve as a formative evaluation of the effects of the actions taken.

*School leadership teams or district administrators often initiate schoolwide inquiry.*

Schoolwide action research focuses on school improvement in three areas. First, it seeks to improve the organization as a problem-solving entity. With repeated cycles, it is hoped that faculty members will become better able to work together to identify and solve problems. Second, schoolwide research tries to improve equity for students. For example, if the faculty studies the writing process in order to offer better instructional opportunities for students, the intent is that all students benefit. Third, schoolwide action research tries to increase the breadth and content of the inquiry itself. Every classroom and teacher is involved in collective study and assessment. In addition, faculty members may involve students, parents, and even the general community in data collection and interpretation and in the selection of options for action.

A school executive council or leadership team composed of teachers and administrators often shares the responsibility for keeping the process moving. These leaders spur the collecting, organizing, and interpretation of the data, disseminate on-site data and applicable professional literature for collective analysis and study, and support the actions selected for implementation by the learning community.

**Outside support.** School leadership teams or district administrators often initiate schoolwide inquiry because of their affiliation with a consortium that promotes action research as a major school improvement strategy. Through exposure to consortiums such as the Center for Leadership in School Reform in Kentucky or the League of Professional Schools in Georgia, school leaders read about schoolwide inquiry, attend awareness sessions, or discuss it with peers who are using it. They then work to apply schoolwide inquiry in their home settings.

**Data utilized.** The data gathered from studying the school site and the effects of actions taken may be quantitative, qualitative, or both. The data collection can be as simple as counting types of writing elicited from students or as complex as a multi-year case study. Faculty members might divide the labor as in the case of collaborative action research. They might also reach out to other schools studying similar problems and trying the same or different solutions.

———————— ✂ ————————

*The audience for the results of schoolwide action research includes the total school faculty.*

For greatest effect, the data should be collected regularly, and evaluation of actions taken should be formative. Relying on summative evaluations such as yearly norm-referenced tests will lessen the dynamism of the process. Standard tests, however, can be used to corroborate the results of the formative studies. In almost all cases, multiple assessment measures are needed (Calhoun 1992, Glickman 1990, Holly 1992).

**Audience.** The audience for the results of schoolwide action research includes all the primary participants, at least the total school faculty. The faculty may decide to expand this audience to include students, parents, the general community, and the school board.

**Side effects.** Collective action may be the most complex type of action research, requiring participation from all members of the faculty. This complexity, however, generates important side effects: the faculty learns to build collegiality and to manage the group process. Teachers reflect on aspects of curriculum and instruction they might not have if they had worked alone.

Schoolwide action research may feel messy and uneven, and conflict may arise during the first few cycles, but this is to be expected when a diverse community is learning to apply a complex process. Collecting schoolwide data on an instructional initiative requires trust and mental and physical collaboration. Marshalling the efforts of all both takes and provides energy. Sharing the results from individual classrooms requires patience and understanding toward self and others.

## REFLECTING ON ACTION RESEARCH

In recent years many teachers and administrators have engaged in productive curricular and instructional improvement through each type of action research. Part of the promise inherent in the action research format is support of the current movement toward site-based decision making. In many cases, collaborative relationships have increased between school personnel and members of central district offices, intermediate agencies, and university personnel. Using schoolwide action research has increased the problem-solving capabilities of schools, and even districts.

As knowledge about the process accumulates and we explore action research, we will be better able to guide our school improvement efforts. Assuming that the trend toward action research continues and more and better studies about its effects are produced, we will be able to make more informed assessments of its influence on student opportunities to learn.

These results should be positive, for action research has the potential to generate the energy and knowledge needed to support healthy learning communities. Our challenge as educators is to make this potential a reality.

# REFERENCES

Allen, J., J. Combs, M. Hendricks, P. Nash, and S. Wilson. (1988). "Studying Change: Teachers Who Became Researchers." *Language Arts* 65, 4: 379–387.

Calhoun, E. F. (1992). "A Status Report on Action Research in the League of Professional Schools." In Lessons from the League: *Improving Schools through Shared Governance and Action Research:* Vol 2. Athens, Ga.: Program for School Improvement, College of Education, UGA.

Carr, W., and S. Kemmis. (1983). *Becoming Critical: Knowing through Action Research.* Geelong, Victoria: Deakin Press.

Corey, S. M. (1953). *Action Research to Improve School Practices.* New York: Teachers College Press.

Glickman, C. D. (1990). *Supervision of Instruction: A Developmental Approach.* Boston: Allyn Bacon.

Holly, P. (1991). "Action Research Within Institutional Development: It's Becoming Second Nature to Us Now." Paper presented at the annual meeting of the American Educational Research Association, Chicago.

Holly, P. (1992). Comments made during an Action Research Workshop in Ames, Iowa.

Joyce, B. R. (1991). "Doors to School Improvement." *Educational Leadership* 48, 8: 59–62.

Lewin, K. (1947). "Group Decisions and Social Change." In *Readings in Social Psychology,* edited by T. M. Newcomb and E. L. Hartley. New York: Henry Holt.

Lewin, K. (1948). *Resolving Social Conflicts: Selected Papers on Group Dynamics.* New York: Harper and Row.

Oja, S. N. and L. Smulyan. (1989). *Collaborative Action Research: A Developmental Approach.* London: Falmer Press.

Rogers, D., R. Haven-O'Donnell, S. Hebdon, and F. Ferrell. (1990). "Lessons on Relating Research, Reflection, and Reform from Three Researcher/Practitioner Projects." Paper presented at the annual meeting of the American Educational Research Association, Boston.

Sagor, R. (1991). "What Project LEARN Reveals about Collaborative Action Research." *Educational Leadership* 48, 6: 6–10.

Schaefer, R. J. (1967). *The School as a Center of Inquiry.* New York: Harper and Row.

Sirotnik, K. A. (1987). "Evaluation in the Ecology of Schooling." In *The Ecology of School Renewal: The Eighty-Sixth Yearbook of the National Society for the Study of Education,* edited by J. I. Goodlad. Chicago: The University of Chicago Press.

Strickland, D. S. (1988). "The Teacher As Reseacher: Toward the Extended Professional." *Language Arts* 65, 8: 754–764.

Tikunoff, W. J., and J. R. Mergendoller. (1983). "Inquiry as a Means to Professional Growth: The Teacher as Reseacher." In *Staff Development: Eighty-Second Yearbook of the National Society for the Study of Education,* edited by G. A. Griffin. Chicago: The University of Chicago Press.

Whitford, B. L., P. C. Schlechty, and L. G. Shelor. (1987). "Sustaining Action Research Through Collaboration: Inquiries for Invention." *Peabody Journal of Education* 64, 3: 151–169.

# Exemplary Project

*The Effectiveness of Spalding Instruction
for Spelling Performance*

Margo S. O'Neill

In this proactive action research I sought to assess the effectiveness of Spalding instruction for enhancing the spelling achievement of young elementary students. Spalding instruction is a total language arts strategy that provides sequential, multisensory instruction in spelling (including phonics and handwriting) as well as reading and writing composition. Its premise is that young children will become better readers and writers by becoming better spellers because of the mental skills they acquire while spelling.

My action research was carried out at Villa Montessori School, a Phoenix-based charter school operating since 1995. Before that Villa had been a private Montessori school for thirty years. Since becoming a charter school, Villa has attracted mostly lower-socioeconomic families and students with learning limitations.

The action research took place from August to February, 2003–2004. Five of our six elementary teachers (one teacher chose not to participate) taught their students spelling using Spalding instruction. Each of the three grade levels (first, second, and third) received weekly spelling lessons via Spalding. As the Education Director (principal) I charged each teacher with keeping a journal to record the days and times of the Spalding lessons. I also observed every teacher and class in operation several times. One hundred and thirty-two students in all took part in the action research.

From September 2003 until February 2004, on about the same day each month, we gave spelling tests to the students using the Morrison-McCall Spelling Scale, and I determined and recorded grade equivalent scores. Then I calculated changes for each student by subtracting his or her August score from his or her February score. I also administered a phonogram dictation test in early March to assess how many phonograms each student had mastered.

Virtually every student, those in special education, those about average, and those who were already advanced showed positive gains. Only five students did not show progress. In my ten years as elementary teacher and three years as Education Director, I had never experienced such near universal student improvement in spelling. Still, due to the newness of Spalding, Villa teachers were not yet experienced enough to use assessment data to make their own instructional improvements. I saw that more teacher training targeted to improve teacher expertise in assessment would be needed during the next phase of our action research on Spalding instruction in spelling at Villa. The most important insight I gained, however, is that students' effective spelling skills do improve their abilities in reading and writing.

---

SOURCE: "The Effectiveness of Spalding Instruction for Spelling Performance", by Margo S. O'Neill (2004) College of Education, Arizona State University West.

# Exemplary Project

*The Business Managers' Network: Action Research
to Improve Business Capacities of Colorado Charter Schools*

Lori Grant

The serious lack of competent business knowledge in Colorado charter schools is, I believe, the largest reason of charter-school failure in the state; it far outweighs charter closures due to poor teaching and low student achievement. Colorado charter school business managers do not often make fiscal data useful for local decision making, lack knowledge about the accrual requirements in the Colorado "Chart of Accounts," and do not properly take advantage of their school's tax-exempt status. Moreover, their understanding of sound accounting practices is usually minimal. In a few cases fraud has caused a school's demise; in many cases financial mismanagement has shortened the life of the school.

In order for charter schools to be successful with students, they must be able to take care of business. Unfortunately, before this action research very little accurate financial knowledge was being exchanged between Colorado charter business managers. What information was being shared often was incorrect. In order to increase the effectiveness of Colorado charter school business managers, I thought that it would be important to create new ways for them to share accurate knowledge about sound business practices.

With that objective in mind, Brian Anderson, Katie Norton, and I created The Business Managers' Network and collaborated in doing action research on it. We designed the network to communicate about business matters regularly, ask pertinent questions of one another, seek and share timely accurate answers, keep up-to-date with statewide changes, and increase their shared knowledge about charter school finances. We hoped that network members would learn about fiscal duties required of Colorado charter school boards, and how to articulate those requirements tactfully to their board members.

We gathered network members together twice a month for one school year to distribute valid information and for shared exchanges and group problem solving. We also developed a Web site to facilitate ongoing communication among network members between face-to-face meetings. We hoped that by creating opportunities for an active communicative network that the business practices in the state would improve. We believed, too, that a cohesive network could become a powerful political force in dealing with legislative issues facing Colorado charters.

As part of our collaborative action research we gave pre- and post-questionnaires about business knowledge to network members. We assessed members' satisfaction

*(Continued)*

(Continued)

with the meetings and the Web site with another questionnaire, and we interviewed one-on-one a sample of members about how the network might become more effective. An outside researcher, Karen DeSchryver, evaluated the network in conjunction with the Colorado Department of Education.

The data indicated that in one year The Business Managers' Network had become a valuable institution for providing accurate and useful financial information to network members. Most member's valid information about Colorado charter business matters had increased, and their attitudes about the value of the network had become more positive. The external researcher observed that during an important Colorado legislative session when budget cuts in education were on the table, business network representatives provided accurate and up-to-date facilities financing information to the state's Joint Budget Committee, which became influential in heading off a seven-million-dollar reduction in capital construction funds for charter schools and in preserving that money for subsequent years.

In 2004, two years after the action research had started, the Colorado League of Charter Schools and the Colorado Department of Education gave their strong support to ensure continuation of The Colorado Business Managers' Network.

SOURCE: "The Business Managers' Network: Action Research to Improve Business Capacities of Colorado Charter Schools", by Lori Grant (2004) College of Education, Arizona State University West.

# Exemplary Project

*Improving Schoolwide Communication Through a New School Web Site: Responsive Action Research*

## Heidi Mitchell

When parents in Northwest Phoenix entrusted their children to our suburban elementary charter school, they wanted to believe that their children would be safe, nurtured, and treasured. They sought assurances, too, that their children would be learning well and being properly socialized. Thus, communication between parents and the school became critical for building constructive home-school partnerships. Yet, that sort of trusted communication, or rather lack thereof, was identified by many parents before this action research as one of our school's top weaknesses. Thus, in this action research I set out, as an objective outsider, to study issues that were hampering parent-teacher dialogue, and worked closely with all members of the school-community to establish better channels of communication.

After my preliminary study, I met with administrators, staff members, teachers, parents, and students to gather systematic information through one-on-one interviews, question-naires, and focus-group discussions. Later, members of each group brainstormed with me ways to reduce the communication problems that we had jointly pinpointed. Based on those multiple interactions, I decided to design a brand new Web site for the school. I later met again with members of the five groups to review and revise the new Web site and to make improvements in it. During that process, school participants pointed out the former Web site's deficiencies, arguing that its security features had been cumbersome and unnecessary and that its out-of-date, misleading content had reduced its effectiveness. Most wanted an entirely new Web site. In short, the old school Web site had been rejected by parents, teachers, and students alike and was not being used by more than ten percent of the school community.

My action research process generated a cornucopia of new and creative ideas. Teachers, for example, wanted Web sites for every single class in the school; an idea that parents readily accepted. Parents and students asked for continuous twenty-four hours, seven days access to curricula, report forms, homework assignments, and reading lists. Students wanted easy-to-reach links to homework-helper sites and more frequent teacher feedback and help. Parents wanted an online, e-mail directory so that they could communicate directly with certain teachers and administrators. They also asked for ways to contact "homeroom mothers" and easy avenues for their volunteering for classroom-helper activities. Some parents wanted a family-forum index so that parents' hobbies, interests, and skills could be easily shared.

In short, the new Web site was well accepted by over ninety percent of participants. And my action research design and procedures were positively accepted by nearly every-one. I observed, too, that the problem-solving discussions we had, during which we pin-pointed alternative features of the new Web site and during which we brainstormed improvements, succeeded in increasing school-community cohesiveness and helped administrators, teachers, and students adopt an attitude in support of continuous school improvement, an unexpected benefit of the action research.

SOURCE: "Improving Schoolwide Communication Through a New School Web Site: Responsive Action Research", by Heidi Mitchell (2007) College of Education, Arizona State University West.

# PART III

## *Implementing Action Research*

Defining and understanding alternative types of educational action research offer mental exercise that is prologue to the central question of this book. What challenges and pitfalls do educators face as they implement action research? This section includes six published articles and nine unpublished LEE Exemplary Projects that provide a plethora of answers to that question. These 15 examples more than double the number of implementation studies presented in the first edition and form the heart and soul of this revision.

The first article is by Eleanor Perry, the inspirational leader and administrative manager of the LEE program. Before commencing her career in higher education, Perry served as an elementary principal in southern Oregon. She describes how she implemented an improvement strategy as principal of 5–11-year-olds of mostly lower socioeconomic families. Perry explains how she engaged parents, students, and teachers in schoolwide change, by integrating the OD strategies of STP problem solving, and Force Field Analysis with staff development workshops and action research. She reflects on how what she learned that year influenced her teaching designs in higher education. By reading her article, we can understand why the LEE program took on its design and why the 13 LEE Exemplary Projects in this book inform us so well about practical action research.

The next three Exemplary Projects respectively, on school leadership, teacher coaches, and school dropout reduction, offer "Goliath-like" examples, both small and large scale, of Perry's wish to create school climates where all "Davids" can be successful. Thomas-Wilson describes a schoolwide strategy for preparing teachers to assume leadership in carrying out administrative tasks in a South Carolina charter school. Her action research demonstrates that enhanced adult teamwork and cooperation can foster both faculty cohesiveness and student success. Apolito shows how external coaches for a host of Ohio schools can help teachers raise students' academic achievement. Effective coaches form partnerships with school administrators, offer teachers professional development work-shops, and develop cohesive teacher teams to raise students' reading and math test scores. Gaitens demonstrates how an on-line school can success-fully raise high school graduation rates of at-risk young adults. Her intervention focused on remedial coursework, workforce skill training, counseling and outreach, and individualized assistance in developing postschool opportunities.

The next two Exemplary Projects on improving elementary and mid-dle school students' math achievement offer specific case studies on Johnson and Kromann-Kelly's goal of using action research to assess and improve classroom instruction. Darroch shows how valid uses of the Singapore Math curriculum by fully involved teachers can raise the stan-dardized math scores of sixth, seventh, and eighth graders.

In the next article, Emily Calhoun explains how cooperative action research can transform a school staff into a learning community. She pro-vides an example of how a faculty designed action research on the com-mon student learning goal of improving reading comprehension. The faculty carried out such action research tasks as: (1) collecting data about student reading, (2) specifying reading performance goals for students, (3) identifying school resources to enhance student reading, and (4) amass-ing relevant information from the literature on reading. Calhoun describes how that project unfolded during one school year.

Jordan's Exemplary Project describes how as a middle-school teacher he used a schoolwide change to improve his students' math achievement. The school change entailed moving from co-educational to sex-segregated classes in the core subjects. Jordan focused his action research on develop-ing instructional practices that he especially tailored to boys' and girls' dif-ferent learning styles in math. His project demonstrates how schoolwide change and individual teacher research can build off of and contribute to each other.

The next article by Caro-Bruce and McCreadie describes lessons learned from three years of action research in one school district. Their his-torical overview is an inspirational story. Educators who strive to carry out their own districtwide action research can learn a great deal by reflecting on the historical events that took place when over 100 teachers and admin-istrators became involved in action research in the Madison, Wisconsin Metropolitan School District.

In the next Exemplary Project, Rodriquez-Elkins demonstrates how an Nevada-based Charter School Education Consortium implemented proac-tive action research on teacher recruitment and training to support educa-tional improvement processes in five very different schools.

The last three articles by Salisbury et al., Cheney, and Arnold describe practical action research in an assortment of public schools. Salisbury and colleagues zero in on elementary schools, Cheney works in a middle school. Arnold focuses on a high school. The last two Exemplary Projects by Kreienkamp and Laughlin are case studies of proactive action research that nicely complement the Salisbury and Cheney articles.

Salisbury and her colleagues report on a collaborative action research effort in two elementary school districts. Their action research was proactive in that the participating teachers started with innovative strategies for including students with disabilities in regular K–5 classrooms. They then collected qualitative and quantitative data to document and improve upon the efficacy of their strategies. Kreienkamp also implemented proactive action research in an elementary school. Her project shows how simple and straightforward some action research can be. She focused very narrowly on teaching math facts to six–nine-year-olds, demonstrating that just by increasing time on task a small amount, she could improve her students' math achievement.

Cheney describes a responsive action research project with sixth, seventh, and eighth graders and their parents. The students had serious emotional and behavioral problems. The educators, with the help of the parents, collected data on the students' strengths and weaknesses, and after reviewing those data, generated goals and interventions for each student. Next, teachers and parents carried out the interventions and together they studied the effects. In a project also focused on parents, Laughlin demonstrates how powerful four hours of parent training in her reading curriculum can be in helping them understand ways to foster self esteem and reading readiness in their children.

In the final article, Arnold writes like Perry about his involvement in action research as a principal. Arnold intervened as a high school principal in cooperative action research with three teachers, one each in art, geometry, and physics. The proactive actions of each of the three teachers focuses on integrating the curricula of their three subjects.

# 5

Creating a School for David

*A Principal's Narrative*

Eleanor A. Perry

## INTRODUCTION

Like the biblical story of David and Goliath, educational leaders frequently face gigantic challenges in creating a climate where all children can be successful in multicultural and diverse socioeconomic communities. Often norms in and outside the schoolhouse door need to be altered. Administrators must find ways to educate adults as well as children so that both might grow and contribute to the common good of our society. This qualitative study recounts one school's year-long trek to pull a high-poverty community together.

## WHAT WE DID

### The Situation

As a second-year principal, I was assigned to a school in southern Oregon. Only six schools in the entire state had a lower socioeconomic status. One hundred-fifty students (5-11 years old) attended this school. Eighty-four

SOURCE: "Creating a School for David: A Principal's Narrative", by Eleanor A. Perry (2000) *Journal of School Leadership*, 10 (3), 264–282. Reprinted  with permission from Rowman & Littlefield Education.

percent of the students received free or reduced lunches. There was an 86% annual student transient rate and a high teacher turnover. Parent involvement was low. Teachers were unhappy.

The Superintendent chose me to replace a veteran principal who had alienated the teachers, staff, and community by implementing major changes during the previous summer without any input or feedback from key stakeholders. The teachers returned from summer vacation to find themselves enmeshed in whole language, multi-age groupings, cooperative learning, and full-class inclusion. Parents, as well, were outraged. The veteran principal's stance was that he was simply following the new educational reform law that called for these changes.

My task was to bring the community back into the school and the school back into the community. The Superintendent charged me with that responsibility because I had a background in organization development focusing on team building, communication, decision making, and problem solving. Little did I know when I took the assignment how critically important each of those skills would be during the coming year.

My first experience with the community occurred in the spring prior to my assignment. The Superintendent told me to simply attend a parent meeting, introduce myself, and listen to concerns. I quickly learned that nothing in this school was "simple."

I knew parent involvement was traditionally low in this rural community and expected to meet with a handful of die-hard parents. To my amazement, the cafeteria was packed with adults who were visibly agitated. Unattended children ran in, under, and around the tables. The current principal tried to control the audience long enough to introduce me but was interrupted by shouts, multiple questions, and a general hum of side conversations. One large woman loudly warned me not to waste her time by speaking too long because she still had hay to bale before the sun went down. Considering her comment, I spoke only long enough to tell them my name, where I currently was principal, and that I looked forward to working with them in the fall.

Focus quickly turned back to the veteran principal who side-stepped questions about classroom assignments for the fall and the continuation of whole language, cooperative learning and inclusion. I made a mental note of several parents who seemed to dominate the group. These were the first people I wanted to meet during the summer.

The next day I slipped away from my own assigned middle school and visited the elementary campus again. When I walked into the tiny front office, the secretary briskly told me there was a child destroying the principal's office. She sternly told me to take care of the situation because the administrator was nowhere to be found.

I discovered disarray in the principal's office and a child calmly looking out the window with his back to me. After several moments of silence, I told him I was new in the neighborhood and asked him if he knew anybody that could show me around. I didn't want a grown-up tour. I wanted to see the really good spots in the school. He jumped at the opportunity to be my guide. Of course we had to clean up the principal's office before we could go.

I learned from this third-grade youngster about where kids hid from the principal, what teachers were "easy," and how to shimmy down a gym rope that hung from the ceiling. We returned to the office hand-in-hand. I had a new friend and a bewildered secretary.

Based on these first experiences with the internal and external publics of my new school, my summer plans changed dramatically. My focus now (in addition to hiring six of nine new teachers) would be to meet key parents, determine what they liked best about the school and what they most wanted to see changed. I was a researcher. This would be easy. It was simply a matter of collecting data, analyzing it, providing feedback to the community, and implementing change. It was a perfect textbook scenario, or so I thought.

Fortunately, there was a strong talent pool to fill the six teacher openings. I chose a blend of new and veteran teachers who had training and experience in whole language, cooperative learning, multi-age grouping, and inclusion. As each candidate advanced through the administrative team screening, I brought in the current teaching staff to meet the finalists. They provided input into the selection of their new teammates. This was a new experience for them and one that proved beneficial in the long run.

The two returning classroom teachers quite easily became mentors and role models for the new first-year and veteran teachers. Bonding started before contracts were even signed. We needed this type of collegiality among the teaching staff if we were to implement any change within our community. The third returning teacher was an itinerant reading specialist. She did not readily adjust to a collaborative staff environment. I did not consider her behavior an immediate threat and therefore chose to move forward without her participation. Ultimately, this proved to be an unwise decision on my part.

The new teaching staff (minus one) brought excitement and a renewed energy into the school. We met often during the summer to plan how we could bring the community back into the school. Word spread quickly in this small rural town.

Support staff still on summer vacation were the first to drop by school. They were curious about the new principal and teachers. I met with each person and asked my two important questions: "What do you like most about your school?" and "What needs to be changed?" Quickly they became caught up in our enthusiastic attempt to reach out to parents.

The support staff helped us understand the culture of a high-poverty community. We learned that an event featuring food and casual clothes would attract the most people. The teachers and staff decided to plan a school picnic. Local grocers donated food. Stores provided school supplies for door prizes. I donated film. My third-grader's mother was a freelance reporter for the local newspaper. She provided free publicity for the event.

Our theme, "Welcome Back," was simple on the surface, but carried strong implications. It clearly set the tone for community renewal. This was evidenced in a change in the parents' behavior.

Parents started to stop by school. They heard the new principal was interested in listening. They wanted their chance to be heard. Parents provided feedback on what worked in the past and what they wanted to see changed. Much of what they said echoed the sentiments of the teachers and support staff. Many complained about sudden change. One likened it to taxation without representation. They felt the age spread in K–3 blends was too large to effectively reach all children. Whole language and cooperative learning were a mystery to parents, as well as to the returning teachers who had received no training in implementing those strategies. Parents of gifted and special needs children questioned the validity of full school inclusion.

By the time our picnic day arrived, I had a fair idea of what mattered most to our internal and external publics. Patterns of concern focusing on what's best for kids had emerged. The picnic would be our vehicle to drive home several key points: (1) we care, (2) we listen, and (3) we create collaborative change for the sake of increased student achievement. Every member of the teaching and support staff had to deliver the same message to all people attending the picnic. We did this by setting up a learning stations raffle. This is how it worked.

Parents received a "learning card" when they arrived. There was room for five stamps on their cards, one stamp for each letter of the school name. They received a stamp for each station they visited. Locations included individual classrooms to meet the teachers, the cafeteria to meet the support staff who served the picnic food, the gym for the evening's greeting and raffle, and the library where I snapped free family pictures, a major luxury rarely experienced by many who attended. To be eligible for the five raffle stamps then, families needed to visit more than one classroom, even if they had only one child in the school. We felt this would introduce them to our welcome message in a variety of venues.

As I met parents in the "photo" library and took their family pictures, I told them that we would not have traditional parent conferences at the end of the report card period. Instead, they could pick up their portraits in two weeks at the next school event—goal-setting conferences. I explained that we valued their input on what and how their children learned. The goal setting conference would be the first step for parents, students, and teachers to work together to carefully craft annual goals for each child in our school. The idea was overwhelmingly well received.

The picnic and goal setting put us two weeks into the school year. We were confident that positive trust-building had started within our community. Life, however, was not as calm as it seemed. This became clear at our first staff development session.

The school district allowed one hour each Friday morning for teachers' staff development meetings. At the first meeting, the district Director of Personnel made a formal presentation to our school's teachers. His message was loud and clear. Due to increased state legislation focusing on rigorous academic standards, teachers were expected to maintain a high degree of student mastery, especially in the basic subjects of reading, writing, and mathematics.

The teachers were visibly shaken by the forcefulness of the Director's presentation since standardized test scores were historically low in this school. The district would not accept the rationale that the students came from a low socioeconomic status, nor would they recognize the high family transient rate. Teachers were advised to take ownership of any child whom they had for one year or more. They would be held accountable based on standardized test scores. This accountability system would prevail regardless of the pedagogical philosophies embraced by the teachers.

At the end of this session, teachers provided written feedback to me in the form of: "I learned . . ." and "I wish. . . ." I compiled the data, arranged the information in logical order and distributed it back to the teachers by the following Monday morning. This process helped check for understanding and validated the needs and wants of the individuals. The data also helped monitor the progress and success of our efforts.

Written feedback from teachers who attended this first session indicated they learned about current legislation, but wished they were not so confused about specific state expectations. They also expressed frustration regarding the use of standardized tests as a measure of student achievement. One angry teacher sarcastically wrote, "I learned what I had suspected was lacking in my instruction—teaching children *how* to take tests." Another wrote, "I wish we could figure out a way to avoid testing kids to death and a way to deal more effectively with transient students."

At the next meeting teachers identified four topics they wanted to investigate: (1) the relationship between the students' socioeconomic status and testing results, (2) how data collection and reporting might be used to better understand the problems, (3) the possibility of skills grouping, and (4) strategies to move from concrete to abstract in teaching important concepts.

It was only the first month of school yet the written feedback at the end of this session reflected great waves of agitation among the staff. Teachers wrote: "I need to find another job," and "I'm overwhelmed and in over my head." Another wrote, "Whoa! What do I do? I need strategies to work with the wide range of skill levels here." Others, while expressing a more positive tone, still indicated concern such as, "I learned that overall we are doing a great job, but I wish we had more time to look over the assessment information." Still another teacher indicated that she wished they had more knowledge on how the testing statistics were compiled so that the information could be used for their program planning.

Tensions rose. Teachers were torn between valuing their own self-knowledge as educators and facing the cold reality of the students' low test scores. I asked them to generate lists showing students who needed some form of academic or social counseling. They identified more than 90% of the student body. Oddly enough, the children with the most severe problems on those lists were all named David.

Much like Sizer's (1984) Horace, this study's David is a composite. He represents all our students who were living in run-down shacks, busses, and dilapidated cars—and those were the more fortunate ones. Some camped out under the bridge; others looked for warm shelters along the street. Not all children in this study came from financial poverty. Most, however, experienced some sort of deprivation including social, emotional, and cultural poverty.

I told the teachers there was one special way they could help David. They needed to stop talking about frustrations and start articulating problems, because problems could be solved, frustrations could not. At that point, they took their first big step to move beyond the "tension" stage and started to become a community of problem solvers.

The teachers started to discuss what they thought their current situation was. First, they believed we had serious problems that only could be solved by involving *all* people who came in contact with the children. Collectively, they agreed to rearrange their schedules so that all support personnel could also attend the staff development meetings. This meant that all part-time educational assistants would come in early on Fridays and leave at noon. That decision required all teachers to cover some lunch duties and afternoon recesses—certainly a less than desirable arrangement for the teachers. It is important to note, however, that it was the teachers' choice to do this. Without their dedication to the effort, the process would not have been successful. In other words, the teachers believed they had serious problems in their school that could only be solved by involving all people who came in contact with the children on a daily basis. They were willing to be flexible regarding their union contracts and use of their personal planning time for the sake of finding ways to help children like David succeed.

Next, the teachers and I invited parents to the staff development meetings but few came. We wondered if our efforts to build trust within the community had not been as strong as we originally thought. This feeling of uncertainty brought back tensions within our school. We were on a constant emotional roller coaster. Every time we saw a glimmer of light, we faced another setback. Nonetheless, we moved forward to identify specific targets, determine factors that might help or hinder our progress, and design a plan to reach our goals.

## The Target

At the first joint meeting, teachers and support staff divided themselves randomly into three groups of no more than six people each. It was important that they self-selected their group members. This process provided a comfort level conducive to open communications and trust. Instinctively they made an effort to equally balance the membership of each group to include both teachers and support staff at varied grade level assignments and years of experience.

Teachers shared with the staff what the Director of Personnel had described regarding assessment. Then each group brainstormed their own perceptions of the current situation. They identified possible targets and noted how they might reach those specific goals (see Figure 1). The major focus centered on reading improvement.

At the group level, written feedback unilaterally supported this process and indicated a bonding within the groups since they now had a chance to share common "feelings and concerns." One participant wrote, "I liked the feeling of community today." Another added, "We need to take care of each other." A third shared, "There was a more relaxed feeling here. I know it can't be all the time, but most of the time would be nice."

At the individual level, one person wrote, "I learned the importance of sharing philosophies and ideas—I learn more about *me* every time we share." Still there were others who were not ready to individualize and acknowledge successful bonding. One wrote, "I wish people could be more honest and open." Another suggested, "Whoever has a problem should go to the source and not get an undercurrent going. Nothing gets solved." Two commented on workload noting that "We need to narrow our focus. It is impossible to do everything that's required of us so therefore we do very little well. . . . I wish our dimension of 'wants' was reduced to absolute needs."

Staff development meetings took on a tone of sharing. Teachers brought reading strategies to the sessions. Some advocated direct instruction using phonics drills. Some described whole language techniques that perked children's interest in reading. They took turns relating how they successfully used those methods in other school settings.

Teachers also assumed specific roles including facilitator, recorder, process observer, reporter, and encourager. They were learning how to attend to content tasks as well as improve their interpersonal skills.

**Figure 1**    Our S-T-P Strategy

(S)ITUATION

(1) High poverty
(2) Low test scores
(3) No data on transience
(4) Inconsistent pedagogy

(T)ARGET

(1) Preschool
(2) Formal reading program
(3) Reading continuum

(P)ATH

(1) Share materials
(2) Become more focused
(3) Re-think mixed aged grouping

Support staff were not readily willing to assume leadership roles. Teachers encouraged them, however, to participate whenever they felt comfortable doing so. In that respect, we developed a group agreement that dictated our expectations for group behavior. We agreed that *h*onesty, *p*ositive attitudes, and not taking things *p*ersonally were most important to us. We called it our HP-squared attitude. This was another giant step in alleviating real and perceived tensions. Now we had a behavioral framework for quick reference when situations became tense. It was not uncommon to hear someone quip in the hallway, "Did she shift into her HP-squared attitude when things got tough at that meeting? Sure was different from last time we were together."

We worked hard to refine what our literacy situation and targets should be. We tried to describe our philosophies toward how to teach reading, analyze the lack of consistency in reading materials used in different classrooms, and determine how we could develop a reading continuum where children could seamlessly move from "learning to read" to "reading to learn." How could we do this with so many different opinions on the "best way" to teach reading?

The more the teachers and staff engaged in open communications, the more complex the issues became. Their written feedback at the end of a session in November looked as though people attended two different meetings. For instance, one person wrote, "I learned that we are in a state of confusion. The children aren't learning. . . . Why?" On the other hand, a person indicated, "Although we are all different people, we are all in-tune with solving problems." And yet another wrote, "We need to stop talking and start fixing."

As principal, I felt torn. I tried to understand the different personalities on the staff, encouraged them to collaborate with each other, and attempted to motivate them to draw invisible parents into the conversation. I was troubled by a gnawing, deep-seated concern about parent involvement. I remembered what one person wrote: "I wish the parents of some of our children cared about them as much as we do." I knew I had to work harder to provide a safe environment for parents to participate in problem solving. Antagonism was growing toward the parents we worked so hard to bring into the school in August.

I was constantly juggling my own personal need to engage everyone in the problem solving process while facing the reality that time was slipping away from us. Already holidays were distracting us and we were yet to identify what factors would help or hinder us from reaching our goals for improved reading.

It seemed as though my staff sensed my frustration. The depth of their written feedback to me before winter vacation gave me the strength to continue on. One told me, "Problem identification is fairly easy; solving methods are the challenge!" Another pointed out that "we all have a strong commitment to making needed changes here." One comment, however, motivated me more than any others. It simply stated, "Today I felt the joy of working as a team on a common goal." No one could have given me a more cherished gift of understanding and acceptance. I knew then that I could lead this process to fruition. We had come a long way, we would ultimately help our children become proficient readers, and we would involve more parents along the way.

At the final December staff development session, I introduced the staff to Force Field Analysis (FFA). The first step in FFA, picking our highest priority target, was the most difficult for us. Group members often had strong feelings about what was most important. I stressed the need for group consensus and assured members that no identified ideas would be lost in the process. This renewed the group's enthusiasm. They narrowed their lists of possible targets until they agreed to focus solely on increased student achievement in reading. They believed that was the most critical, immediate issue they faced.

As a second step, the group brainstormed all forces that might enhance their journey toward, or deter them from reaching their targeted goals. There was no discussion during that exercise other than asking clarifying questions. Individual forces included people's feelings and attitudes toward the target while group forces focused on norms, roles, and proce-dures. Although the list (see Figure 2) identified over three times more hin-dering forces than helping forces, the teams maintained their dedication to the process and attacked their problems head on. It seemed that open com-munication linked them together as a true problem solving organization and gave them strength.

As a third step, the group chose the forces that might hinder their progress the most. They decided to explore the possibilities of removing the following obstacles: (1) lack of sharing resources, (2) our multi-age grouping practices, and (3) the school's overall lack of focus. This was a major step that tested our HP-squared attitudes.

We learned being honest with each other meant we also had to engage in deep self-reflection that sometimes was painful. Were the teachers hoarding materials? Did we only communicate on the surface? Was isola-tionism our norm except for the one-hour staff development session each week? Did changing classroom structures mean that the teachers them-selves had failed at multi-age grouping? Was I pulling the staff in too many directions? How could we remain positive as we deeply questioned our own self-worth as educators?

Again, people's individual feelings and concerns interfered with the overall scope of the planned, systematic change process. I reminded all participants that the success of this process directly rested on their ability to respect the decision of the group. Individuals did not need to fully agree on the forces chosen, but they had to reach consen-sus and be willing to support the effort by not impeding the team's progress.

In the final step of the Force Field Analysis process, the group priori-tized the new shorter list of hindering forces based on how feasible it was

**Figure 2**    Our Force Field Analysis (FFA)

| HELPING | HINDERING |
|---|---|
| Enthusiasm | Time |
| Good resources    . . . | Lack of sharing |
| Desire to improve | Poverty |
| Good team | Lack of training |
| Free to share ideas    . . . | Multi-age grouping |
| Sense of unity | Interruptions |
| | Over worked |
| | Over committed |
| | Too much information |
| | Constant change |
| | Philosophical differences |
| | No preschool program |
| | No parent involvement |
| | No retention |
| | 5-year-olds not ready to learn |
| | Low reading expectations |
| | Lack of district direction |
| | . . . Lack of focus |
| | High staff turnover |

to remove each force. They worked on changing their own behaviors. A pre-vacation house-cleaning day resulted. Everyone dug through their cabinets, closets, nooks, and crannies. They piled stacks of unused materials in the cafeteria. Then the entire staff gathered to pick out resources that best suited their students. Upper primary teachers who advocated phonics-based learning took basic kindergarten reading primers. A primary teacher picked several upper-level chapter books for one of her voracious readers. Maybe it was the holiday spirit, or maybe it was the realization that honesty, positive attitudes, and the ability to put personalities aside helped break the isolation barrier. Whatever the reasons, the staff was sharing resources, preparing to rethink multi-age grouping, and I was coming to grips with a singular school focus: increased reading achievement.

By January, the full staff self-initiated a declaration supporting the problem-solving process we had used at our staff development meetings. They requested that all future sessions be dedicated to resolving the issues at hand. Wholeheartedly, they agreed that they were well on their way toward shaping their thoughts into a plan of action. They did not want to lose the momentum we had gained. I honored their request. Then they started to develop a plan of action.

## The Plan

Each week the teams worked to refine their target and develop a path to achieve their goal. They prioritized issues. I suggested that Action

Research might be a way to narrow the plan's focus. The staff was receptive to this idea. I introduced the five fundamental steps of Action Research at the next staff development session.

First, in reviewing their progress to date, the group realized they already had identified key issues by using the FFA process. They easily reaffirmed that the problem was a need to increase student achievement in reading. As a tightly knit group of self-proclaimed problem-solvers, they quickly agreed to devote the rest of the school year staff development sessions to their Action Research project.

Second, at staff development sessions, they devised ways to collect data from a variety of sources within their surroundings. They created timelines and assigned people responsibilities to collect data regarding the students' test scores, transient rates, and poverty status. They explored current research on improving student reading in high poverty communities. Then they collected data regarding current student information.

Third, they continued to use the staff development sessions to analyze their data. They identified main themes and sorted the data into logical supportive evidence matrices.

Fourth, they informally reported the results of their efforts at the weekly staff development sessions. Those reports led them to choose a grant proposal format as their way to formally report their findings. Now they were ready to develop a plan for implementation of what they learned during their investigation for the purpose of school and classroom improvement.

The fifth step was to complete a grant proposal seeking funds for resources to support increased student learning at our school. The staff used their data sets to actively pursue federal grant money to support their identified goals of (1) establishing an on-site preschool, (2) implementing a formal reading program, and (3) developing a reading continuum. The preschool would introduce children of poverty to the joys of reading, expose them to readiness behavioral activities prior to entering kindergarten, and train parents in reading techniques and parenting skills. The formal reading program would include instructional materials, opportunities for literary events such as library visits and author visits, and staff-parent training sessions on reading instructional strategies. The reading continuum would identify scope and sequence, assessment tools, and resources needed to support the flow of the curriculum from kindergarten to fifth grade.

As their plan grew, they also grew professionally and personally. Feedback became more and more positive. One person wrote, "I learned, 'WE CAN DO IT!' I wish to continue the positiveness of this morning." Another wrote, "We finally have some closure. I wish we had this earlier." A first-year teacher exclaimed, "I learned we have more agreement now than disagreement, YAHOO!" A veteran teacher expressed a definite attitude change. She wrote, "Now I can look forward to next year." Nonetheless, feedback still reflected a sense of apprehension and that is understandable. Change can be a scary thing. One teacher wrote, "I feel like I am looking at this new reading continuum through a dusty window." An educational assistant noted, "I learned it's not just us who have things to learn!" Together, one by one, they built the trust to say out loud, "I don't understand." Perhaps, that was one of the biggest steps they collectively took in changing the norms of the school.

The teams became more confident and were able to communicate their new understandings with parents. In doing so, they became educators of adults as well as children. The more the parents understood, the more they became involved. It wasn't until then that we started to learn why parents had not come to the earlier staff development meetings. We found that many were innately leery of bureaucracy. Some did not feel comfortable in an environment surrounded by "edu-jargon." Others were embarrassed to attend because they did not have appropriate school clothes. Transportation was an issue for others. Learning certainly had come full cycle, yet the process was very slow. Our work was cut out for us. We needed to keep embracing parents so that they, too, would be change agents.

Results of this planned, systematic change effort were threefold. First, the dysfunctional staff became more cohesive as they targeted a common goal. Second, they altered their norms of isolationism by working together as a group. Third, and of great importance, based on the data they collected during the action research phase of this plan, the school's federal grant proposal was accepted.

Although it may take 3–5 years to show academic growth on the standardized reading tests, the staff is now experienced in identifying problems and removing hindering forces that stand in the way of reaching their goals.

## WHAT STRATEGIES WE USED

Specifically, we used two Organization Development problem-solving strategies to alter the norms of our school's culture and to lead our community through change for purposes of increased student achievement. In this section, I describe how the Organization Development strategies of S-T-P (Situation-Target-Plan) and FFA (Force Field Analysis) were integrated with staff development and action research.

### Organization Development (OD)

Businesses have used OD strategies since the 1940s to strengthen their organizations. It was not until the 1960s that the notion caught on in the educational arena (see Schmuck and Perry, 1994, for a detailed historical background of OD). Many educational theorists try to succinctly capture the essence of OD. Perhaps Schmuck and Runkel (1994) painted the clearest picture by defining OD as a way to accomplish planned, systematic change. The intent here is not to oversimplify a complex series of interpersonal actions, but merely to provide a basic definition for further exploration and application.

OD strategies help participants organize their thoughts, express them in a risk-free environment, and work toward common goals. For instance, we used Schmuck and Runkel's OD strategy called S-T-P (Situation-Target-Plan) to create planned change in our school. In structured exercises, the teachers and staff identified their perceptions of the existing unsatisfactory *situation* (S), suggested more desirable goals or *targets* (T), and created a systematic plan (P) that would remove (or at least decrease) the gap between the S and T. Then they applied Lewin's force field analysis (FFA) to identify the issues that would help or hinder them from reaching their goals.

S-T-P, as explained by Schmuck and Runkel (1994), is part of a six-step problem-solving process:

| | |
|---|---|
| 1. Determine the current situation and desired target. | S and T |
| 2. Brainstorm ways to reach the target. | P |
| 3. Decide what forces will help or hinder your progress. | FFA |
| 4. Develop an action plan. | Plan |
| 5. Implement the plan. | Act |
| 6. Evaluate your efforts and make adjustments as needed. | Adjust |

During the S-T-P process, we conducted a force field analysis (FFA). FFA is a useful tool for quickly identifying what pressures need to be removed to reach a desired goal. Weisbord (1990) noted that, "(FFA) is effective as a group exercise because it helps people see all at once what can be done, and builds group support for follow-through" (p. 97). There are four steps in the FFA process:

1. Pick one high priority target (T).
2. Brainstorm all forces that might help or hinder reaching the targeted goal.
3. Choose up to six forces that might hinder progress the most.
4. Prioritize the six forces.

S-T-P and FFA helped our staff get ready to travel toward becoming a community of self-sustained problem solvers. Staff development served as the vehicle that helped them get there. Then action research carried them successfully to their new destination—a self-renewing organization whose main focus was increased student achievement.

## Staff Development

Vojtek's (1992) review of staff development literature drew her to the conclusion that staff developers were the critical link to organizational change. She wrote, "They are repeatedly being called to facilitate innovations which are designed to lead to effective school renewal and institutionalized school reform" (p.1). DuFour's (1991) work supports Vojtek's premise. He makes three observations: (1) the best place for school improvement to happen is at the local level, (2) to improve schools, the focus must be on people improvement, and (3) the principal is the key player in effective staff development leading to more proficient schools.

Sparks (1994) stresses that staff development alone does not lead to increased student achievement. He argues that Organizational Development must be a major school focus as well. I believed we needed to go a step further to reach our goals. Action research became a major piece of our change process.

### Action Research

Action research, unlike traditional research that simply reports findings, has as its purpose to improve education in the school that is conducting the research on its own practice. Sagor (1992) explained that action research "is conducted by people who want to do something to improve *their own situation* . . . they want to know whether they can do something in a better way" (p. 7). He noted that this is different from traditional research where the scientific researcher looks at "what *others* are doing or should be doing." Today many teachers are becoming involved in action research, studying their own work instead of being studied by outside "experts" (Cochran-Smith and Lytle, 1993). Principals and other educational leaders, too, must find practical ways to study issues that confront them and their schools. We found that action research was one way to meet our needs. It fit our desire to create change in our school. In using action research we learned how to (1) state our problems, (2) collect data, (3) analyze the data, (4) report the results, and (5) design an action plan that fits the needs of our school.

## WHAT I LEARNED

As the principal of this small rural school my responsibility was to serve as an instructional leader and vision-setter. I exercised this responsibility by assuming the roles of facilitator and motivator. Maintaining the neutral role of facilitator sometimes caused me great anguish. It was also difficult to separate the deep-seated organizational problems from the personalities within the school. For example, it was difficult to continue the project when the group identified the school's lack of focus as one of the three main hindering forces. I took that revelation as a personal affront to my leadership abilities. As the process continued, however, I learned that to be a successful educational leader, sometimes you must swallow your pride, put your ego aside, and be open to how others see the situation—a hard lesson for anyone to learn.

I also learned not to avoid confrontation. At the year-end district meeting, the Superintendent asked me to present the itinerant reading specialist to the School Board which routinely recognized retiring teachers.

Our staff came to the meeting to help our reading teacher celebrate her retirement. The Board granted her an opportunity to address them. She read a prepared statement explaining why she was retiring. In her statement, she lambasted the time we "wasted" at staff development meetings playing games and sitting around talking instead of using that time productively. She argued that what the teachers needed instead was a formal staff development program where qualified reading experts would provide strategies for direct implementation into the classrooms. She read direct quotes from early data feedback I had provided to the staff supporting her notion of how dysfunctional we were. Some of the teachers had confided in her about their concerns of process over product. She openly shared those comments with the Board as well. When she finished, the room was silent. My teachers and I were frozen. She quietly walked to the front of the room, received her retirement plaque, and returned to her seat.

I wished I had had a crystal ball to foresee what damage the itinerant reading specialist's distant attitude would ultimately reap. Perhaps, I should have tried harder to bring her into the conversation, probed for a better understanding of her position, and worked more collaboratively to meet her needs. When early on she removed herself from the project, I should have seen that as a red flag of impending doom. I learned that no matter how well-trained we think we are, we often come to the job ill-prepared, or at least only partially prepared, to facilitate change.

Schmuck and Runkel (1994) wrote "schools and colleges are social organizations. Without human collaboration and commitment, they are only wood, concrete, and paper. Typically, educational improvement requires less change in the paper and more change in the patterns of human action" (p. 1). Now, as a professor, I prepare future educational leaders who need skills to modify human behavior for the sake of creating increased student achievement. I often question how well prepared I am to carry out the task Schmuck and Runkel describe.

My university leadership preparation program made a gallant attempt to train me in many areas: business, finance, evaluation, supervision, organization theory, and law—to name a few. Developing planned, systematic change, however, appeared to be more theoretically embedded within existing courses rather than actively practiced.

Fortunately, in my doctoral program of studies I chose an elective in organization development taught by Richard Schmuck and Philip Runkel. Their keen insight and patient mentoring helped me use Organizational Development strategies in my principalship. Because of my studies with them, I was able to facilitate the development of a climate in my school that laid the foundation for increased trust and team building. That atmosphere ultimately increased the school's capacity for becoming a community of self-sustained problem solvers.

In my new role as a professor working with future educational leaders, I introduce OD strategies. The students learn how to apply those strategies so that teachers, staff, and parents can work together to systematically bring about planned change for the Davids of our world.

I firmly believe that all leadership programs must allow time for students to explore the OD skills of communication, problem solving, decision making, and constructive confrontation. Those skills are critical to an educational leader's success. Without them, there will be no school for David. There will only be the "wood, concrete, and paper" Schmuck and Runkel described earlier.

I encourage my students to question why staff development, OD, and action research are treated as separate entities as though life exists devoid of connections between knowing and doing. As we move toward a better understanding of integrating curriculum for students, I point out that it makes sense to also integrate learning experiences for the adults in our schools.

I share with my students our year-long journey as a school. I show them how they can integrate staff development principles, OD strategies, and action research methods to reduce the norms of isolationism within a school for the sake of improved student achievement. Based on what I learned as a principal, I now use the following model to demonstrate how to create collaborative school improvement (see Figure 3).

**Figure 3**    Our Collaborative School Improvement Model

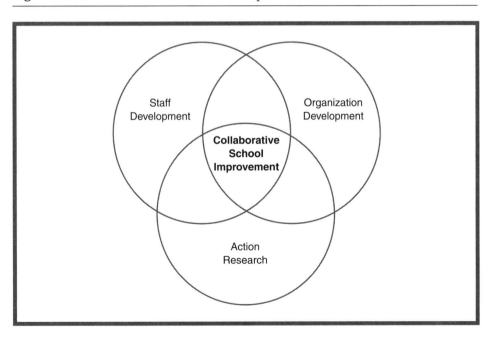

This model shows how a school administrator using *Organizational Development strategies* can facilitate planned, systematic change in a sustained effort to alter the dynamics of a social system. It encourages educators to go a step beyond traditional *staff development* by valuing the importance of involving the entire school community in a problem solving decision making process culminating in an *action research* project.

By integrating these three areas (i.e., OD strategies, staff development, and action research), I show my students how an educational leader's chances of successfully constructing an environment for increased student learning is greatly enhanced.

While teaching these concepts, I continue to picture the faces of our school's Davids, as they struggled with wanting to learn how to read. Then I look at the faces of my leadership students. I wonder if traditional preparation programs provide enough foundation for the challenges they will soon face. I wonder if the staff development, OD, and action research tools I provide will make a difference. For all too soon, it will be their turn to create a school for David.

## REFERENCES

Cochran-Smith, M. and Lytle, S. (1993). *Inside/Outside: Teacher research and knowledge.* New York: Teachers College Press.

DuFour, R. (1991). *The principal as staff developer.* Bloomington: National Education Service.

Sagor, R. (1992). *How to conduct collaborative action research.* Alexandria, VA: Association for Supervision and Curriculum Development.

Schmuck, R. and Perry, E. (1994). Organizational development and consultancy in education. In T. Husen and T. N. Postlethwaite (Eds.), *International encyclopedia of education.* London: Pergamon.

Schmuck, R. and Runkel, P. (1994). *The handbook of organization development in schools* (4th ed.). Prospect Heights, IL: Waveland Press.

Sizer, T. (1984). *Horace's compromise: The dilemma of the American high school.* Boston: Houghton Mifflin.

Sparks, D. (1994). A paradigm shift in staff development. *Journal of Staff Development, 15* (4), 26–29.

Vojtek, R. (1992). *Integrating staff development and organization development: An empirical study of staff developers.* Paper presented at the Annual Meeting of the American Education Research Association, San Francisco (April).

Weisbord, R. (1990). *Productive workplaces: Organizing and managing for dignity, meaning, and community.* San Francisco: Jossey-Bass.

# Exemplary Project

*Proactive Action Research to Build Leadership*
*for a Charter School's Success*

Lillian Thomas-Wilson

Wthin this twenty-first century of school reform and educational innovation, charter schools have emerged as cutting edge models in the public sector. They are leading the way in demonstrating how local school control and strong parental involvement in student learning can strengthen students' motivation and achievement.

Still, charter schools, like other more traditional public schools, face the challenge of selecting and training their own administrative leaders and professional managers. Indeed, the continuous self renewal and growth of charter schools will depend on the quality of their leadership. Charter schools will have difficulty surviving, even for another five years, if there are no new, vigorous leaders ready to replace the early innovators and contemporary managers. Unfortunately, too few experienced school administrators today want to risk the challenges and pitfalls of running a brand new charter school.

I faced that realization when I started my own charter school in South Carolina in 2002, leading me to design a proactive action research project about developing a "Team Leadership Strategy" focused on establishing professional cooperation to take the lead in ensuring our success and continuous improvement as a cutting edge charter school.

My action research focused on designing a training program for the future leaders of our school. I carefully recruited particular staff members with leadership potential, and over four years I gradually prepared them for formal leadership in the school. My report on the action research explains what I did to select the particular individuals, and how I trained them to carry out various administrative tasks in the school. My report explains what I did during each year of the four-year evolution to facilitate the new leaders' independence in working effectively with our students, staff, and parents. Throughout the action research I assessed the new leaders' weaknesses, strengths, discomforts, and comforts, while making available to them training events and workshops to increase their understandings and skills.

The main result of the project was enhanced teamwork, cooperation, and effectiveness in our charter-school leadership and student success. I hope that by reading about my action research, other charter school administrators and new charter school boards will find ways to plan their own strategies for developing future charter school leaders.

SOURCE: "Proactive Action Research to Build Leadership for a Charter School's Success", by Lillian Thomas-Wilson (2006) College of Education, Arizona State U. West.

# Exemplary Project

*Examining the Impact of External
Building Coaches on Teachers*

Betsy Apolito

Since The No Child Left Behind Act (NCLB) of 2001 mandated state achievement testing, a negative gap between federal targets for students' reading and math performance and their actual tested achievements have continued to increase in Ohio schools. Schools in which students continually do not meet those federal targets receive the undesirable status of "improvement required," thereby requiring them to sponsor ways to reduce student deficits and to demonstrate new programs to upgrade student performance. This action research focused on some Ohio schools designated in 2003 with "improvement required" status, and a special intervention entailing external-building coaches charged with helping teachers and administrators raise the reading and math achievement scores of their students.

The specific target groups were fifteen external building coaches and twenty-three Ohio schools (sixteen elementary, five middle, and two high schools) in which the coaches intervened. The coaches' mission was to upgrade teachers' capabilities to deliver effective instruction in reading and math to all students. Coaches aimed at helping teachers tailor their instruction to students' individual needs and learning styles, cooperate with one another in teams to maximize each teacher's strengths, use short-cycle student assessments to measure continuously their formative progress, and use "standards-based curriculum" data at each grade level to test students' summative performance in reading and math.

After several years of action research on the processes and results of external building coaching, we came up with three conclusions well supported by our data; External coaches successful in helping teachers raise students' reading and math scores: (1) conscientiously worked collaboratively with the school's administrators to develop a cohesive intervention team in which the administrators also acted effectively as coaches; (2) tactfully introduced professional development workshops to help teachers understand the "standards-based curriculum" appropriate to their students' grade level; and (3) diligently sought to establish cohesive teacher teams in which the members carried out continuous assessments of student performance in reading and math.

---

SOURCE: "Examining The Impact of External Building Coaches on Teachers", by Betsy Apolito (2006) College of Education, Arizona State U. West.

# Exemplary Project

## Implementing Strategies to Reduce Dropout Rates of At-Risk Youth in an Online Learning Environment

### Jill Gaitens

This action research, on what I entitled "The Connections Program," used online instruction, based on traditional research about high-school dropout prevention, to increase graduation rates and postsecondary opportunities for at-risk young adults, typically older than 18. In late 2005, I wrote a proposal to the Arizona Department of Education to fund implementation of the Connections Program; after four months my school successfully received a grant of nearly $200,000 to implement and do action research on Connections.

Although the on-line school in which I worked already had a well-designed academic curriculum, The Connections Program added: (1) remedial coursework in reading, writing, and math, (2) special training in "Arizona Workforce Skills," (3) transitional-postsecondary counseling to help students deal with foster home movements, parenthood, and substance abuse, and incarceration, or any other special challenge they faced, and (4) individualized assistance in academic test taking, study skills, and preparation for postsecondary opportunities, such as higher education, vocations, military service, and miscellaneous transitional assistance.

By fall 2006, after about nine months of implementing The Connections Program, our action research data showed that (1) on the AIMS test (Arizona Instrument to Measure Standards), 70% of Connections' students, overall, who had previously failed it, now could meet or exceed most of the state's standards; (2) in particular, 79% of Connections students met or exceeded reading standards, 76% met or exceeded writing standards, and 55% met or exceeded math standards; (3) Connections' students increased their online participation 31% over the previous year; and (4) the dropout rate of Connections' students decreased from 13% in 2005 to 2.5% in 2006.

With those results our Connections Program received a similar funding amount for the 2006–2007 school year, and it became eligible for renewed funding until 2012, provided the action research results continue to be favorable.

SOURCE: "Implementing Strategies to Reduce Dropout Rates of At-Risk Youth in an Online Learning Environment", by Jill Gaitens (2006) College of Education, Arizona State U. West.

# Exemplary Project

*Singapore Math: Action Research on a Curriculum Change,*
*Student Achievement and Teacher Efficacy*

Barbara J. Darroch

This proactive action research focused on implementing a new math curriculum in an Arizona elementary school. The project dealt with changing the math curriculum and training teachers to teach the new curriculum effectively.

I carried out the action research at Benchmark Elementary School, a charter school, located in the Paradise Valley School District, near Phoenix. From 2001–2003 Benchmark teachers became increasingly concerned with weak math performances of many of their fourth graders as measured by the AIMS test (Arizona Instrument to Measure Standards).

A Benchmark committee (I as the administrator and two teachers) read results of the Third International Mathematics and Science Study (TIMSS), an ambitious international study on student achievement. In a sample of forty-one countries the committee found that Singapore students earned first place in math while U.S. students scored far below the mean. Upon further study our committee discovered that Singapore Math had been organized well to motivate students with its captivating word story problems. They saw that the Singapore curriculum progressed logically, delved into a range of numerical concepts deeply, and carefully connected one concept to the next. They saw, too, that Singapore Math taught a skill and followed it up with attractive stories, thus accomplishing several objectives: it allowed students to see new concepts from different perspectives, required them to solve problems with different operations, called for skills students had learned in previous lessons, and provided them some review while introducing new work.

The target group for our action research was 80 third and fourth graders and their six teachers. Our methods included (1) before and after structured questionnaires for students and teachers, (2) systematic observations of the teachers when they were receiving training, and (3) before and after Stanford Nine Math tests for the students.

Our data analysis showed that those teachers who authentically and validly implemented the Singapore Math curriculum fostered positive student attitudes toward math and helped their students increase their Stanford Nine Math scores. Over time, the Benchmark committee and the third and fourth grade teachers saw the new curriculum as a success. Postschool year faculty discussion, however, revealed that more training and support of teachers would be necessary for the Singapore curriculum to flourish with the students. The Benchmark committee concluded that curriculum improvement depends more on teacher effectiveness in implementation than it does on the curriculum content.

SOURCE: "Singapore Math: Action Research on a Curriculum Change, Student Achievement, and Teacher Efficacy", by Barbara J. Darroch (2004) College of Education, Arizona State U. West.

# Exemplary Project

## Increasing Math Achievement
## of Title 1 Middle School Students

### Tatyana Chayka

Today our world is largely shaped by mathematics and science. Modern communications, entertainment, financial activities, law enforcement, medicine, sports, and transportation all make heavy use of math. Moreover, the need for citizens to use accurate, logical, precise, and rigorous thinking is more important now than ever before. We, the faculty of The Academy of Math and Science (AMS) in Tucson, Arizona seek to ensure that our students in all grades learn the math skills necessary for their future success. The official mission of AMS reads, "We are a charter school dedicated to providing students with a top quality education; we emphasize math and science, while also providing a superior education in all aspects of a well-rounded school curriculum."

With its startup in 2000 AMS began to address the need for a high-quality academic school on Tucson's west side in a neighborhood with families of low socioeconomic status. For its initial six years it has been designated as a Title 1 school by the Arizona Department of Education. By the summer of 2006 AMS employed 18 teachers with many years of experience in national and international schools.

During the summer of 2004, I chaired an instructional committee at AMS, which identified weak student performance in math as a curriculum focus for improvement. We found that the majority of our newly arriving Title 1 students were transferring to AMS performing several years below grade level in math. Working collaboratively with two of the committee members, I designed a proactive action research project targeted at the ninety-two students of our middle school (grades six through eight). During the 2004–2005 school year we initiated two main instructional changes in math: increased instructional time and small-group intensive tutorials.

To our middle-school students' schedules we added an extra math class per week, where students practiced math concepts with which they were having difficulty. In addition, our middle-school teachers selected seven to nine students at each grade level to receive special math tutoring from AMS's support staff. Those tutorials met for two hours each week, taking the place of those students' electives. Other special small-group instruction, aimed at sixth graders, who were far below their grade level in math, was given by teams of support teachers and regular classroom teachers who removed a few low-performing students at a time and gave them individually tailored instruction and feedback.

*(Continued)*

(Continued)

Results of the proactive intervention in math were quite positive. Whereas in fall 2004, 34% of AMS middle-school students failed the math standards, by spring 2005 less than 17% failed. The success rate moved from 66% to 83% in less than nine months. The most significant change occurred with the lowest achieving students, where most of the efforts of the interventions were focused, with 21% failing in the fall and only 2% failing in the spring. Results of the continuing action research were even more striking when analyzed over the two-year period from 2003 to 2005. Whereas 54% of AMS middle-school students failed the math standards earlier, only 8% tested below par two years later. Overall, AMS students' scores on the math section of the Arizona Instrument to Measure Standards in 2006 placed them among the top ten schools in Tucson.

SOURCE: "Increasing Math Achievement of Title 1 Middle School Students," by Tatyana Chayka (2005) College of Education, Arizona State U. West.

# 6

# Action Research for School Improvement

## Emily F. Calhoun

S eeking to understand and acting on the best we know. That describes
how most educators hope to live and grow as professionals. It also
describes action research. For the past 10 years, I have used that statement
to introduce action research to school teams, administrators, and other
educators in central offices, intermediate service agencies, and departments of education.

A more formal definition of action research is continual disciplined
inquiry conducted to inform and improve our practice as educators.
Action research asks educators to study their practice and its context,
explore the research base for ideas, compare what they find to their current
practice, participate in training to support needed changes, and study the
effects on themselves and their students and colleagues.

For 60 years, action research has been an avenue for creating professional learning communities whose members engage in problem solving
and for attaining individual and collective goals. As Lewin (1948) wrote,
action research can

> transform . . . a multitude of unrelated individuals frequently
> opposed in their outlook and their interests, into cooperative
> teams, not on the basis of sweetness but on the basis of readiness to

SOURCE: "Action Research for School Improvement," by Emily F. Calhoun (2002)
Redesigning Professional Development, 59 (6), 18-24. Reprinted with permission.

face difficulties realistically, to apply honest fact-finding, and to work together to overcome them. (p. 211)

My experience with action research has convinced me of its potential to transform professional development. Action research can change the social system in schools and other education organizations so that continual formal learning is both expected and supported. It can replace superficial coverage with depth of knowledge. And it can generate data to measure the effects of various programs and methods on student and staff learning.

## ACTION RESEARCH AT WORK: A TEACHER'S STORY

Katie's school was involved in an initiative called "Every Child Reads." Sponsored by the Iowa state department of education, the initiative aimed to change the context in which participants engaged in professional development, help them become more closely connected to scholarship in reading, and support them in generating knowledge and increasing their capacity as learners and leaders. Over a three-year period, participating school facilitation teams (composed of teachers, the principal, and, when possible, district office and intermediate service agency staff responsible for supporting school improvement) became a statewide professional learning community engaged in the study of literacy.

Participants attended 14 days of workshops and received additional technical assistance at their school sites. They studied current practices in their schools and classrooms; examined research related to literacy development; selected and used evaluative instruments to assess literacy; organized and used data to make decisions about effectiveness; learned how to implement new practices; and learned to provide staff development to colleagues as they engaged in these same actions.

Katie implemented the picture word inductive model (PWIM), a new teaching strategy for her, and studied her kindergarten students' vocabulary development as a part of learning to use this model. The picture word inductive model is an inquiry-oriented language arts approach that uses pictures containing familiar objects and actions to elicit words from students' own vocabularies. Teachers use it to lead their students into inquiring about word properties, adding words to their sight-reading and writing vocabularies, discovering phonetic and structural principles, and using observation and analysis in their study of reading, writing, comprehending, and composing. The picture word cycles (inquiries into the pictures) generally take from four to six weeks at the kindergarten level (Calhoun, 1999).

At first, Katie thought the learning tasks might be too demanding for her students. But as she tried the model and studied what her students did in response, she changed her mind. Katie's data collection showed that her students had achieved a mean gain of 16 sight vocabulary words during their third PWIM unit (in November), and a mean gain of 27 words in their sixth unit (ending in mid-March). These results confirmed for Katie the effectiveness of the picture word inductive model.

Katie also collected detailed data on each student's word knowledge as he or she began the unit and again at the end of the unit. The data allowed her to analyze the word-reading strategies that individual students were using: sight vocabulary, decoding, analogies, common spelling patterns, and context clues (Ehri, 1999). As she analyzed the data for each student and across students, Katie made many instructional decisions, such as which phonics principles needed additional explicit instruction, when more modeling was needed to support using context clues, which students needed small-group work on phonemic analysis, and who needed special attention to encourage independent decoding.

Studying specific domains of student performance and her own instructional practice has become a way of life for Katie.

## THE POWER OF ORGANIZATION-WIDE SUPPORT

Katie's use of action research occurred as part of a structured initiative sponsored by a state department of education. This initiative illustrates how education leaders in states, districts, and schools are attempting to make action research a dominant way of doing business-building an organization context that supports inquiry by school staffs working as a whole and by smaller groups and individuals pursuing their particular avenues of study. The development of inquiring communities is what distinguishes action research from school improvement approaches that focus on the implementation of specific initiatives, such as a new curriculum or a new mode of assessment.

Although I am an advocate of carefully conducted action research whether it is individual, collaborative, or organization-wide, I put my professional energy and time into supporting schoolwide and organization-wide action research (Calhoun, 1994; Joyce, Calhoun, & Hopkins, 1999). This action research option has the power to transform the organization into a learning community.

My experience is that regular use of multiple sources of data to inform us about student performance or our own performance is often threatening at first, because it requires that we juxtapose our practices and our students' performance against exemplary research-based practices and high levels of student performance attained in similar settings. The resulting confrontation and social turmoil, however, may be natural accompaniments to substantive change.

The good news is that when groups have adequate organization support in using data as a source of information to guide practice, leadership generally surfaces within the group. These leaders provide examples of using classroom data to make instructional and curriculum changes and model informed decision making and problem solving in action. Their schools begin to use on-site data and the external knowledge base as sources for continually assessing the effectiveness of actions and current practices.

This emerging leadership often signals a change in the social system of the school. It doesn't come easily in most settings, but with opportunity and leadership from school and district administrators, it happens. Along with benefits for students, educators feel more professional.

## USING A STRUCTURED ACTION RESEARCH MODEL

Educators who wish to use action research for professional development or school improvement should select a structured process to use in the school, district, or region. Many resources are available. Although all action research approaches encourage disciplined inquiry, reflection, and the improvement of practice or expansion of knowledge, they do vary in purposes and emphases.

My own approach (Calhoun, 1994) focuses on the schoolwide or district-wide pursuit of student learning goals. It emphasizes using action research to change how the organization works so that educators study student and staff learning continually and pour information from the external knowledge base into the collective study and action-taking process. Glanz (1998) provides a number of tools useful for administrators and leadership teams as they study school effectiveness and student performance. Sagor (1992) emphasizes the development of collaborative action research teams who identify issues or problems, study the context of those problems, collect data, take actions, and engage in discourse and reflection around the results of those actions. And Hopkins (in press) emphasizes changes in classroom practice through careful study by individual teachers as researchers.

After selecting a resource or action research model, those leading the effort need to learn to use it in their work and determine how to support its use within their organization. If no one in the initiating group has experience and skill in using action research, perhaps faculty members at the local college or university can provide technical assistance.

If the group wishes to use action research to support school improvement as well as individual professional development, the chief administrators in the school or district need to be on board-preferably as members of the initiating group. In most settings, school or district staff members will need to change the way they use data, study student and staff learning, and use the external research base. These changes are unlikely to occur if principals, district office staff members, and the superintendent do not participate and help lead the effort.

## THE SCHOOLWIDE ACTION RESEARCH MATRIX

Figure 1 provides an example of how schools might structure their action research around a common student learning goal. In providing technical assistance to sites working to implement action research focused on student achievement, I often recommend that they use this Schoolwide Action Research Matrix as a guide for structuring collective inquiry and action. The matrix includes a place to identify the student learning goal that a staff selects for its current collective focus and six sections to describe the content of collective study and action. Educators build their school or district action plans and staff development plans around the actions outlined in each of the six matrix sections.

## The Schoolwide Action Research Matrix—One Example

**School Focus:** *To improve reading comprehension* (Academic student learning goal in a curriculum area)

**Figure 1**

| Learners (Students) | | Learning Environment (District/School) | | |
|---|---|---|---|---|
| **ON-SITE INFORMATION:** (Information at the district/ school level) | **1. Current student information** <br><br> **Gates-MacGinitie scores, grade 9:** <br> Only 25% of students scored at GLE 9.0 or higher <br><br> **State tests:** <br> Matched comparisons, student performance decreased from grade 8 to 10: <br> 1998–1999, 12% <br> 1999–2000, 10% <br> 2000–2001, 14% <br><br> **Teacher, parent, and business leader perceptions:** consensus that students are not prepared | **3. Student performance and response we would like to see** <br><br> • Students able to comprehend and learn from the texts being used in courses <br><br> • No loss from 8th to 10th grade on state curriculum tests <br><br> • More benchmarks will be developed | **4. Information about the current learning environment in our district/ school** <br><br> • Summer school <br><br> • Tutorials <br><br> • Buddy program <br><br> • Special education <br><br> • Reading aloud <br><br> • Group work <br><br> • Extra time for assignments <br><br> • Computer tutorials | **6. Learning environment we would like to see** <br><br> • Increased staff development on designing classroom activities and homework assignments <br><br> • Increased student access to tradebooks <br><br> • More tutors <br><br> • A course for accelerating literacy for struggling students |

*(Continued)*

**Figure 1** (Continued)

| Learners (Students) | Learning Environment (District/School) | |
| --- | --- | --- |
| | **2. External information about learners/students** | **5. External information about the learning environment** |
| **EXTERNAL INFORMATION: (Study of literature, standards, & best practices)** | • Data from the state testing program from other high schools with similar demographics; found 3 schools with better performance<br><br>• NAEP Executive Summary and test Items<br><br>• District curriculum standards | Collective study of Four selected texts:<br><br>• Moore et al. (1999). *Adolescent Literacy: A Position Statement*<br><br>• Stahl (1999). *Vocabulary Development* (pp. 8–13)<br><br>• Richardson (2000). *Read It Aloud: Using Literature in the Secondary Content Classroom*<br><br>• Showers et al. (1998). "A Second Chance to Learn to Read" |

## CURRENT STUDENT INFORMATION

Scores on both norm-referenced tests and state curriculum exams told the staff that their students were performing below expected levels. For example, the staff reviewed data comparing their students' reading performance on the state curriculum tests in 8th grade with the performance of the same cohort in 10th grade. In the three years studied, the mean percentiles in reading had decreased 12 percent, 10 percent, and 14 percent from their 8th grade levels.

Staff members also collected data about perceptions. Teachers identified many instances where students would have been able to manage the assignments from their courses had they had better literacy skills. And according to data from the past three years of school climate questionnaires, dissatisfaction with students' reading and writing performance had been a persistent problem identified by parents (42 percent), the business community (60 percent), and school staff members (75 percent).

## EXTERNAL INFORMATION ABOUT LEARNERS

The staff reviewed data on student reading performance in high schools with demographics similar to theirs. Out of 21 high schools studied, they found three where students were performing at much higher levels in reading and writing on state tests administered in 10th grade. The principal had insisted that the staff look at these data because he wanted teachers to recognize that some schools with similar student populations were achieving better results.

To gather information about the literacy standards that students should be achieving, the staff also reviewed their district's new curriculum standards document and the executive summary and sample items from the National Assessment of Education Progress in Reading (Donahue, Voelkl, Campbell, & Mazzeo, 1999).

## STUDENT PERFORMANCE GOALS

Staff members decided that they wanted to improve the reading performance of all their students to the point where students could at least manage the secondary education that was planned for them-the basic high school curriculum.

Using the state tests, they set one of their first targets: Students would not lose ground in their scores on these tests between 8th and 10th grade. Staff members, however, were not ready to set other benchmarks or indicators of performance. The facilitators agreed that it might be useful to begin by studying what worked to improve reading performance and how much this performance could be improved in a semester or year. Then, the staff would set further benchmarks for improvement.

## INTERNAL INFORMATION ABOUT THE LEARNING ENVIRONMENT

Next, the facilitation team organized the teachers to identify the programs, initiatives, and instructional practices that they were currently using to address the literacy problem. Organization efforts already in place included summer school programs, after-school and lunchtime tutorials, a "buddy program" in which high school students read with elementary students once a week, and special education programs. In addition, individual teachers identified what they were already doing to help struggling students, such as reading materials aloud, using computer programs, giving students extra time for assignments, and using cooperative learning. The teachers agreed, however, that they had no systematic program or plan for accelerating the reading and literacy development of the struggling readers and writers.

## EXTERNAL INFORMATION ABOUT THE LEARNING ENVIRONMENT

The facilitation team had a resource collection of about 20 articles and chapters and four books. From this, the team selected four items for in-depth study by the staff. At staff meetings during the next two months, the teachers worked in cross-department groups to discuss and analyze each item. Using structured response sheets (Sparks, 1999), they identified curriculum ideas, instructional strategies, and assessment techniques that would be applicable in their courses, as well as ideas about organizing the learning environment more effectively in terms of staff deployment, class size, changes in course availability, and scheduling. A facilitation team member worked with each group.

## LEARNING ENVIRONMENT GOALS

The facilitation team studied what groups had derived from their analyses and put together a tentative action plan for the staff to review. The plan included actions at the school level, actions all teachers would take, and actions for departments. Actions included

- Providing a series of staff development sessions on designing classroom activities and homework assignments, including modeling and discussing successful strategies for gaining meaning from text.
- Increasing student access to high-quality, non-fiction tradebooks at a range of reading levels (in classrooms, the school library, and community libraries).
- Recruiting more tutors, providing a better support system for them, and increasing the amount of time tutoring is available before and after school.
- Developing a course for accelerating literacy for those students who are reading two or more grade levels below their placement. The course would be 90 minutes per day, replace elective courses, and focus primarily on the reading and writing of informative prose. Both teachers and students would study progress assiduously.

## SOME RESULTS

A group of teachers volunteered to teach the literacy course. A consultant helped the group design it and learn the new teaching strategies that were needed. The teachers selected students for the course on the basis of a combination of standardized test scores and teacher judgment, serving the poorest readers first. During the first semester, the teachers enlisted the students in the formative evaluation process. For example, each student kept a "word box" that contained cards with vocabulary words that he or she was learning.

It became immediately apparent that the standardized test scores were *overestimates* of the actual reading levels of many of the students. About half of them were not even sure of the "high-frequency, useful little words" that are often learned in the first year of school.

At the end of the first semester, a re-administration of the standardized test indicated that about half of the student scores had risen about two grade level equivalents, and by the end of the second semester, most of the students were making gains and had learned how to learn more effectively, Teachers and students are continuing to refine and improve the class.

## THE POTENTIAL FOR CHANGE

As with other types of school improvement efforts, school and district staff members who attempt to make effective use of action research will encounter barriers to change. They may have difficulty providing time for the staff to work together, finding and supporting staff members who are willing to lead such work, and designing collective work that improves student learning, professional expertise, and staff leadership capacity simultaneously.

Its a challenging task to help staff structure action research into their work and the work of the organization. Yet we know that improvement in education requires us to change the typical, ineffective practice of professional development.

The good news is that we have options and models. When used as an organization-wide process for school improvement, action research changes the context and provides a way of organizing collective work so that professional expertise is tended and extended, helping to build a strong professional learning community, Whether action research is used as a school improvement tool or as an individual professional development option, staff members who draw on the current research base, add to their current knowledge, and create new knowledge-in-action can make instruction in the school or in the classroom more intentional and effective for student learning.

## REFERENCES

Calhoun, E. F. (1994). *How to use action research in the self-renewing school.* Alexandria, VA: ASCD.

Calhoun, E. F. (1999). *Teaching beginning reading and writing with the picture word inductive model.* Alexandria, VA: ASCD.

Donahue, P. L., Voelke, K. E., Campbell, J. R., & Mazzeo, J. (1999). *NAEP 1998 reading report card for the nation and states.* Washington, DC: U.S. Department of Education.

Ehri, L. C. (1999, April). Phases of acquisition in learning to read words and instructional implications. Paper presented to the annual meeting of the American Educational Research Association, Montreal, Canada.

Glanz, J. (1998). *Action research: An educational leader's guide to school improvement.* Norwood, MA: Christopher-Gordon.

Hopkins, D. (In press). A *teacher's guide to classroom research* (3rd ed.). Buckingham, England: Open University Press.

Joyce, B., Calhoun, E. F., & Hopkins, D. (1999). *The new structure of school improvement: Inquiring schools and achieving students.* Buckingham, England: Open University Press.

Lewin, K. (1948). Action research and minority problems. In K. Lewin, *Resolving social conflicts; Selected papers on group dynamics* (compiled in 1948). New York: Harper & Row.

Moore, D. W., Bean, T. W., Birdyshaw, D., & Rycik, J. A. (1999). *Adolescent literacy: A position statement.* Newark, DE: International Reading Association.

Richardson, J. S. (2000). *Read it aloud! Using literature in the secondary content classroom.* Newark, DE: International Reading Association.

Sagor, R. (1992). *How to conduct collaborative action research.* Alexandria, VA: ASCD.

Showers, B., Joyce, B., Scanlon, M., & Schaubelt, C. (1998). A second chance to learn to read. *Educational Leadership, 55*(6), 27–30.

Sparks, D. (1999). The singular power of one goal: An interview with Emily Calhoun. *Journal of Staff Development, 20*(1), 54–58.

Stahl, S. A. (1999). *Vocabulary development.* Cambridge, MA: Brookline Books.

# Exemplary Project

*Action Research on Middle School Mathematics
Instruction Differentiated by Student Gender*

Joshua Jordan

In this action research I aimed, as a math teacher, to increase students' math achievement by teaching differently to segregated groups of boys and girls. I carried out the project during the 2004–2005 school year at Westwind Middle School Academy, a Phoenix-based charter school, serving seventh and eighth graders, most of whom came from troubled, lower-class urban families.

In preparing for the 2003–2004 year, Westwind's Board decided to try to enhance students' academic performance by moving from coeducational classroom instruction to sex-segregated classrooms in the core subjects. After one year, however, Westwind students had failed to demonstrate the achievement gains that, according to the literature, were so prevalent in other sex-segregated schools. Westwind students' test results on the Arizona Instrument to Measure Standards (AIMS) in math were not significantly improved in spring 2004 from what they were in spring 2003.

During summer 2004 I planned new classroom practices for my instruction that would, I hoped, cater specifically to boys' and girls' different learning styles in math. After I read extensively in the literature on single sex instruction and reflected on my 2003–2004 teaching experiences, I came up with the following checklist to guide my 2004 lesson planning:

**Boys:**

Competition, to include races, timed tasks, and contests between teams.

One-at-a-time directions, to give very brief preview of overall result of directions, then break them down into one step at a time. Directions should be clear, concise, and repeated with visual clues, modeled outcomes, and ample wait time for each step.

Terminology, conducive to competition.

Gender-relevant attention-getters, such as cut to the chase, quick examples or a demonstration.

Fewer story problems, especially when introducing new concepts.

**Girls:**

Collaboration, such as peer tutoring, whole class projects, and frequent class discussions.

Big picture directions, to give detailed preview of the overall results of the directions, then break them down into multiple steps (two to three at a time). Directions should

*(Continued)*

(Continued)

be clear, concise, and repeated with gestures, modeled outcomes, and ample time for completion.

Terminology, conducive to cooperation.

Gender-relevant attention-getters, such as life examples, demonstrations, real-world events.

More story problems, especially when introducing new concepts.

During the first semester, fall 2004, as I tried a series of new practices based on that checklist, I also solicited students' reactions by (1) having them reflect on their own math learning styles by completing a thirty-item *Student Learning Preferences Questionnaire*, (2) conducting interviews about their perceptions of the math instruction, (3) keeping my own reflective journal in which I recorded my observations of the students, (4) forming small groups to keep weekly journals about math, and (5) videotaping several of my whole-class teaching sessions.

Results of those five data collection methods indicated to me that (1) boys prefer to work out problems on the board, research how math is used in real life, and practice problems independently; (2) girls prefer to take notes, for me to remain in the front of the room, and do homework every night; (3) boys tend to play rather than work in cooperative groups, whereas girls seem to work naturally well when cooperating, and, more than the boys, to stay on task; (4) girls typically are self starters, while boys often need considerable prodding and pushing; (5) when voting on solutions, boys are assertively outspoken, while girls strive to please one another; (6) boys need directions one at a time. Otherwise they hear the first step and miss the rest, leading them to complete the first step at the expense of knowing what to do when they have finished. Girls tend to do better with directions that are chunked into two or three steps at a time. They seem to get bored when directions are given one at a time; (7) girls like to play math games, but boys love them; and (8) the closer I followed my gender-specific lesson plans, the smoother each period would go.

I measured seventh and eighth grade students' math achievement with my own criterion-referenced pre- and posttests throughout the year and eighth grade student' achievement with the Arizona Instrument to Measure Standards (AIMS) math test at the end of the year. Girls did considerably better than boys on all unit posttests averaging 79.7% as compared to 68.6% for the boys, but by the end of the year, girls averaged 63.6%, while the boys averaged 68.6%, indicating that the boys retained a little more math than the girls overall. In general students' performances on the yearlong pre- and posttests showed great improvement overall. The seventh grade boys mean score rose 20.8%, while the eighth grade boys mean score rose 18.1%. The seventh grade girls improved 11.4%, while the eighth grade girls showed the greatest improvement of 33%. In spring 2004, 90% of Westwind eighth grades failed to meet the standards on the AIMS math test, while in spring 2005 that failure score was cut in half: 45% of Westwind eighth graders failed. After nine months of my special sex-differentiated teaching 50% of eighth graders met the AIMS standard and 5% exceeded it. And the eighth grade boys did just as well as the eighth grade girls in 2005. Westwind eighth graders, furthermore, made significantly greater gains in 2005 than other eighth graders in Arizona. In 2004 37% of all Arizona students fell below the AIMS standard, as compared with 19% in 2005, an improvement of 18%. Compare that to the 45% improvement at Westwind and we can call my intervention successful.

SOURCE: "Action Research on Middle School Mathematics Instruction Differentiated by Student Gender", by Joshua Jordan (2005) College of Education, Arizona State U.West.

*7*

# What Happens When a School District Supports Action Research

## Cathy Caro-Bruce and Jennifer McCreadie

I n 1990, 10 staff members of this [Madison Metropolitan] school district sat around a table intensely discussing their action research questions. The two facilitators, feeling the excitement and uneasiness that come with stepping into unfamiliar territory, encouraged, probed, and reassured the eight elementary school teachers as they worked through the process of inquiring about their topics. Another 12 middle school teachers and 12 elementary principals participated in action research the following year. In 1992–93, we were joined by four additional facilitators, and almost 40 elementary and middle school teachers were split among four action research groups. Over 40 teachers became action researchers during 1993–94, and 10 facilitators led five groups.

How did action research grow in this district? How can a district support and sustain a large number of teachers and principals interested in participating in this experience? Several critical elements have nurtured the growth of classroom action research in the Madison Metropolitan School District, and the implications may be helpful to other districts interested in establishing an active action research program. In this chapter, we will describe the background and context of how action research has

SOURCE: Reprinted by permission of the Publisher. From Susan E. Noffke, Robert B. Stevenson, (editors), *Educational Action Research: Becoming Practically Critical*, New York: Teachers College Press, © 1995 by Teachers College, Columbia University. All rights reserved.

grown in the district; the organization and process being used to help teachers and principals work on their questions; the value of the experience as perceived by the participants; and some lessons we have learned about implementing classroom action research in our school district. This is Madison's story, but aspects of it could easily apply to other districts.

The Madison Metropolitan School District is located in Madison, Wisconsin, the state capital and home of the main campus of the University of Wisconsin. This is a city where education has been valued and supported by the community. With approximately 24,000 students, the district has 29 elementary schools, nine middle schools, and four high schools. The teaching staff comprises approximately 2,100 elementary, middle, and high school classroom teachers.

## BEGINNINGS

Classroom action research did not arrive in Madison for the first time in the fall of 1990. Rather, commitment, patience, and making the most of opportunities contributed to its development over time. For 2 years, beginning in 1985, a staff development specialist in the district sought funding to try this idea. She had heard about action research at a teacher center conference and thought it would be an interesting and stimulating staff development activity. After justifying the use of a pocket of research money to fund released time (to pay substitute teachers), she embarked on this independent project. Seven teachers from kindergarten through high school participated the first year, five teachers during the second year. Although teachers felt the experience was worthwhile, as with many initiatives, it was seen as this individual's project.

When this staff development specialist left the district after the second year of action research, she hoped that what she had begun would be sustained. At this stage, a partnership was born, which continues, bringing together the authors of this chapter, a staff development specialist and the coordinator of research and evaluation for the district. In the fall of 1987, with a little knowledge, a strong inclination, a collection of books and articles, and notes from the previous facilitator, we designed a 6-hour course to introduce district staff to the concept of teachers researching questions important to them. We thought that if we could build some knowledge of and interest in the process, teachers would sign up when money could be found to support them. When just two people registered, we canceled the workshop.

During the 1987–88 school year, we presented information about action research to a district leadership group and to elementary principals. Action research was met with mild interest, and several suggestions were made for possible sources of money for released time, which we felt was essential to attract and sustain participants. We went to the schools where special money had been allocated to support racial integration.

Teachers were interested in action research, but their money had already been designated for other projects, and they were hesitant to take on yet another commitment.

————————— ❧ —————————

*Teachers were interested in action research, but were hesitant to take on yet another commitment.*

At the same time, some dramatic changes in the demographics of the school district's student population were being recognized. Dialogue increased among staff about trying to meet the needs of more diverse, more challenging students. Teachers were finding that what used to work in their classrooms was no longer appropriate or successful. Some district funds were directed toward schools with high levels of special needs. In the beginning, the efforts were designed by individual schools, but it became apparent that district resources had to be organized more effectively. Minority student achievement became a district priority. Continuing to seek funding, we talked with principals at schools that had minority student achievement grants, but their money was committed to other efforts. Our determination and search were eventually rewarded, however.

For 2 years, the district had been supporting a project called "Cultural Differences and Classroom Strategies." Elementary school teachers had been participating in this effort to help teachers increase the repertoire of instructional strategies they used to meet a variety of needs of students from different socioeconomic and ethnic backgrounds. The third year of this project (1990–91) was to be spent helping teachers to implement the ideas they had been discussing and to learn what was making a difference to students' success in school. Action research had the potential to enable teachers who had participated in the Cultural Differences and Classroom Strategies project to explore these ideas more deeply. The Cultural Differences and Classroom Strategies planning committee supported the idea and allocated funds for the project.

Finally, there was a source of funding and an organizational connection to action research. The budget would cover the cost of substitute teachers for a total of 6 full days of released time (a combination of half- and full-day meetings), materials (notebooks, references, and journals), and printing (handouts and final report).

## THE ACTION RESEARCHERS

In the spring of 1990, we described action research to all elementary principals and asked them to encourage teachers to consider participating. Information and an application form were sent to all elementary teachers in the district (about 800). Eight teachers applied, and they became our first group. We felt that we were finally on our way, although at the time it was not clear what that meant.

The 1990–91 year was a learning experience every step of the way. At times, it seemed that we were barely staying ahead of the group.

—————— ✂ ——————

*What initially seemed like a blow later turned into an opportunity.*

—————————————

Numerous hours were spent planning the next session, analyzing what took place at the previous session, and continuing to educate ourselves about action research. But the time was invaluable in what we learned.

We learned, for example, that if teachers settled on a question too quickly, they might narrow their focus and choose topics that might not sustain their interest over the year. Yet, if they did not decide on a question after several meetings, the likelihood of completing a quality project within the time frame was lessened. Journals, we discovered, cannot be a required activity. For some teachers, it was a helpful way to record their thinking over time; for others, it was merely a task to be completed and to feel guilty about when they didn't. We learned the value of having more than one teacher from a school participate in the group. When back at their schools, these teachers could talk about their questions and were able to support each other through various stages of their projects. As we learned more about the action research process, we gained confidence in what we were doing.

We began to look ahead to the following year. Since we had worked with a group of elementary teachers, we thought it would be worthwhile to offer this opportunity to middle school teachers. We were curious about whether middle school teachers would be interested in this kind of experience, and how it might differ from our work with elementary teachers. At about that time the Cultural Differences and Classroom Strategies budget was cut in half. With that decision went half the funding for released time for teachers. However, what initially seemed like a blow later turned into an opportunity.

At a middle school principals' meeting, we described classroom action research and asked the principals to support one or two teachers from their school budgets (e.g., Minority Student Achievement, Talented and Gifted, School Improvement Planning funds). If they would commit half of the costs for each teacher, the Cultural Differences project budget would cover the other half. The response was enthusiastic. Principals indicated that many teachers were attempting to look at their instruction and curriculum from different perspectives, and the principals appreciated the importance of supporting those efforts.

A casual comment by the assistant superintendent for secondary education during our presentation to a meeting with middle school principals took action research into an exciting and entirely new direction for our district. As she watched principals become enthusiastic about the possibilities, she announced, "We should have action research for administrators, and I already have my question!" Everyone chuckled, and we smiled and promised to "follow up with you on that suggestion." What resulted from that brief exchange was the formation of the school district's principals' action research group. The assistant superintendent for elementary education followed up by writing a memo encouraging principals to participate. He discussed it with each principal as he met with them for their conferences at the end of the year. We believe that his personal contact and encouragement were persuasive. Although skeptics in the district told us there was no way a group of principals would participate, when the application forms were returned, 14 principals had signed up. The 1991–92 action research groups ultimately consisted of a classroom action research group of 12 middle school teachers from seven middle schools and a principals' action research group of 12 elementary principals.

## AN ACTION RESEARCH CULTURE

Teachers' and principals' action research has gradually become part of the culture of the Madison Metropolitan School District. During the winter of 1992, a panel of teachers and principals shared their action research questions and experiences with the Education Committee of the Board of Education. The presentation was designed to inform the Committee about this project, but also to start to build a financial commitment to action research. The response was enthusiastic, with one committee member asserting, "This should not be a question of how can we let people participate in action research, but how can we not have everyone doing this!" It was time to look ahead to the next year (1992–93).

Having facilitated a small group of elementary teachers the first year, and recognizing that we were novices at what we were doing, we thought it would be appropriate to offer the experience to another group of elementary teachers the following year. When we discussed this with our group of middle school action researchers, they responded, "But we've been talking this up at our school," and "I know other middle school teachers who are interested in participating."

*It had become clear that interest in action research was growing.*

It was time to rethink the direction for action research in the district. It was apparent that this project had moved beyond the pilot stage and needed to be integrated into the future directions of the district. After several discussions with the assistant superintendent for instruction, it was decided to offer classroom action research to elementary and middle school teachers. When 41 applications were returned, we were overwhelmed! This number represented teachers from 11 elementary schools and seven middle schools. The only way that we could support so many teachers in this process was to involve more facilitators. A few teachers dropped out during the summer, but with the addition of teacher-facilitators, the district still had to support half the costs for 40 teachers.

It had become clear that interest in action research was growing through a combination of factors, including publicity sent to all district teachers and administrators, encouragement from principals, informal discussions with past participants, and dissemination of the write-ups of teachers' work to the schools.

## ORGANIZATION AND PROCESS

The structure and process we use with our action research groups have been developing along the way and we expect that they will continue to evolve. The two of us work as a team, representing staff development and research and evaluation in our district. This combination of interests and backgrounds is a strong partnership for action research. We bring the skills, knowledge, and experience of our separate specialties to our groups, and we learn from each other. Through our collaboration, we feel that we gain as much and have at least as much enthusiasm for action research as any group member. However, by the third year, we came to feel that it was time to share the leadership, because of both the increasing numbers of participants and our desire that action research not be dependent on individuals. The two of us enjoy working together and appreciate the support of a colleague in planning and conducting the process, so we suggested that pairs of teachers facilitate two of the groups, while we would lead the other two groups. We shared with other facilitators all of our references and materials about the structure, process, and organization of this project, but encouraged flexibility and adaptation to suit their own styles and the needs of their groups. We are pleased to see the kinds of change and innovation other facilitators and their groups bring, and are excited about this new level of involvement in action research.

*Attendance and discussion are part of the responsibility of any team or group member.*

### Goals and Expectations

As we began to facilitate action research, based on experience with other groups, we established three general expectations for all participants: (1) that they would attend meetings regularly; (2) that they would participate in discussions; and (3) that they would write about their projects. These expectations have proven to be valid and we have continued to use them. Attendance and discussion are part of the responsibility of any team or group member. They are also the kind of investment that yields maximum benefits from the process. The importance of writing has been affirmed over and over and will be discussed later.

Goals of the action research project in this district have continued to be that:

- Each participating teacher will identify the problem or question s/he will pursue.
- Participating teachers will be encouraged to examine and assess their own work and then consider ways of working differently.
- Participating teachers will work collaboratively with each other, with course facilitators, and with other staff members in their schools.

Action research in our district is a process that takes the full school year (or sometimes more) from beginning to end. We start by getting to know each other, introducing the process of action research and the structure of the meetings, distributing materials, and explaining our expectations. The materials distributed include a binder, a journal notebook that we don't require but recommend that everybody at least try, articles, copies of other teachers' reports, and handouts ranging from a list of group members to a project time line to tips for giving constructive feedback. Participants have told us that they perceive us as organized, nonthreatening, and enthusiastic, and that they appreciate the opportunity the district is providing them. During early sessions, we present some information and resources. We are quite talkative and directive in the first meeting or two, after which we draw the participants into more active roles and eventually diminish our own roles.

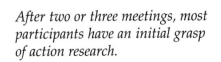

*The group support and interaction . . . are an integral part of the action research process.*

## The Group Process

The group support and interaction that occur throughout the year are an integral part of the action research process. We believe that group members need to feel at ease with each other in order for this to be successful. Therefore, we begin the year, and early sessions, with informal "warm-up" activities in which people gradually get to know each other and become more comfortable with the group. Over the course of the year, meetings vary according to topic and stage in the process, but the basic structure allows for each member to have 10 to 15 minutes to talk about his/her question and get support, encouragement, references, and suggestions from the rest of the group. At every meeting, participants share their questions, concerns, frustrations, and progress. This process enables all participants to become interested and involved in each other's projects. We emphasize the need to facilitate others' learning by asking questions that help individuals to think more deeply or in different ways about their questions rather than just offering solutions to problems they present. Participants are creative and thoughtful in their interactions with colleagues. The generosity, caring, and investment of individuals in each other's projects are apparent.

We agreed that our second-year groups of 12 to 15 were too large. Dividing each group into two discussion groups deprived members of the opportunity of being involved in everyone's research. Based on 2 years of experience, we felt that 8 to 10 was the optimal group size, which we confirmed in the third year. This group size allows every participant significant opportunity to participate, while still exposing all to a range of topics and issues.

*After two or three meetings, most participants have an initial grasp of action research.*

Through a variety of articles and readings, including examples of action research done by teachers in Madison and elsewhere, our action researchers begin to get a sense of what action research is and can be. This enlightenment may come during the first meeting but more often takes longer. After two or three meetings, most participants have an initial grasp of action research. Some participants feel constrained by traditional research paradigms. These can be intimidating, even aversive to some teachers, while they are comfortable and desirable to other participants. Visits to the group meetings by previous years' action researchers give new participants the opportunity to hear what others' experiences have been and to ask questions about concerns or interests. Other resource people are invited to visit meetings as requested by the group members or as they seem worthwhile to us. Examples of such visitors include faculty members from the University of Wisconsin who can share their experiences with action research at other institutions and sites, and action researchers from elsewhere.

## Finding the Right Question

Beginning with general topics of interest, participants develop possible questions to pursue. Through a series of exercises, participants generate criteria for "good" action research questions. Participants each write a question about some topic of interest, which is not necessarily the question they will end up with. Then each participant reads a question aloud and the group listens carefully without comment. Based on writing their own questions and listening to others, participants generate criteria for "good" action research questions. Groups fairly consistently suggest certain characteristics. Such criteria include a question that: is clear and concise; is "doable" or manageable; will yield observable or measurable evidence; is meaningful to the action researcher and others; will make a difference to the researcher and others; has some tension and cannot be answered yes or no; and will sustain the researcher's interest or passion over the course of the year. The group and facilitators help each member to refine individual questions, a process that can happen almost instantly or take months.

The group is introduced to a variety of research methods so that participants can make informed choices about data collection techniques that suit their questions. Triangulation, gathering data from a variety of sources using a variety of methods over time, is stressed to help the participants choose approaches for gathering their own data. We emphasize that the data-gathering methods chosen should be relatively easy for the researcher to use in the course of normal classroom activities with the resources available, as well as appropriate to the question being asked.

Throughout the action research process, participants discuss problems, issues, concerns, insights, and observations emerging from their inquiry. The process can be never-ending as action researchers iteratively plan, act, observe, reflect, plan, act, and so on. However, we do require that they pull together their experiences in this project and their findings to date at the end of the year. In the course of the year's meetings, we schedule considerable amounts of "work" time in which action researchers do library research, read, develop data gathering instruments, analyze data, confer with colleagues—whatever is most useful to them at the time. They eventually come to the struggle of analyzing data, making sense of the muddle, and, finally, write about their questions, inquiry, and findings.

## But I Haven't Written a Paper Since I Was an Undergraduate . . .

Although writing a report is intimidating to some action researchers, it is a clear expectation of this project from the start. We emphasize that they will have plenty of support and help from us and from each other as we progress through the year. Group members are generally excited about the opportunity to read or hear about other teachers' research, and recognize the importance of their own contributions. While we encourage alternative means of communicating about action research projects, written reports are still an expectation, and they are the most widely disseminated form of information about the inquiry conducted. Participants in action research enjoy the opportunities it gives them to be learners, as well as to be respected and sought as professionals and experts with knowledge and experience to offer. Creating and disseminating reports enhances the professional image and self-concept of these educators. But this is not the only reason for writing. We have found that participants feel proud of the accomplishment of completing their projects and have a greater sense of closure after writing reports than before. Some participants also feel that they come to a sense of clarity or understanding through writing that they did not achieve earlier in the process, even though they had already learned from their action research and reached some findings or conclusions. While writing may not be intrinsic to action research, the participants and facilitators in this project have seen enough benefits to warrant the continuing expectation of a written report. Despite this emphasis on writing and reports, it is also clear that this is often a starting point for further reflection and not a conclusion in any sense.

*Creating and disseminating reports enhances the professional image and self-concept of these educators.*

## The Value of Action Research

At some time during each meeting, we ask participants to give us oral or written feedback about the process. This evaluative information helps us to identify needs of individuals and the groups and to modify plans, if necessary, to meet those needs. At the end of the year, participants share with us their perceptions about the value, effectiveness, and substance of action research and about its applicability to their work.

Action researchers in this district have conducted systematic inquiry into questions or issues that are important and meaningful to them. They report that they have become more reflective in their practice. They have grown professionally, developing a greater sense of efficacy and professionalism. They also have learned that their experience and expertise are valid and valued. Group members have pursued their questions independently or with partners, but have had the interest, resources, and support of a whole group of colleagues as they pursued their inquiry. Their questions have led to more questions and to further inquiry and learning. Some teachers have found that when they shared their projects with their students, the students became involved and contributed meaningfully to the research.

We are now gathering data from past action research participants about their retrospective perceptions of the experience and the influence that experience has had on their teaching practice. We hope to trace some of the effects that ripple out from action research participants to their colleagues, their students, and their practice beyond the initial year of involvement.

## CONCLUSIONS, OR LESSONS LEARNED (SO FAR), ABOUT IMPLEMENTING ACTION RESEARCH IN OUR SCHOOL DISTRICT

It takes time and effort for a district to embrace action research. While this may not be true in many other settings, some people in this school district are reluctant to support an activity that has a perceived connection to the research of university settings. Some participants need time and different experiences to let go of their negative impressions of traditional research. Some struggle with this problem the entire year, and those who are not participating in action research find it even more difficult. In our district, commitment to action research has grown through sharing the experiences of past participants, making presentations to a variety of groups, holding informal discussions at individual schools, and learning about action research in other professional contexts.

Finding a meaningful context to which action research can be connected is critical. Unless teachers and principals perceive that what they will learn will make a significant difference in the success of their students, the chance of people wanting to become involved is minimal. Connecting the themes of action research to district and personal priorities and future district directions is necessary.

Moving action research from the initiative of individuals to a district commitment is essential. While it is crucial for districts to support pilot projects and encourage risk-taking among their staffs, finding funds and trying to convince others of the worth of new efforts is time- and energy-consuming. When the leadership of a district decides that action research is an important direction, it shifts from the ownership of individuals and then can be evaluated in the context of district priorities.

Funding released time for teachers to do action research results in teachers feeling valued and renewed. It is hard to overestimate the importance of giving teachers time away from their classrooms to meet and talk with their colleagues about issues that are important to them. Mostly, teachers spend many hours in late afternoon or evening classes working on their own professional growth. While the action research meeting time did not have the same kind of impact on principals because they do have regular opportunities to meet as a group, the principals spoke often about the importance of creating time to discuss meaningful issues with their colleagues, away from their buildings. (The opportunity to earn credits from the district for professional advancement, from the state to meet recertification requirements, and from the university is another incentive and reward for participating in action research.)

> *It is hard to overestimate the importance of giving teachers time . . . to meet and talk with their colleagues.*

Sharing the costs with the school leads to increased commitment and interest by principals. When principals started sharing the cost of released time, they more actively supported teachers pursuing action research questions. They were also more willing to designate funds, knowing the district was contributing to expenses.

The more layers of support, the more likely action research will succeed. The layers of support for participants in the action research process include the group of colleagues from around the district in their action research group, another teacher-participant from the same school, past participants from other groups, and facilitators working with individuals. Facilitators of the action research process have found support from their collaborative efforts with co-facilitators, University of Wisconsin professors, colleagues elsewhere, and other action research facilitators. These different layers have all served a variety of purposes in strengthening the process, the skills, and the quality of the experience of all those involved.

## THE FUTURE

Action research has a strong base of support in this district, including its incorporation into the district's strategic plan, Madison Schools 2000. As of the end of the 1992–93 school year, about 100 teachers and principals have participated in action research projects in the district and the number is growing. We don't know how many more undergraduates, student teachers, cooperating teachers, supervisors, and active professionals have been involved in or touched by action research through university programs.

One of the possibilities we envision for the future is a Madison area action research network. Staff members from the school district and university faculty members formed a partnership to organize and support the first Madison Area Action Research Network Conference in the spring of 1993, at which area teachers, student teachers, and principals presented their work to colleagues. Interest in building an action research network was discussed at that conference. We are eager to explore with others ways of disseminating the action research experience and findings. We also look forward to a time when several studies will have been done on the same topic, building bodies of practitioner knowledge in specific areas.

We plan to continue to meet with other action research facilitators, in our project and beyond. We hope to encourage more action researchers to become facilitators of action research, and we are happy to share our experiences with others who want to start action research groups or projects. Other groups we would like to see emerge include action research groups within schools, as well as action research on a single topic or question, either within or across schools. Two special topic groups were formed for 1993–94: re-structuring the ninth grade and technology in the curriculum. We would like to see a group of action researchers continue beyond the current framework of one year, ending with a report. Group members could represent mixed grade levels, roles or responsibilities, and topics or subject areas. Madison high school teachers haven't yet had an opportunity to form an action research group, but we hope they will become involved soon. Principals and other administrators should have further opportunities to conduct action research in this district. Others may suggest topics, in addition to those we can imagine. The possibilities are endless.

We hope that the concept of action research will evolve in this district, both with our involvement and independent of us. We believe that it has tremendous potential to stimulate the professional growth of those involved, to acknowledge and create teachers' individual and collective knowledge and wisdom, to solve problems and enhance instructional practice, and to provide leadership in the profession.

# Exemplary Project

*Professional Development as a Tool to Enhance
Teacher Quality in Charter Schools*

Ricci Rodriquez-Elkins

Charter schools often do not receive assistance and support from their local districts, and since they may recruit professionals in fields other than education as new teachers, they must have access to alternative college programs for teacher preparation and certification. Those two charter-school needs lead to the development in 2000 of the Charter School Education Consortium (CSEC), a Nevada-based organization with five schools, a charter support unit (similar to a district office support staff), the Sierra Nevada College of Education, and a few privately funded groups dedicated to increasing student achievement in charter schools.

In 2000 the five schools of CSEC were: (1) a rural high school serving sixty-three students, who were, before this school opened, transported by buses to schools over two hours from their homes, resulting in a dropout rate of over 80 percent, (2) a K–8 school for students with attention deficits, behavioral disorders, and emotional disturbances; its enrollment stood at 280 students, (3) a math and science academy that served 264 racially and ethnically diverse college-bound sixth to tenth graders, (4) a remedial high school of 373 dropouts who required reentry support, individualized instruction, and credit recovery, and (5) a K–5 Montessori elementary school with 115 special-needs students.

The CSEC received a federal grant (2000) to expand its options in recruiting and preparing nonteachers to receive their licenses as Nevada elementary and secondary teachers. It recruited seventeen highly qualified college graduates who would work toward certification in bilingual and special education, reading, math and science education, and agree to be available to teach in one of CSEC's five schools. The grant allowed CSEC to offer its recruits two, forty-five hour college course in Child Development and Classroom Management, as well as two followup supervision visits of each new teacher by a college representative during his or her first teaching year. For this action research CSEC added three two-hour workshops (Learning Communities, Action Research, and Individualizing Instruction) along with an intensive, once-a-week, supervisory meeting between a teaching mentor and a recruit. The proactive action in the action research ended in spring 2002 after the recruits' first teaching year.

The data I collected in this action research design from 2001 to 2004 showed that the CSEC proactive intervention did not only produce a new crop of very competent teachers,

*(Continud)*

(Continued)

but it also lead to enhanced academic achievement in their students. Project records showed that all seventeen recruits participated fully in all project components from summer 2001 to December 2003. In spring 2003, however, three participants decided to accept job offers outside the CSEC, two in education and one in business. By summer 2003 fourteen recruits who had completed the program had signed contracts to teach full time in one of the five consortium schools; all taught successfully during 2003 and 2004. By fall 2004 thirteen of those fourteen were employed with a continuous contract in CSEC.

My data from specially designed questionnaires, interviews, and observations showed that over the course of their two years of teaching, all thirteen improved in their classroom communication skills, ability to establish positive classroom climates, use of research-based instruction, ability to maintain positive control and discipline, treatment of students of diverse ethnicities and races fairly, and skills at working cooperatively with colleagues in committees and teaching teams. Most importantly, regular faculty of all five schools reported that the new recruits made documented: (1) uses of student feedback to improve their classroom practices, (2) uses of assessment data to enhance student achievement, and (3) actual gains in student achievement test scores.

SOURCE: "Professional Development as a Tool to Enhance Teacher Quality in Charter Schools", by Ricci Rodriquez-Elkins (2004) College of Education, Arizona State U. West.

# 8

# Using Action Research to Solve Instructional Challenges in Inclusive Elementary School Settings

Christine L. Salisbury,
Linda L. Wilson, Tabetha J. Swartz,
Mary M. Palombaro, and Jami Wassel

As the field of special education becomes more acutely aware of the problems associated with implementation of educational mandates, there is an emerging consensus regarding the limitations of traditional "top down" approaches to policy making as an effective means of building quality programs (Darling-Hammond, 1990; Richardson, 1990). Traditional approaches to policy development assume that university-based research and development efforts produce technology and knowledge which can be readily transported and consumed by the "field" to solve problems faced by practitioners. However, the success of this approach has been limited, at best (Berman & McLaughlin, 1978; Odom & Warren, 1988). Furthermore, standards and regulations that attempt to specify how policy must be implemented in local settings have often been ignored or reinterpreted by "frontline" practitioners in a fashion which

SOURCE: "Using Action Research to Solve Instructional Challenges in Inclusive Elementary School Settings", by Christine L. Salisbury et. al., (1997) *Education Treatment of Children*, 20 (1): 21–39. Reprinted with permission from the publisher.

distorts the underlying goals of the policy (Goodlad & Lovitt, 1992; Weatherly, 1979). New strategies are needed that acknowledge the importance of contextual conditions which affect the actual implementation of integrated and inclusive programs.

One such strategy derives from recent work on teacher-directed inquiry, or "action research" (Evans, 1991; Gideonese, 1990; Houser, 1990; Sagor, 1990) as a basis for addressing implementation issues at the building and classroom level. Action research is an approach that recognizes and supports the expertise and knowledge of practitioners as those most knowledgeable about local contexts and conditions. It further assumes that practitioners are ideally suited to design solutions for the challenges arising within school and classroom settings.

The rationale for adopting an action research approach is five-fold. First, the approach values and respects teacher knowledge about what the salient implementation issues are at the classroom level. In a very real sense, the practitioner, rather than an outside university consultant, is acknowledged as the local "expert." Second, action research puts data in the hands of teachers in a way that enables them to become more reflective about what is occurring on their teams and in their classrooms. Decisions made from these data sources enhance the likelihood that solutions will be both educationally and socially valid (Voeltz & Evans, 1983). Third, action research provides a viable mechanism for improving the quality of instructional practice. Fourth, if done collaboratively, the inquiry process breaks down the isolated nature of teaching and improves communication across classrooms and schools. Finally, the dialogue, study, and evaluation that transpires within an action research approach can serve to improve the intellectual environment in which teachers work. Action research is particularly well-suited as a strategy for addressing implementation issues related to the inclusion of students with disabilities in general education classrooms. Because each child brings to the classroom unique learning and support needs, it is imperative that solutions be developed that are practical for the specific classroom context and individual child. Professional educators are uniquely positioned to appraise the situation, hypothesize why issues exist, propose tenable solutions, implement these strategies, and evaluate outcomes of their efforts. Action research offers teams, as well as individuals, a viable strategy for solving problems and improving professional practice.

*Action research offers teams a viable strategy for solving problems and improving professional practice.*

The purposes of this article are two-fold. First it describes the major components of the Collaborative Innovations Project, a federally funded research project that utilized action research methodology to study issues related to inclusion. Second, examples of interventions designed and directed by practitioners to promote the inclusion of students with moderate to profound disabilities in general education classrooms are shared.

# COLLABORATIVE INNOVATIONS
# PROJECT METHODOLOGY

## Setting

Two school districts, one in New York and the other in Pennsylvania, are involved in the Collaborative Innovations Project, a federally funded research project designed to promote the inclusion of students with moderate to profound disabilities in general education settings. These districts are briefly described below.

**Johnson City Central School District.** This district in south central New York serves a community of 17,000 predominantly blue collar, middle class, Caucasian (96%) residents. The district consists of two elementary schools, one middle school, and one high school. All students involved in this project were enrolled in the district's two inclusive elementary schools. In many respects, such as size and composition of the student population, the district is typical of other suburban-rural communities in the region. However, the district is also quite unique. Nationally recognized for its validated Outcomes Driven Developmental Model (Alessi, 1991), the district incorporates many practices endorsed in the effective schools literature within an organizational framework of outcome-based education (Purkey & Smith, 1983; Spady, 1992). Their efforts over the past decade to fully include students with mild to profound disabilities in general education classrooms (Hollowood, Salisbury, Rainforth, & Palombaro, 1994; Salisbury, 1991; Salisbury, Evans & Palombaro, 1992; Salisbury, Palombaro, & Hollowood, 1993) further distinguish this program from others with similar demographic characteristics. As a result of its reputation for progressive educational practices, there has been an influx of families with special needs children to this district. This, in addition to shifting local economic conditions, has created challenges to this district's commitment to inclusive educational services (cf., Salisbury & Chambers, 1994). Staff and administrators expressed the need for a problem solving approach, such as action research, that would help address "second generation" inclusion implementation issues and take into account current and changing local realities.

**Fox Chapel Area School District.** Located in a suburban community northeast of Pittsburgh, this district serves six municipalities that represent a diverse socioeconomic picture. Residents of the Fox Chapel district are predominantly Caucasian (97%), relatively young (average age = 39 years), and economically stable (median family income = $53,294, range $26,000–$130,000 across municipalities). The school district serves about 4,000. Its four elementary schools serve children in grades K–5. Project staff are supporting teachers and administrators in two of these schools. One school serves approximately 361 students, 38 of whom receive special education and related services. The second building serves approximately 540 students, 36 of whom receive a range of special education and related services.

The Fox Chapel Area School District is recognized nationally for the high achievement levels reached by its general education students (average = 93rd percentile). Within this backdrop of achievement and progress, the district recently began efforts to integrate and include students with the full range of disabilities within their home schools. At the inception of our work with these two schools, children with disabilities were based in general education classrooms and received special education and related services both within the classroom and on a pull-out basis. While cognizant of the district's commitment to inclusive schooling, individual schools and teachers had many questions about the implementation of inclusion and what practices should look like at the classroom and building level.

## Participants

Both school districts had teachers from a variety of disciplines involved in the project, as well as administrators from the elementary buildings. Table 1 reflects the number and distribution of participants from two years of project operation.

**Table 1**    Action Research Project Participants

| Area | Fox Chapel Year 1 | Fox Chapel Year 2 | Johnson City Year 1 | Johnson City Year 2 |
|------|------|------|------|------|
| General Education | 3 | 6 | 4 | 5 |
| Special Education | 3 | 6 | 4 | 6 |
| Speech & Language | | | 1 | |
| Administration | 2 | 2 | 2 | |
| Art | 1 | 1 | | |
| Music | 1 | 2 | | |
| Library | 1 | 1 | | |
| Physical Education | 1 | | | |

The student population of direct interest to this funded project was students with moderate to profound disabilities in general education contexts. Tables 2 and 3 provide descriptive information about the target children served in these schools by these practitioners.

## Measures

Five types of information were collected by project staff to understand the context of these schools and classrooms, as well as the performance levels of the target students. This information was used to inform our work with teachers and to assess our efforts in these schools.

**Table 2**    Selected Characteristics of Target Children (Year 1)

| Target Children | Chronological Age (mos.) | Gender | Grade | Adaptive Behavior Age Score[1] (mos.) | Diagnosis |
|---|---|---|---|---|---|
| 1 | 125 | F | 4 | 58 | Emotional disturbance |
| 2 | 91 | M | 2 | 23 | Mental retardation |
| 3 | 124 | M | 4 | 110 | Emotional disturbance |
| 4 | 80 | M | 1 | 4 | Multiple disabilities |
| 5 | 102 | M | 3 | 9 | Mental retardation |
| 6 | 91 | F | 2 | 5 | Multiple disabilities |
| 7 | 92 | M | 2 | 16 | Autism |
| 8 | 109 | M | 3 | 36 | Autism |
| 9 | 112 | F | 3 | 15 | Multiple disabilities |
| 10 | 125 | M | 3 | 51 | Mental retardation |
| 11 | 141 | M | 5 | 77 | Neurologic impairment |
| 12 | 118 | M | 3 | 56 | Mental retardation |
| 13 | 115 | F | 2 | 42 | Mental retardation |
| 14 | 75 | M | K | 51 | Developmental delay |
| 15 | 80 | M | K | 51 | Developmental delay |
| Mean | 105.33 | | | 40.27 | |
| SD | 19.83 | | | 29.52 | |

**Ethnographic fieldnotes.** In Year 1, fieldnote data were initially collected on the general ecology of the schools and the nature of services and supports provided to target students. This information was used to help project staff better understand the dynamics of each school context and the resources available for students with and without disabilities. Once action research (AR) groups were established, data collection focused on implementation of the AR projects and the performance of target students in school settings. This focus was retained throughout Year 2 of the project.

The ethnographic method involves the collection of detailed fieldnotes written during or immediately after each scheduled observation to reconstruct the observed experiences as accurately as possible. In order to ensure that observations were both representative and balanced, a systematic, rotating schedule of observations across contexts was employed so that important school and classroom activities could be described on a regular basis.

**Table 3**    Selected Characteristics of Target Children (Year 2)

| Target Children | Chronological Age (mos.) | Gender | Grade | Adaptive Behavior Age Score[1] (mos.) | Diagnosis |
|---|---|---|---|---|---|
| 1 | 122 | F | 3 | 61 | Mental retardation |
| 2 | 79 | M | K | 26 | Autism |
| 3 | 104 | M | 2 | 58 | Learning disability |
| 4 | 74 | M | K | 34 | Autism |
| 5 | 132 | M | 4 | 56 | Mental retardation |
| 6 | 125 | M | 4 | 65 | Mental retardation |
| 7 | 124 | F | 5 | 96 | Learning disability |
| 8 | 100 | F | 3 | 6 | Multiple disabilities |
| 9 | 102 | M | 3 | 34 | Multiple disabilities |
| 10 | 111 | F | 4 | 14 | Multiple disabilities |
| 11 | 77 | F | 1 | 6 | Multiple disabilities |
| 12 | 101 | M | 3 | 37 | Autism |
| 13 | 119 | M | 4 | 48 | Autism |
| 14 | 84 | F | 1 | 48 | Multiple disabilities |
| 15 | 82 | M | 1 | 37 | Multiple disabilities |
| 16 | 71 | M | K | 42 | Multiple disabilities |
| Mean | 100.44 | | | 41.75 | |
| SD | 20.45 | | | 23.29 | |

**Semi-structured interviews.** Individual, semi-structured interviews were conducted by project staff at the beginning and the end of each school year with participants of each action research group. Interviews were designed to allow the teachers to talk about their experiences with action research and its impact on the inclusion of students with disabilities in general education classrooms and activities. Each interview lasted about one hour, was audio-taped, transcribed verbatim, and incorporated into the project's data base.

**Action research spring institute transcripts.** Interviews and fieldnotes were supplemented with verbatim transcripts generated by participants from both districts during two spring AR institutes. These institutes provided teachers and administrators with opportunities to observe each others' schools and classrooms and share their research. Each spring institute was video-taped, transcribed verbatim, and added to the data base. Transcripts of the research institutes provided additional testimony about the research projects, as well as evaluative comments about the usefulness of action research and its direct and indirect impact on the inclusion of children with disabilities in general education classrooms.

**Child performance measure.** The Scale of Independent Behavior (SIB) (Bruininks, Woodcock, Weatherman, & Hill, 1984) was used to measure individual student performance in the areas of motor development, social development, language, and self-help skills. The SIB was completed by project staff for each target student using direct observation and conversations with teachers and parents. The Scale was administered in the fall of each year. Adaptive behavior scores are included in Tables 2 and 3.

**Classroom context.** The Classroom Environment Scale (CES) (Moos & Trickett, 1987) was distributed to project participants in the fall and spring of each project year to obtain an assessment of the classroom contexts in which target students were enrolled. The CES is a self-report measure that consists of nine subscales that describe teacher-student and student-student relationships and the organizational structure of a classroom. The nine subscales tap three underlying dimensions: Relationships, Personal Growth, or Goal Orientation, as well as the System Maintenance and Change dimensions. Scoring is additive, with one point allotted for each True/False answer scored in the direction of the key. The sum is then referenced against the normed group average of 50. The psychometric properties of the CES have been reported in the literature, and these studies indicate the instrument is both valid and reliable (Moos & Trickett, 1987). Table 4 depicts scores for each school (classrooms aggregated) across the nine subscales of the CES.

Analysis of the CES data revealed that teachers' perceptions of classrooms across the two school districts were similar. Teachers perceived classrooms to have attentive students who were interested in the activities of the classroom. The classes were also perceived as being task oriented but having minimum competition between students for grades and recognition. Order, organization, and rule clarity seemed to be important to the classrooms across the schools. Teacher report data on the CES indicated that the Fox Chapel schools appeared to have more teacher control and were perceived as less innovative in their use of classroom strategies than Johnson City schools.

## Procedures

All teachers in each building were made aware of the project through announcements and flyers. During the initial year of the project, selection of final participants was based upon (1) administrative nomination, (2) the presence of children with moderate or severe disabilities in their classrooms, and (3) interest. Participating faculty representated a range of disciplines and experiences with children with disabilities (see Table 1).

**Table 4**    Classroom Environment Scales Form R-Standard Scores

| Subscales | Fox Chapel | | Johnson City | | |
| --- | --- | --- | --- | --- | --- |
| | School 1 | School 2 | School 1 | School 2 | School 3 |
| | Classrooms N=23 | Classrooms N=15 | Classrooms N=8 | Classrooms N=19 | Classrooms N=4 |
| Involvement | 60 | 59 | 61 | 57 | 52 |
| Affiliation | 50 | 53 | 59 | 54 | 55 |
| Teacher Support | 50 | 54 | 59 | 56 | 54 |
| Task Orientation | 54 | 47 | 45 | 50 | 47 |
| Competition | 42 | 31 | 28 | 33 | 22 |
| Order & Organization | 51 | 53 | 53 | 47 | 45 |
| Rule Clarity | 58 | 56 | 55 | 50 | 54 |
| Teacher Control | 57 | 55 | 46 | 50 | 47 |
| Innovation | 49 | 54 | 61 | 57 | 49 |

Once selected, these teachers and their administrators received two days of inservice training from a consultant experienced in conducting action research in inclusive contexts. Content of the training included information about the conceptual basis for action research and guided practice related to the major steps in the research process (developing a research question, planning data collection, identifying supports, collecting and analyzing data, taking action and reflecting on their findings). Teachers and administrators formed action research groups around shared issues and concerns. Some of these groups extended across schools, while others were within school groups. Table 5 reflects the range of questions addressed by participants in both districts across years 1 and 2 of this project.

Based upon evaluation data from participants in Year 1, project staff adapted the inservice training in Year 2 to more directly address the "how tos" of collecting, analyzing, and interpreting text-based data. In addition, this inservice included opportunities to see examples and to learn about previous action research projects. Participants concluded the inservice by forming action research groups around shared issues. Unlike year 1, none of these groups crossed school lines and several individuals elected to undertake projects on their own.

In both years, participants received technical and social support for the action research process through the availability of a project staff person who served as a "critical friend." A critical friend is defined as a

**Table 5**     Action Research Questions Explored by Participants Each Year

| *Fox Chapel (Year 1)* | *Johnson City (Year 1)* |
|---|---|
| How should job roles/functions be redefined for classroom teachers, specialists, and aides to support inclusive education? What are the best practices for these roles? | What practices can be used to promote inclusion of students with severe emotional challenges? |
| How do we blend resources at the building level to support inclusion? | What are the stresses of practicing inclusion, and how can we deal with them such that we can maintain our commitment to inclusion? |
| What practices in this school and in other inclusive schools are proving effective in managing disruptive and other problematic behavior? | What techniques are being used in other inclusive schools to maintain communication among service providers? |
|  | How can we develop an effective classroom team in our own classroom? |

| *Fox Chapel (Year 2)* | *Johnson City (Year 2)* |
|---|---|
| How can we increase the time available for collaboration planning/ teaming? | How do we collaborative teachers ensure that appropriate and intentional learning is occurring even when we cannot be with our students? What are the roles of the teacher, collaborative teacher, and special education aides in our inclusive elementary setting? |
| How can we increase the active participation of students with disabilities in general education activities? | How can we make our classroom more inclusive? |
| How can we monitor the implementation of IEP-related instruction? | How do we successfully utilize cooperative grouping to include all children with various needs? |
| What are the outcomes of inclusion for children with and without disabilities in our school? | How do we develop a curriculum-linked assessment (rubric) that will enable us to design instruction for the full range of student needs in our classroom? |

subjective "third party" who is knowledgeable and provides constructive support while keeping the practitioner-researcher's interest at heart (Sagor, 1992). The role of the critical friend was that of facilitator, consultant, and research colleague. The critical friend did not direct the practitioner action research projects, but responded to the needs of the practitioner-researcher for guidance in the selection and development of data collection techniques, data analysis strategies and procedures, and development of project reports. The critical friend was available to the practitioner-researchers throughout the project, and made regular visits to each classroom/school to provide needed resources and support. Responsibilities of the critical friend included keeping fieldnotes or anecdotal records of requested activities during the day (e.g., class, lunch, recess, transitions between classes), providing current information about research topics, and/or helping teachers make contact with other programs involved in inclusive practices.

On a weekly or bi-weekly basis, the critical friends provided typed transcripts of fieldnote data involving classroom events, AR project implementation, or individual student performance. Participants worked independently or with project staff to identify meaningful themes and/or units within the data, and to "make sense" of these themes through a comparative sorting technique (Patton, 1990). Responsibility for interpreting the themes rested with the participants. Participants then made decisions about what to change in their classroom practices, what additional information they might need, and/or what supports they would need from the project to implement their desired changes.

Monthly meetings were scheduled to further support the practitioners in their efforts to conduct action research. The critical friends were available at these meetings to respond to the requests and needs of the research groups. In addition, some groups used these blocks of time to delve deeply into their data transcripts and refine their research plans. In tandem with the spring action research institute each year, participants were afforded regular opportunities to reflect on current practice, develop specific interventions, analyze data, and discuss outcomes and applications of their research. Substitute teacher funds were provided through the project to release teachers for AR meetings during school hours.

## ACTION RESEARCH PROJECT FINDINGS

Given this backdrop of information, the following section provides two examples of AR projects designed and implemented by practitioners in these two districts. Because this information was drawn directly from their final AR group reports, reported findings include both our narrative summaries of their work and the first person accounts of the AR group members.

## Example One: Active Participation of Students

This AR group consisted of three general education teachers, one special education teacher, and two "special area" teachers (art and music). These teachers began with a global issue of, "How can we increase the active participation of students with disabilities in general education activities?" Their project goal was to develop strategies and adaptations that would encourage these students to become more active partici-pants in the classroom. Several of the group's members designed an intervention to help one student [Bill] with moderate learning difficulties become more meaningfully included in aca-demic instruction. His particular need for sup-port was highlighted in the ecological (baseline) fieldnotes collected by project staff and shared with team members during Year 2.

*Their project goal was to develop strategies that would encourage these students to become more active participants.*

The primary goals for Bill were to increase his responses to direct ques-tions and provide sufficient success such that cues could be faded and he would respond spontaneously. The intervention involved increasing the number and type of direct questions posed throughout the day with rein-forcement delivered for correct responses. Data were collected daily across academic and non-academic settings. The number of questions asked of Bill and the nature of his responses to those questions (correct, incorrect, no response) were recorded on a data sheet designed to yield frequency counts of Bill's answers across subject areas. Participants of this group communicated with all adults supporting Bill to ensure that the goal was implemented and reinforced consistently. Conferences were held with Bill's parents to discuss his progress.

Initial analysis of the data collected by teachers, displayed in Figure 1, showed that Bill was initiating more responses on his own, and was responding when asked a question. At mid-year, his level of responding was higher than in October, sustained through February, but declined by later April. Staff and parents attributed this pattern of response to physical factors. Interview data from his parents were consistent with teacher per-ceptions and reports.

> I think that's a classic thing with him. He gets tired as the year goes on and starts to exhibit a little bit more oppositional and a little bit more avoidance type of behaviors. (Bill's mother)

Using their data as a guidepost, these participants decided to continue with their intervention plan because Bill had become a more active partic-ipant in the classroom. Project staff provided support to this AR group by documenting observations of Bill within the context of the classroom, at lunch, and during recess. They also provided journal articles to the group focusing on students with disabilities in the primary grades.

**Figure 1**    Bill's Active Participation Record

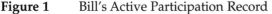

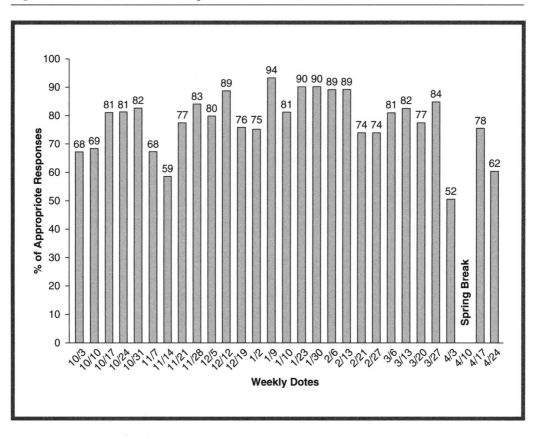

Through analysis of the fieldnote and teacher collected data, this group reported that the knowledge they gained through the AR process affected their classroom practice and thinking about inclusive schooling. Specific observations included the following:

- Inclusion cannot exist without making accommodations and adaptations.
- A "blanket cure" is not possible because all students have different needs that need to be addressed.
- Inclusion is a team approach among all "contacts" [everyone] that encounter an individual student.

When asked to recommend ways in which they might use the process differently in the future, they summarized their feelings in the following ways:

- The research process needs to be spiraled from elementary to secondary schools.
- The strategies and adaptations that helped make Bill successful need to be used in the following grade level to assure continued success.

## Example Two: Making a Classroom More Inclusive

Unlike the previous example where the group focused on an individual student, the participants of a second AR group focused on the question, "How can we make our classroom more inclusive?" The group consisted of one general education teacher and one collaborative (special education) teacher. They selected this question because they felt that students with disabilities were out of the classroom attending "pull-out" sessions too much of the time during the day, and that teaching was fragmented. They made the following observations prior to beginning their project:

- Students with disabilities or those identified as "at risk" were not included in many of the classroom activities.
- The flow of teaching/learning was frequently interrupted.
- Peers did not see the students with special needs as part of the class.
- Peers did not see the students with special needs as "learners."
- They had drifted from past practices such as co-teaching, push-in service, adapting curriculum (because it had become easier to pull out and teach separately), heterogeneous groupings for students, and co-planning.

Their AR project design involved having the critical friends collect fieldnote data on target children and instruction within the classroom. These data were typed and given to the teachers who then held discussions with their team and experimented with various schedule configurations and classroom arrangements. In addition, they took the time to reflect and discuss successful past practices. Because the fieldnotes conveyed a running account of classroom activity, rather than judgments about individual staff, they provided a dispassionate, "bird's eye" view of what transpired in the class. This vantage point was seen as a particularly useful source of feedback to everyone, including the paraprofessional staff. Their findings and reflections included the following:

- We had time to examine classroom practices, the classroom environment and the daily schedule. We were able to design a working schedule that allowed us to include all students in more of an inclusive environment. That is, by pushing children into the regular education classroom, the collaborative teacher was able to effectively do reading intervention in a classroom setting with a mixed group of children. Having children come into the general education classroom for instruction was less stigmatizing than pulling them out. We related well to all regular education children in the classroom, forming new relationships with peers and support staff.

- An unplanned outcome occurred when the paraprofessionals asked to read the fieldnotes taken by project staff. They read them and were able to use the information to evaluate their interactions with students. A change in attitudes and expectations of students took place almost immediately.

For example, an aide was able to objectively view how dependent a particular student was on her. Another example was that another aide was able to see how a specific student was physically present for an activity, but not an active participant.

- Some co-teaching took place such as in reading groups. There was more involvement of all team teachers in planning, such as choosing literature or reading activities. The collaborating teacher was more able to interact and instruct all children in the classroom. There was greater flexibility in teacher roles and role release. Children looked on the collaborating teacher more as a "teacher" and not just "someone who comes to take me out." By having the collaborating teacher in the classroom, many children and support staff have much more support and expertise available to them.

- Because children were "pulled in" rather than "pushed out," children had fewer places to go, changes to make, and less teachers to deal with, giving them more stability.

- Changes in the physical set-up of the classroom also occurred such as where students sat at tables and where reading groups took place. In addition, the classroom schedule was examined and changed to allow for weekly meetings with the paraprofessionals during the school day. The occupational and physical therapist also were able to join them.

- We would have liked to have taken more time to read all of the field-notes and reflect on them at greater length. We should have taken more time to discuss fieldnotes with support staff and related service providers such as speech, occupational and physical therapists.

### Evaluation

**AR process.** As groups designed, implemented, and revised their work, we were interested in evaluating two aspects of the AR process: AR project implementation and the social validity of the process itself. Specifically, we were concerned with evaluating the extent to which participants used the data they collected or were given to make decisions. Our fieldnote data from interactions with and observations of AR groups and meetings indicate that teachers made better use of their text-based data in Year 2, in large part due to the more focused training on how to code, segment, and "make sense of" the information. Teachers did, however, experience difficulties finding the time to cull through the transcripts and be reflective within the constraints of day-to-day school life. Because the types of data collected varied with specific projects, teachers were exposed to the challenges of reconciling qualitative and quantitative information about children and classroom practices. This was a professional "stretch" for many that added an important dimension to their discussions. The following quotes reflect practitioner reports related to these findings:

I think the stuff that you guys did with the observations was very beneficial. And I think it became more beneficial as I became more involved with the program. I wasn't as defensive about what I was reading (Art teacher).

I think I am more refreshed and more focused when I come back from these things (half-day data analysis sessions) than I was before . . . I feel better when I come back and have other ideas (3rd grade teacher).

I think being involved in AR is a boost . . . enlightening to me in that, not only am I aware that I need to change some behaviors of my own, but also that this is a part of a study that's being done and that I can be part of changing things in the much more general sense (5th grade teacher).

Second, we were interested in how participants felt about engaging in the AR process and serving as researchers of their own professional activity. The semi-structured interviews and spring institute transcripts served as primary vehicles for obtaining feedback on the social validity of the AR process. A total of 93 interviews were conducted over the two year period (3 teachers chose not to participate in the interviews). In addition, each action research team was responsible for writing up the results of their action research projects. Included in these written reports was a section in which they, as a group, were asked to reflect on the usefulness of the AR process.

These textual data were coded and analyzed using AQUAD (Huber, 1990). Codes used reflected prevailing themes that emerged from a preliminary analysis of the Year 1 baseline (ecological) data, derived using a modified, constant comparative method (Patton, 1990). Validation of these themes occurred through the use of triangulation and member check procedures.

The following quotes from these varied sources provide commentary on the social validity of the process:

This project has forced us, but has also allowed us the time . . . to talk about what the stressors are, and actually sitting down and saying, "All right. This is what we're up against. How are we going to fix it? What are we going to do about it?" It's been very effective (2nd grade teacher).

It makes me more aware of the problems than I was before because we never really were included. And now I don't feel like I'm pushing in or interfering. I mean, I'm working with these students and I can do something to help (Librarian).

**Group and individual outcomes.** Because the AR projects were directed at improving professional practice related to the inclusion of students with disabilities, we were also interested in determining how successful these intervention efforts were. Data from their 16 written final reports attest to varying levels of success in achieving desired changes in practices and student outcomes. We believe our need to assume a supportive, rather than directive posture with these groups directly affected the degree of change experienced by these groups. On the other hand, because we made no attempt to dictate what needed to change and how it should occur we believe that participants felt more empowered to direct the course of their projects and to adopt strategies that "fit" within the constraints of their set-ting (e.g., library, art, 3rd grade, kindergarten). Supplemented with inter-view data on what they perceived to be the most salient outcomes of their efforts, we also saw evidence of positive personal change resulting from the process of reflection itself. Taken together, we believe the Collaborative Innovations Project has achieved some measure of success in fostering the adoption of the AR approach and in helping teachers improve their own professional practice.

Comments from teachers support these findings:

*AR is definitely affecting our instructional practices because it's giving us more time to sit down with my aide and the new special ed teacher and purposely plan for our classified children . . . Definitely the instruction for all the kids is becoming more intentional (3rd grade teacher).*

*I can't imagine him (classified child) not in my classroom next year. He's just so much a part of my teaching now and a part of that class that it's gonna be hard. That's how it's affected me. AR has helped with that, giving me support, and helping us develop as a team (3rd grade teacher).*

*I can be completely intentional with all that I do with the kids that have IEPs because I know about the IEPs specifically, and what needs to be done, what's expected. We've had a chance to talk together, brainstorm . . . You have many more sources of information and everybody's getting the same story, being more consistent . . . The child is being much more successful (2nd grade teacher).*

## CONCLUSIONS

Action research is a viable strategy for improving professional practice related to the meaningful incorporation of students with disabilities in general education classrooms. As support personnel to the process, one of the most difficult aspects is maintaining a non-directive ("outside expert") posture. The underlying principles required that we allow practitioners to identify priorities, select interventions from an informed base of informa-tion, and implement the strategies in ways that made sense for their class-room climate. While we believe there may have been more efficient and effective approaches than those selected by some of our AR groups, we firmly believe that these participants "owned" the solutions and were more likely to sustain and generalize the process over time than if we had imposed solutions from outside.

To successfully implement AR requires administrative support, a shift in practitioner orientation towards more reflective practice, and resources to help generate contextually relevant information upon which pedagogical decisions can be based. To embrace an action research approach, educators must develop a comfort level with not "having all the answers" up front, and be willing to solve problems through a process of classroom-based inquiry. Our preliminary findings suggest that this can be achieved at the elementary level in schools representing different economic and pedagogical characteristics.

## NOTE

1. Scales of Independent Behavior

## REFERENCES

Alessi, F. (1991, April). ODDM: The gentle bulldozer. *Quality Outcomes Driven Education,* 11–18.

Berman, P., & McLaughlin, M.W. (1978). *Federal programs supporting educational change. Vol. VIII: Implementing and sustaining innovations.* Santa Monica, CA: Rand Corporation.

Bruininks, R.H., Woodcock, R.W., Weatherman, R.F., & Hill, B.K. (1984). *Scales of independent behavior: Woodcock-Johnson psycho-educational battery, part four.* Chicago, IL: The Riverside Publishing Company.

Calhoun, E.F. (1994). *How to use action research in the self-renewing school.* Alexandria, VA: Association for Supervision and Curriculum Development.

Darling-Hammond, L. (1990). Instructional policy into practice: "The power of the bottom over the top." *Education Evaluation and Policy Analysis,* 12, 233–241.

Evans, C. (1991). Support for teachers studying their own work. *Educational Leadership,* 48 (6), 11–13.

Gideonese, H.D. (1990). Organizing schools to encourage teacher inquiry. In R. F. Elmore (Ed.), *Restructuring schools: The next generation of education reform.* San Francisco: Jossey-Bass.

Goodlad, J., & Lovitt, T. (1992). *Integrating general and special education.* New York: Merrill.

Hollowood, T.S., Salisbury, C.L., Rainforth, B., & Palombaro, M.M. (1994). Use of instructional time in classrooms serving students with and without severe disabilities. *Exceptional Children,* 61(3), 242–253.

Houser, N.O. (1990). Teacher researcher: The synthesis of roles for teacher empowerment. *Action in Teacher Education,* 12(2), 55–60.

Huber, G.L. (1990). AQUAD: *Computer-assisted analysis of qualitative data; principles and manual for the software package AQUAD 3.0.* Schwangau, Germany: Huber. (Trans. Renata Tesch).

Moos, R.H., & Trickett, E.J. (1987). *Classroom environment scale.* Palo Alto, CA: Consulting Psychologists Press, Inc.

Odom, S., & Warren, S. (1988). Early childhood special education in the year 2000. *Journal of the Division for Early Childhood, 12,* 263–273.

Patton, M.Q. (1990). *Qualitative evaluation and research methods.* Newbury Park, CA: Sage.

Purkey, S.D., & Smith, M.S. (1983). Effective schools: A review. *Elementary School Journal, 83*(4), 427–452.

Richardson, V. (1990). Significant and worthwhile change in teaching practice. *Educational Researcher, 19,* 10–18.

Sagor, R. (1990). What project LEARN reveals about collaborative action research. *Educational Leadership,* March, 6–10.

Sagor, R. (1992). *How to conduct collaborative action research.* Alexandria, VA: Assocation for Supervision and Curriculum Development.

Salisbury, C. (1991). Mainstreaming during the early childhood years. *Exceptional Children, 58,* 146–155.

Salisbury, C. & Chambers, A. (1994). Longitudinal costs associated with the provision of inclusive educational services. *Journal of the Association for Persons with Severe Handicaps, 19*(3), 215–222.

Salisbury, C.L., Evans, I., & Palombaro, M.M. (1992). *Outcome data on an inclusive elementary school: Johnson City in perspective.* Presentation at the national conference of the Association for Persons with Severe Handicaps. San Francisco, CA.

Salisbury, C.L., Palombaro, M.M., & Hollowood, T.M. (1993). On the nature and change of an inclusive elementary school. *Journal of the Association for Persons with Severe Handicaps, 18*(2), 75–84.

Spady, W.C. (1992). It's time to take a close look at outcomes-based education. *Outcomes, 11*(2), 6–13.

Voeltz, L.M. & Evans, I.M. (1983). Educatonal validity: Procedures to evaluate outcomes in programs for severely handicapped learners. *Journal of the Association for Persons with Severe Handicaps, 8*(1), 3–15.

Weatherly, R.A. (1979). *Reforming special education: Policy implementation from state level to street level.* Cambridge, MA: The MIT Press.

# Exemplary Project

## Math Fact Memorization in a Highly Sequenced Elementary Mathematics Curriculum

### Kelli Kreienkamp

This action research focused on math fact drill as part of a structured, sequential math curriculum for early elementary students. The setting for this project was a K–8 midwest, suburban charter school with a specially tailored curriculum of core knowledge and direct instruction. During the school year of this project, the school's special student populations included: 12.3% low income, 17.3% minorities, and 5.3% special needs.

As I designed this action research, I assumed that young students must commit basic math facts to memory if they are to advance in conquering more complex algorithms, concepts, and problems. My research-based assumption was that although elementary students must learn a developmental series of math skills to succeed in middle school and beyond, in the beginning stages of the early grades they must be able to retrieve simple math facts quickly from memory, in order for them to become successful at mastering subsequent higher level math concepts and problems.

The student participants were members of two early elementary classes. The year of this project the school administration grouped students in core subjects, like math, according to their instructional ability; thus the two target classes had multiage populations. My experimental class had 16 first, second, third, and fourth graders, ten of whom used a specially constructed addition packet, while six used the subtraction packet. The control class, taught by a colleague of mine, had 12 second, third, and fourth graders with eight using the addition packet and four using the subtraction packet. Both classes had a few special needs students; my colleague and I considered the two classes to have had similar rates of math learning in the past.

The primary difference between the two classes for this action research was that with my class, I conducted math fact drills five times per week, while my colleague conducted math fact drills three times per week (the usual plan for our school) with her class. My objective in creating those action differences was that the two extra sessions of practice per week would facilitate the experimental students in my class to master math facts more quickly than their control counterparts in the other class.

At the start my colleague and I gave all twenty-eight students math pretests to gather baseline data. Our addition and subtraction tests had one hundred facts each. After collecting the pretests, we averaged the number of correct items for each class. At the end of our six weeks trial, we gave students the same tests. Again, we averaged the number of correct items for each class. Next we calculated the percent gain for each group: results were 19% gain for the experimental class and 7% gain for the control class.

Our data indicated that the more our students were drilled about math facts the greater were their gains in mastering math facts. My colleague and I presented our results to the other elementary teachers in our school at a regular staff meeting. Six weeks after that meeting, most of our colleagues had begun to implement math fact drills daily. By the end of the school year that change in our curriculum plan had become institutionalized.

---

SOURCE: "Math Fact Memorization in a Highly Sequenced Elementary Mathematics Curriculum," by Kelli Kreienkamp (2006) College of Education, Arizona State U. West.

# 9

## Using Action Research as a Collaborative Process to Enhance Educators' and Families' Knowledge and Skills for Youth With Emotional or Behavioral Disorders

### Douglas Cheney

The past 20 years have seen an explosion of activities in research and practice regarding collaboration between teachers, administrators, related service providers, paraprofessionals, and family members. Several factors influenced this activity following the passage of Public Law 94–142. By mandating collaboration through the work of multidisciplinary teams, this law provided a structure for practitioners and parents to develop and monitor the individualized education plan (IEP) of students with disabilities.

Following the implementation of PL 94–142, multidisciplinary teams were challenged to broaden their scope so that members could fulfill several necessary educational functions. For example, teacher assistance

SOURCE: "Using Action Research as a Collaborative Process to Enhance Educators' and Families' Knowledge and Skills for Youth with Emotional or Behavioral Disorders" by Douglas Cheney (1998) *Preventing School Failure,* 42 (2): 88-93. Reprinted with permission of the Helen Dwight Reid Educational Foundation. Published by Heldref Publications, 1319 Eighteenth St., NW, Washington, DC 20036-1802. Copyright © 1998.

teams (Chalfant, Pysch, & Moultrie, 1979), mainstream assistance teams (Fuchs, Fuchs & Bahr, 1990), and prereferral teams (Johnson & Pugach, 1991; Pugach & Johnson, 1988) focused on providing (a) support to general education classrooms to decrease referrals to special education, (b) support to general and special educators to implement IEP goals, (c) assistance to teachers to include students with disabilities in general education classrooms, and (d) forums in which educators and specialists could work cooperatively to develop interventions, rather than relying on prescriptive programs from external consultants.

---- ❧ ----

*Recent work has validated the efficacy of collaboration for educators working with children with disabilities.*

Central to all of these endeavors has been the skill of collaboration, defined as a process that leads to the attainment of goals that cannot be efficiently achieved by any one agent (Bruner, 1991). Collaboration means to work with one another, to cooperate, and to work jointly to produce the results that all desire. Collaboration requires mutual respect, trust, and cultural sensitivity. Open exchange of information, flexibility, understanding, common language, and realistic expectations are essential components of collaboration. Collaboration results in outcomes that are valued and supported by families and professionals alike (Cheney & Osher, 1997; DeChillo & Koren, 1995; Karp, 1993).

Recent work has validated the efficacy of collaboration for educators working with children with disabilities. For example, collaboration offers a cost-effective intervention to reduce educators' feelings of isolation and decrease rates of attrition by offering opportunities for work-related problem solving and support (Cooley & Yovanoff, 1996). It has also been suggested that the process of peer collaboration has reduced referrals to special education, increased the confidence of practicing teachers to develop classroom interventions, and improved their affective outlook toward their students and classroom (Pugach & Johnson, 1995).

Pugach and Johnson (1995) concluded that teachers working collegially to intervene with specific student problems should be able to restructure their school to accommodate schoolwide collaboration. This restructuring would require administrative support and a structure within which teachers collaborate frequently on problems, generate educational strategies, and improve their ability to use new and varied strategies.

One collaborative process with great utility in schools is the action planning and research (APR) process. APR has been used to study schoolwide problems and develop strategies to improve learning communities. Three phases of inquiry have been suggested to guide inquiry in APR: (a) selecting a problem or area of interest; (b) collecting, organizing, and interpreting on-site data related to the problem; and (c) taking action based on the information (Calhoun, 1994). Together these phases constitute the APR cycle. Recently the cycle has been used in schoolwide projects to improve collaborative problem solving by educators (Salisbury, Evans, &

Palombaro, 1997) and to promote inclusion of students with moderate to profound disabilities in general education classrooms (Salisbury, Wilson, Swartz, Palombaro, & Wassel, 1997). By using the APR process, teachers generated and evaluated interventions that increased instances of physical, social, and instructional inclusion of students.

In recent projects conducted in New Hampshire, APR was used with elementary and middle school teachers to address the complex social, emotional and academic problems presented by students with emotional or behavioral disorders (Cheney & Barringer, in press; Cheney, Manning & Upham, in press; Cheney & Muscott, 1996). School staff and families worked together in educational support teams whose major goals were the enhancement of their knowledge, skills and strategies for working with students with emotional and behavioral disorders. The collaborative teams were composed of general and special educators, administrators, specialists and parents, when possible.

This approach enhanced individual team members' skills by supporting a format for learning new information, making decisions on how to apply the information, implementing classroom and schoolwide interventions, and evaluating the impact of their work on student and staff performance. One purpose of working collaboratively in teams was to evaluate the use of a modified action planning research process with the teams, and its consequent effects on the academic and social performance of targeted students. I report here on the use of the action planning and research process by seven collaborative teams in a middle school.

## METHOD

One middle school in southern New Hampshire adopted the APR approach and implemented it on a schoolwide basis. School staff were presented an overview of the approach and offered an opportunity to discuss its implementation, and over 90% of them agreed to participate in team meetings to implement the APR. Families of targeted students were recruited into the project through meetings, phone calls and mailings. Four groups participated in this schoolwide project: 42 educators, 14 students with serious emotional disturbance (SED), 15 students nominated because of emotional or behavior problems (EBP), and the parents of the students with SED. In addition, a cohort of typically developing students were identified to compare with the students with SED/EBP.

The Systematic Screening for Behavior Disorders (Walker & Severson, 1990) was used by teachers to identify students with significant externalizing or internalizing behavior during the first quarter of the school year. Teachers completed the Teacher's Report Form (TRF) of the Child Behavior Checklist (Achenbach, 1991) at the second stage of this screening process. The T scores from the Total Test Score of the TRF were used to classify students as EBP (>60) or typical (–60). Students who were identified as SED under special education law were all classified in the clinical range.

This process for identifying students with challenging behaviors is consistent with arguments that students with SED are underidentified, and that 3 to 5% of school age children exhibit significant emotional or behavioral problems (Kauffman, 1997). During stage one of the screening process, teachers also identified typically developing students in their classes for normative comparison.

### Action Planning

Project staff (a special educator and clinical psychologist) worked with seven teams from the sixth, seventh, and eighth grades three times monthly to implement the APR process (i.e., identifying problems, developing interventions, and evaluating the effectiveness of the interventions). First, the team used a student study format to assess the functioning of targeted students in the school and community. The study assessed students' strengths and weaknesses in four developmental areas: interpersonal, affective, cognitive, and biological. After reviewing the students' strengths and weaknesses, the teams generated goals and interventions for them (see Cheney & Barringer, in press, for an in-depth discussion of the student study format). Finally, teachers and parents implemented the interventions and reported progress to their teams every 1 to 2 weeks (see Figure 1 for the steps in this process).

## CASE STUDY PROCESS AT THE SCHOOL

### Identifying Students and Inviting Parents

The APR process was used for 6 months with 29 students at the middle school. These students included 6 in the sixth grade, 12 in the seventh grade, and 11 in the eighth grade. Six teams addressed student issues, one at the sixth grade level, three in the seventh grade, and two in the eighth grade. The teams were involved in a total of 84 meetings throughout the school year. At the meetings, project staff initially facilitated the process, and then school or family members became the facilitators. Core team members included four general educators, a reading specialist, a guidance counselor, and the principal. Periodic attendance was noted by school psychologists, along with the physical education, health, and art teachers. Parents and students were invited to participate in the APR meetings, and six students, one father, and nine mothers attended APR meetings.

### Assessing Student Strengths and Weaknesses

In step two of the APR process, collaborative team members used a student assessment and planning form to identify strengths and weaknesses of students. The student assessment form required teachers and parents to review and select priorities in the interpersonal, emotional,

**Figure 1** Steps in the Action Planning and Research Process

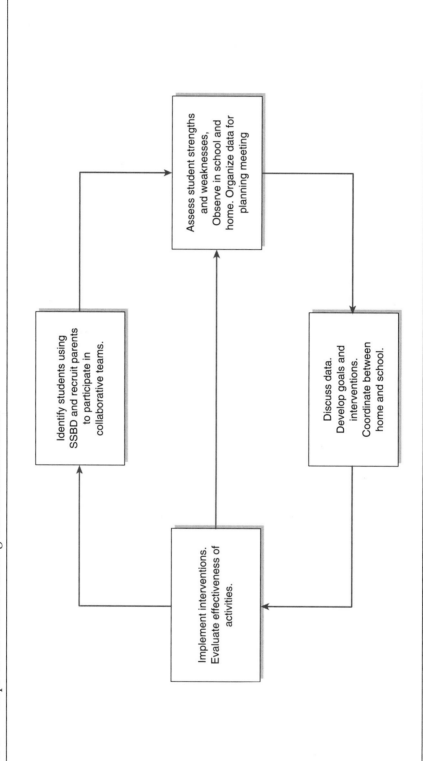

cognitive, and biological areas. (See Figure 2 for representative items in each of these four areas.)

The following strengths are representative examples of team statements used in reviewing the 29 completed assessments: honest, has friends, sense of humor, verbalizes feelings, takes turns and shares, sense of right and wrong, reading and math skills are adequate for grade level, good problem solver, and helps others. Generating these strengths was intended to reduce negative attributions based on problematic behavior and help team members focus on areas to enhance.

Numerous reasons were given for student weaknesses in the APR meetings. One general reason was that the student had been identified as SED (14 instances) and was receiving all educational services in the general education setting. More specifically, teachers used areas of the student study form to identify reasons for reviewing the student in the APR group such as academic (e.g., low math, reading or language skills, grades below C, not working independently), interpersonal (e.g., lacks friends, hostile toward adults, aggressive to others, lacks social bonds), and affective (e.g., easily angered, no enthusiasm, overexcited in groups, temper, doesn't express feelings).

**Figure 2**    Items From the Student Assessment Form

---

Directions: Check areas of concern in front of the item.

**Interpersonal**

Peer Relationships

—— Behavior during structured group activities.
—— Behavior during unstructured group activities.
—— Helping others.

Teacher Relationships

—— Following directions.
—— Asking for help.
—— Hostility toward authority figures.

**Emotional**

—— Verbalizes little or no emotion.
—— Verbalizes only negative emotion like anger or hopelessness.
—— Is overly critical of self.

**Cognitive**

—— Reading skills are adequate for curriculum.
—— Math skills are adequate for curriculum.
—— Hands in assignments on time.

**Biological**

—— Has neurological problems.
—— Takes medications.
—— Has chronic illnesses.

**Developing and Implementing Interventions.** Based on a review of student strengths and weaknesses, two to four objectives were written for each student. Although many suggestions were discussed, a majority vote of group members determined which objectives would be adopted. When in attendance, students and parents gave their views about the need for, and social validity of, the objectives. (Table 1 presents some of the objectives developed.)

**Evaluating Interventions.** Throughout the year, the teams used several sources of data to evaluate the action planning and research process. These sources included (a) standardized rating scales for student problem behavior and social skills, (b) questionnaires about team members' perceptions of collaboration and team effectiveness, (c) weekly narratives on student progress, (d) student grades, (e) student attendance, and (f) parent perceptions of the process.

———————— ✀ ————————

*Teachers . . . perceived improvement in the use of positive social skills.*

**Problem behavior and social skills.** Both the Social Skill Rating System (Gresham & Elliott, 1990) and the Child Behavior Checklist (Achenbach, 1991) were completed in November and April during the APR process. The scores suggested that students with SED/EBP showed

**Table 1**    Representative Objectives Established for Students

**Interpersonal**

    Work with a mentor as a positive role model.
    Receive warnings for unnecessary walking around class and rude comments.
    Use verbal cues and redirection to use positive social skills.
    Increase positive interaction with other peers.
    Ask for help from adults and peers.

**Academic**

    Provide 1/2 hour of daily tutoring for academic support.
    Use an assignment book to monitor and evaluate daily work.
    Use a laptop computer for writing assignments.
    Enroll student in advanced art class.
    Provide space in class to work independently.

**Affective**

    Squeeze a stress ball when anxious during classroom tasks and lectures.
    Work with school counselor at least once a week for guidance/counseling.
    Work with the librarian at least once a week to reduce stress.
    Express wants and needs with teacher and peers.
    Spend daily a.m. time with advisor.

**Familial**

    Teachers and mom will correspond weekly.
    Mom will monitor homework notebook and communicate progress to school.

significant improvements in their social skills based on teacher ratings using the Social Skill Rating System. Total test scores on problem behaviors from the Child Behavior Checklist revealed no significant changes for students with SED/EBP (Barringer & Cheney, 1997). These findings suggest the difficulty of improving scores on a problem behavior checklist for middle school students because of the intractable nature of the behaviors, the students' developmental period, and their lengthy history of behavior problems. Despite the stable nature of the problem behavior, however, teachers still perceived improvement in the use of positive social skills.

**Attendance and grades.** Attendance and grades were broad indicators of the students' progress. Students with SED/EBP and typical students had similar attendance (172.5 days and 171.7 days, respectively). That the students were retained in school throughout the year suggests that they were willing participants and that teachers and parents were monitoring and encouraging attendance. The typical student group had higher grades, averaging a 3.35 grade point average (GPA) on a 4-point scale, whereas the students with SED/EBP had a 2.15 GPA. These students' C average was encouraging in that it was nearly a half-point higher than the national average of 1.7 (Wagner et al., 1991).

**Team members' perceptions of collaboration and team effectiveness.** Two questionnaires were used to assess team members' perceptions of collaboration and team effectiveness, modified questionnaires from Schmuck & Runkel (1985). Findings on teacher perceptions of collaboration and team effectiveness are reported in depth elsewhere (Cheney, Barringer, & Harvey, in review). In general, teachers showed significant increases in their perception of team effectiveness but only slight increases in their collaborative skills. The team effectiveness finding may signify their need to become efficient and task oriented toward developing goals and implementing programs.

**Weekly narratives by teachers and parents.** Through periodic interviews (Cheney, Manning, & Upham, in press) and an independent evaluation of parent and teacher perceptions (Shaeffer, 1996), qualitative data were collected from teachers and parents on the process and outcomes of implementing the APR. These data indicated that teachers were quite satisfied with the student study format and APR process. They commented that the APR process provided the school with a systematic way of looking at children through a collaboration among teachers, administrators, specialists, and parents. One teacher summarized the impact of APR by stating, "The student study approach taught us how to look at kids more holistically and showed us there was more to the student than just educational performance." Another teacher said, "We now have a structured way to look at students in need, through the eyes of the student, the parent and the school staff." Teachers were realistic and stated that the cost of achieving such a formalized process was the investment of a lot of time. At the end of the school year, however, the teachers decided to continue the APR process into the next school year. This is a step toward institutionalizing the process in the school.

———— ⚜ ————

*Involving parents and students as collaborative members in decision making was a highlight of the project.*

Several teachers indicated that involving parents and students as collaborative members in decision making was a highlight of the project. Teachers and parents reported improvements in communications and interpersonal relationships when parents were included in the decision-making process provided by APR. Parents were also quite positive about having a forum to voice their concerns about their children. Several participants indicated that the student study approach helped to decrease isolation and build positive bridges with parents by valuing and honoring their contributions (Cheney, Manning, & Upham, in press). By the end of the school year, teachers, administrators, specialists, and parents agreed that the school should institutionalize the process and carry it forward into the following school year. The school staff also agreed to continue their work on positive forms of discipline and to work on schoolwide social problem-solving strategies.

## CONCLUSION

I have reviewed here the process and related outcomes of using an action planning and research process in one middle school. Although school staff were the most frequent participants in grade level teams using the process, parents and students also became members of the teams. This approach allowed school staff and parents to work collaboratively to solve problems and implement coordinated strategies to support students with emotional and behavioral problems.

Implementing the APR process to address students' social, emotional, and academic problems requires the commitment of administrators and allocation of resources to be successful. For example, a core member of the APR teams in this project was the school's principal who attended over 90% of the meetings and viewed the APR as essential for the staff and families to understand and meet the needs of students with SED/EBP. In addition, this principal, with the agreement of the staff, dedicated six planning periods per week for APR meetings, a major commitment of the precious resource of time. Staff supported this commitment by regularly attending meetings and used the meeting times effectively to develop and implement positive strategies to address complex problems of their students.

The success of the APR process also was supported by a schoolwide vision to educate all students as a community of learners and to obtain the professional development needed to accomplish this vision. Educators and parents implemented activities to meet this vision in assessment, planning and implementation activities and attended APR meetings to refine their skills in the process. The proof of this ownership came in the following school year when the faculty and families continued the collaborative process after supplementary funding for the project ceased.

Finally, involving parents and students in the ongoing APR meetings as collaborative team members was perhaps the most important aspect of the project. By broadening their perspectives and the information they received, team members viewed educational issues more holistically. All involved agreed that listening to and applying ideas of the varied participants in the problem-solving process produced socially valid solutions. This process offered team members a valued and effective method for analyzing complex problems, one they can use in the future to tackle the problems of students with emotional and behavioral disabilities.

# REFERENCES

Achenbach, T. M. (1991). *Teacher's report form of the child behavior checklist.* Burlington, VT: University of Vermont.

Barringer, C., & Cheney, D. (1997). Staff development and the inclusion of middle school students with emotional and behavioral disorders in regular education: Findings from Project DESTINY. In C. Liberton, K. Kutash, & R. Friedman (Eds.), *The 9th Annual Research Conference Proceedings, A System of Care for Children's Mental Health: Expanding the Research Base* (March 6–8, 1996), pp. 347–354. Tampa, FL: University of South Florida, Florida Mental Health Institute, Research and Training Center for Children's Mental Health.

Bruner, C. (1991). *Thinking collaboratively: Ten questions and answers to help policy makers improve children's services.* Washington, DC: Education and Human Services Consortium.

Calhoun, E. F. (1994). *How to use action research in the self-renewing school.* Alexandria, VA: Association of Supervision and Curriculum Development.

Chalfant, J. C., Pysch, M. V., & Moultrie, R. (1979). Teacher assistance teams: A model for within-building problem solving. *Learning Disability Quarterly, 2,* 85–96.

Cheney, D., & Barringer, C. (in press). A transdisciplinary model for students' social and emotional development: Creating a context for inclusion. In J. R. Scotti & L. H. Meyer (Eds.), *New directions for behavioral intervention: Principles, models, and practices.* Baltimore: Paul H. Brookes.

Cheney, D., Barringer, C., & Harvey, V. (in review). Improving teacher knowledge and skills about students with emotional and behavioral disorders. *Teacher Education and Special Education.*

Cheney, D., Manning, B., & Upham, D. (in press). Active involvement of families in the educational support teams of students with emotional and behavioral disabilities. *Teaching Exceptional Children.*

Cheney, D. & Muscott, H. (1996). Preventing school failure for students with emotional and behavioral disabilities through responsible inclusion. *Preventing School Failure, 40*(3), 109–117.

Cheney, D. & Osher, T. (1997). Collaborate with families. *Journal of Emotional and Behavioral Disorders, 5*(1), 36–44.

Cooley, E., & Yovanoff, P. (1996). Supporting professionals-at-risk: Evaluating interventions to reduce burnout and improve retention of special educators. *Exceptional Childen, 62,* 336–355.

DeChillo, N., & Koren, P. (1995). Just what is "collaboration." *Focal Point*, 9(1), 1–6.

Fuchs, D., Fuchs, L., & Bahr, M. (1990). Mainstream assistance teams: A scientific basis for the art of consultation. *Exceptional Children, 57*(2), 128–139.

Gresham, F. M., & Elliott, S. N. (1990). *Social skills rating system.* Minnesota: American Guidance Service.

Johnson, L. J., & Pugach, M. C. (1991). Accommodating the needs of students with mild learning and behavior problems through peer collaboration. *Exceptional Children, 57*, 454–461.

Karp, N. (1993). Collaboration with families: From myth to reality. *Journal of Emotional and Behavioral Problems, 1*(4), 21–23.

Kauffman, J. M. (1997). *Characteristics of emotional and behavioral disorders of children and youth* (6th ed.). Columbus, OH: Merrill.

Pugach, M. C., & Johnson, L. J. (1988). Rethinking the relationship between consultation and collaborative problem-solving. *Focus on Exceptional Children, 21*(4).

Pugach, M. C., & Johnson, L. J. (1995). Unlocking expertise among classroom teachers through structured dialogue: Extending research on peer collaboration. *Exceptional Children, 62*, 101–110.

Salisbury, C. L., Evans, I. M., & Palombaro, M. M. (1997). Collaborative problem-solving to promote the inclusion of young children with significant disabilities in primary grades. *Exceptional Children, 63*, 195–209.

Salisbury, C. L., Wilson, L. L., Swartz, T. J., Palombaro, M. M., & Wassel, J. (1997). Using action research to solve instructional challenges in inclusive elementary school settings. *Education and Treatment of Children, 20*(1), 21–39.

Schmuck, R. A., & Runkel, P. J. (1985). *The handbook of organization development in schools* (3rd ed.). Illinois: Waveland.

Shaeffer, C. G. (1996). *Independent evaluation of Project DESTINY.* Keene, NH: Institute on Emotional Disabilities at Keene State College.

Wagner, M., Newman, L., D'Amico, R., Jay, E. D., Butler-Nalin, P., Marder, C., & Cox, R. (1991). *Youth with disabilities: How are they doing? The first comprehensive report from the National Longitudinal Transition Study of special education students.* Menlo Park, CA: SRI international.

Walker, H. M. & Severson, H. H. (1990). *Systematic screening for behavior disorders: A multiple gating procedure.* Longmont, CO: Sopris West.

# Exemplary Project

*Building Blocks to Healthy Emotions: A Parenting Program
to Improve the Emotional Health of Low-Income Children*

Verree Laughlin

This project focused on teaching low-income parents of Title 1 preschoolers how to use an interactive book and positive reinforcement to improve their children's social-emotional health and to help their children get ready for positive learning experiences in kindergarten. The target group was low-income parents of Head Start preschoolers in Yuma, Arizona (70% Hispanic, 15% Caucasian-white, 10% Native American, and 5% African American). I wrote and illustrated the curriculum for the parents; I entitled it, *Building Blocks to Healthy Emotions*.

I based the action research on three assumptions supported by traditional research on the plight of poor Title 1 preschoolers: (1) Low income families frequently do not know how to prepare their children for positive learning experiences in kindergarten, (2) Kindergarten students who start behind, especially social-emotionally and in pre-reading skills, often do not catch up, and continue to get further behind their peers throughout elementary school and beyond, and (3) Low-income parents can be trained to carry out interactive strategies for promoting healthy social-emotional school-learning behaviors in their preschool children.

The proactive actions in this project included two sets of two, two-hour training sessions for parents implemented over a two-week period. One set taught by Maria Johnson was in Spanish; the other set I taught in English. During week one we each spent fifteen minutes becoming acquainted and getting warmed up, forty-five minutes with a printed lesson on how to encourage healthy self expression and positive interaction with their preschool children, fifteen minutes for informal interaction with a snack, and 45 minutes using my book, *Sparkle: The Interactive Book—A Parental Guide for Building Social Skills*. *Sparkle* is a story about a firefly that lights up when he has feelings. The story is designed to facilitate a discussion between parents and their children about feelings. During week two we spent fifteen minutes with a friendly icebreaker activity, forty-five minutes with a printed lesson describing five strategies for parents to promote self esteem in their children, fifteen minutes for informal interaction with a snack, and forty-five minutes demonstrating ways for parents to use *Sparkle* effectively with their children. Our emphases over the four hours of training were on enhancing parent-child rapport and communication, students' social skills and self esteem, and students' prereading skills.

*(Continued)*

(Continued)

I developed two instruments (a questionnaire and an interview) to administer both before and after the four hours of training. Maria administered the Spanish questionnaire to members of her set, while I administered the English questionnaire to my set. Maria and I also talked with samples of parents from each of our sets, who volunteered to be interviewed. The data showed that overall 85 percent of parents increased their general knowledge about children's social-emotional health, 90 percent of parents increased their understanding of their own children's self esteem, and 95 percent of parents learned how to communicate more openly and supportively with their children, We noted no significant differences among the four ethnic groups, nor were there differences between the two language groups. Our interviews consistently revealed that the participants wanted more than four hours of training, and thought that having more time to discuss and share strategies for using *Sparkle* with one another could be useful.

SOURCE: "Building Blocks to Healthy Emotions: A Parenting Program to Improve the Emotional Health of Low-Income Children", by Verree Laughlin (2006) College of Education, Arizona State U. West.

10

# Action Research in Action

## *Curricular Articulation and Integrated Instruction*

### Douglas E. Arnold

Action research can be a potent tool for school improvement and a catalyst for change. Galax High School developed a project on integrated instruction to increase curricular articulation and connections among disciplines in the school, and to decrease the isolation often experienced by teachers.

Using the action research works of Calhoun (1994) and McKernan (1991), I decided to put action research into action at Galax (Va.) High School. During the 1995–96 school year, three teachers and I developed and conducted an action research project on integrated instruction. As we did not have many examples of articulation among curricular departments, we felt a need existed to increase curricular articulation and connections among disciplines in the school. We also wanted to chip away at the isolation often experienced in teaching and learning.

All too often, teaching and learning in a specific area is thought of as an isolated event with no connections to other areas. Because of this, teachers and students fail to see connections between and among disciplines. Integrated instruction is an "approach to learning that stresses connections and relationships rather than delineations within and across academic" and vocational disciplines (Burns, 1995, p. 3).

SOURCE: "Action Research in Action: Curricular Articulation and Integrated Instruction", by Douglas E. Arnold (1998) NASSP BULLETIN 82 (596): 74–78. Published by SAGE. Used with permission.

## THE PROJECT

The setting of the action research project was the art, physics, and geometry classes at Galax High School, a comprehensive 9–12 high school located in Galax, Virginia.

Rebecca Burns (1995) believes that integrating "instruction affects all of the key components of schooling: organization and management, curriculum, instruction, assessment, and school culture" (p. 21). She stated that the "staff may need to overcome barriers that are rooted in their assumptions about learning and teaching . . . Without a collaborative school culture, shared beliefs, supports for change, facilitating structures, and, most importantly, the desire to change the status quo of teaching and learning at your school, progress toward integrated instruction will be severely hampered" (pp. 21–22).

The collaborating teachers and I realized that necessary conditions for true integration were not possible within an already implemented school master schedule and calendar. We decided to design an integrated unit of instruction and make modifications that would allow the three teachers to collaborate and teach the unit. Our hypothesis was that an integrated unit of instruction shows connections in learning, lessens teacher isolation, and results in greater enthusiasm for learning.

## THE ACTION PLAN

Prior to the development of the integrated unit, the physics teacher and I attended a two-day workshop entitled "Dissolving the Boundaries." The workshop was a professional development activity that focused on decision making in curriculum integration. Rebecca Burns presented information about curriculum integration, different models of integration, and some positive benefits of an integrated approach to teaching and learning. The workshop also presented conditions that, when present in a school, enable the successful integration of curriculum. This workshop served as a springboard for the action research project.

Afterward, I conducted a literature search on integrated instruction to broaden my knowledge. I also established an ongoing dialogue by e-mail with workshop presenter Rebecca Burns.

The three collaborating teachers and I held several informal meetings to discuss the format of the project; to share information about integrated instruction; to plan for the development of the integrated unit; and to discuss the project in general. Finally, we were talking to each other about curriculum instruction, assessment, and possibilities!

*Students as well as teachers lose sight of the interrelation of different subject areas.*

The action research team held an initiating activity, or "kick-off," to explain the unit to all the targeted students, to give a timeline for completion (three weeks), to discuss methods of assessment, and briefly to discuss integrated instruction. The research team wanted to have this initiating activity to introduce students to the concept of integration and to motivate them to participate fully.

The team planned a culminating activity and developed a pre- and post-instruction survey for targeted students and faculty members. The purpose of the survey was to assess attitudes toward integrated instruction.

## OVERVIEW OF THE INTEGRATED UNIT

Students as well as teachers lose sight of the interrelation of different subject areas. In an effort to integrate art, physics, and geometry, students examined the close relationship art has with science and math through "hands-on" activities.

The art teacher, an art specialist and photographer, is knowledgeable in design principles, color systems, and photography, but she felt limited with any scientific explanations and mathematical principles. By teaming with a math and a science teacher, students could be provided with an in-depth understanding of these subjects that they would not otherwise experience.

The physics unit focused on the additive properties of light and primary colors. Students cut circular disks from thin plywood and painted geometric designs on the disks. They drilled holes in the center of the disks and mounted them on a long bolt that could be tightened in the chuck of a drill. Students viewed the revolving disks in various lights to see images and color blends.

In the geometry unit, students planned, designed, and developed a kaleidoscope using geometric layout and photographic principles. After taking color photographs for their individual kaleidoscopes, students printed each photograph 6, 8, 9, or 10 times depending on composition and design. Then they cut each photograph so the angle placed at the center of the kaleidoscope measured 60, 45, 40, or 36 degrees respectively ($n$ = number of photographs; $360/n$ = degree measure of central angles of circle). Students cut the outer edges in a variety of ways depending on the desired effect. Finally, students mounted the kaleidoscopes on foam core boards.

## IMPLEMENTATION

In March 1996, the integrated unit of instruction began in the art, physics, and geometry classes. Prior arrangements had been made to purchase supplies needed to carry out the unit.

The school's master schedule presented a barrier to common planning time for the instruction. The students involved were not

*Student survey results indicated the integrated unit of instruction . . . was a meaningful learning experience.*

teamed to allow for a common group of students in the three classes. In spite of this, the teachers agreed to make the best of it by switching classes to accommodate the students.

As planned, an initiating activity introduced the students to the concept of the unit. After the initiating activity, instruction took place over a span of three weeks. In each of the targeted classes, students and teachers completed a pre- and post-instruction survey to determine attitudes toward integration.

Student assessment consisted of the evaluation of the finished products—the painted disk and the kaleidoscope—and a written test. The written test was given to check for understanding of the underlying concepts the project addressed (measurement, the additive properties of light and color, circular motion, and persistence of vision). Two culminating activities were held at the conclusion of the unit. Both activities were exhibitions of student projects: one at the Galax City School Board meeting and one at the meeting of the Arts and Cultural Council of the Twin Counties. In addition, some student work was displayed in storefronts in downtown Galax.

## EVALUATION

The research team realized there were two major barriers to this project—the lack of common planning time and the lack of a common group of students in the three classes.

Student survey results indicated the integrated unit of instruction was a meaningful learning experience. Most of the students learned about and saw evidence of connections between disciplines. The student surveys revealed positive attitudes toward integrated instruction.

The faculty surveys revealed that the teachers see the value of teaming and curricular connections. Teachers gained a sense of support and belonging by working together on a team for a common instructional purpose, and they modeled working cooperatively.

## DECISIONS

The integrated unit of instruction has sparked interest among some faculty members to expand the scope of the project. The teachers involved in the unit broke out of their isolated cells and built "bridges instead of boundaries" (Burns, 1995, p. 3). The unit helped highlight the intellectual, physical, and emotional isolation of most teachers. It also helped show the connections between disciplines that can lead to collaboration. The unit demonstrated the need for common time—time to learn, to plan, to evaluate—and a common group of students.

From the students' perspectives, the surveys and observations indicate they enjoyed the integrated unit. The students were able to make connections across disciplines and to realize the benefits for instruction when teachers collaborate. Integration focuses on the learning process, not teaching (Burns, 1995).

The problem of integration will be redefined as the action cycle continues. As a faculty, we will continue to explore integrated instruction and its implications for school change. We will encourage new integration teams and support risk taking. We will continue to break down barriers of isolation and unconnected learning and build bridges for collaboration and connections between and among disciplines.

## REFERENCES

Burns, Rebecca Crawford. *Dissolving the Boundaries: Planning for Curriculum Integration in Middle and Secondary Schools.* Charleston, W.Va.: Appalachian Educational Laboratory, 1995.

Calhoun, Emily F. *How to Use Action Research in the Self-Renewing School.* Alexandria, Va.: Association for Supervision and Curriculum Development, 1994.

McKernan, J. *Curriculum Action Research: A Handbook of Methods and Resources for the Reflective Practitioner.* New York: St. Martin's Press, 1991.

# PART IV

*Studying*
*Action Research*

I have selected five thought-provoking articles and Exemplary Projects in all for this section. They each offer important ideas to consider before and after action research is defined, understood, and implemented. They each present critical study and reflective analysis of the processes of educational action research. I have chosen four just for this second edition. The article by Allen and Calhoun appeared in the first edition.

Bergez, a master English teacher and headmaster of his school, shows the power of his students' self-reflection and that of his own for changing classroom dynamics. After doing action research for almost two years, he grew to realize that the process of self-reflection, which he first considered a diagnostic phase of responsive action research, was actually a creative intervention in a proactive design. He learned that the very act of his students' reflecting on their own writing was in itself a major cause of their improved writing.

Espido Bello reflects on the very early phases of action research. As I have warned my action research students, the most difficult challenge of action research is for busy educators to get ready for and to start up their first project. In her article, Espido Bello describes useful guidelines created by different action researchers as they initiated new projects. She points out problems that can arise when choosing appropriate target groups for the action research and when negotiating understandings with them of the content and processes of the project. Her caveats about the pitfalls of starting off on the wrong foot are lessons to heed in doing action research in classrooms and schools.

Capobianco and Feldman enhance our understanding of how to assess the quality of action research. While working with teams of science teachers, they invented two levels of scientific inquiry. They first studied how the teachers carried our collaborative action research with one another. Their first order of inquiry was to assess how the targeted science teachers interacted as they carried out their work with one another. Their second order of inquiry was to assess how they themselves, Feldman and Capobianco, influenced the collaborative work among the targeted teachers. From their dual inquiries they create a framework for promoting high-quality action research.

Allen and Calhoun present an historical overview of schoolwide action research. They summarize what they consider to be the most significant findings about the challenges and pitfalls of implementing schoolwide action research. They argue that while the benefits can be considerable, those benefits will be missed if schools do not invest adequate time and resources in the action research.

Steve Collins philosophically dissects educational action research to create a portrait of its ideal attributes. First is organic collaboration wherein everyone mutually shares research goals and acts interdependently in working to reach them. Second is authentic member participation through cooperation, equalized power, and commonly understood language. Third is an ethical community in which caring participants are interdependent in ideas, language, and relations. Fourth is deep student involvement both to improve effectiveness of the action research and to enhance professional development of the educators. Collins challenges us to reconsider our vision of student participation in schools.

# Exemplary Project

*Self Reflection in Essay Writing: An Action Research Project*

Ronald Bergez

This action research ended at a very different place from where it had started. In the beginning (summer 2004) I designed a responsive action research project in which I would collect data from ninth graders at Tempe Preparatory Academy on their attitudes and beliefs about essay writing. I planned to use the data to critique my writing instruction, change some of my teaching strategies, and evaluate how my students reacted to those changes, especially with regard to their writing attitudes, beliefs, and performance.

By the end of the action research (spring 2006) I realized that I had been engaged actually in proactive action research (not responsive), and that the new practice I had initiated during the 2004–2005 school year was the "process of self reflection about one's writing," both student self-reflection and my own self-reflection as a writing teacher.

In fall semester 2004 I asked 20 students in one of my ninth-grade writing classes to fill out three structured questionnaires, in which they rated factors that make essay writing more or less enjoyable, relationships between essay writing and reading literature, areas about which they felt themselves more or less successful in writing, and specific writing strategies that they had adopted and that they believed were useful. Questionnaire 1 asked them to reflect on how they had planned to write essays in the past, how they went through the process of writing them, and how they evaluated their final products.

The students completed Questionnaires 2 and 3 after they had written essays about "The Federalist Papers" and "Billy Budd" during October and November. Then, during the second semester in winter-spring 2005 the students completed a fourth Questionnaire after they had written an essay about Upton Sinclair's "The Jungle". Items on Questionnaires 2, 3, and 4 focused on writing essays about a specific book, as opposed to the more general and historical emphases of Questionnaire 1, which I gave again to the students as an after measure in spring 2005. Although I originally believed that results from the questionnaires would guide my hopes to improve my writing teaching strategies, I could not find specific ways to change after an initial analysis of them. Perhaps, more importantly, during that same spring (2005) the Tempe Preparatory Academy board assigned me administrative duties to start in Summer, 2005, essentially removing me from classroom teaching in the 2005–2006 academic year.

*(Continued)*

(Continued)

Even in the face of heavy duties as a school administrator, I sought ways to continue the action research. In fall 2005, I arranged for a series of focus-group interviews with 16 students who had participated in the project (four students had left the school). We met in small groups of five or six during free times for the students and me. I raised primarily general questions, such as: (1) Did you feel that you changed your writing as a result of reflecting on essays you had written? (2) Have you continued to use any strategies you learned last year in this year's 10th grade writing class? (3) Did you find it meaningful to have a teacher ask you to reflect on your writing process? and (4) Have you continued your self-reflection when writing essays this year?

Eleven of the 16 students said that they did not think they had changed their actual writing style, but that they had become much more conscious of their style of learning from literature. Three students said very directly that they did not think the action research had changed anything in their writing. Two students were not sure if the project had had any effect on them. Ten students knew that I intended the questionnaires to help them make positive changes in their writing and that they appreciated my doing the project. I understood from the students' comments that whatever I might have tried to do in 2004–2005 did not affect their attitudes, beliefs, or performance about writing. As the calendar moved into winter 2006, I felt a strong sense of discouragement with the project. I had not, in my mind then, carried out effective responsive action research.

With encouragement from Dr. Eleanor Perry, Head of the LEE Program, I turned to the research literature on self-reflection, self-examination, self-appraisal, and self-regulated learning, I uncovered writers who argued that asking students to examine their writing practices can in itself offer a learning benefit. A combination of self-awareness and self reflection about one's learning style can lead to the skill of "metacognition" or "thinking about thinking" through which one can become better able to perform a set of behavioral activities under examination. Perhaps the processes of filling out the questionnaires facilitated new kinds of metacognition in the students; perhaps working on the questionnaires constituted a good in itself, as well as a means to thinking more deeply about one's writing. With those thoughts in my mind, I revisited results of the focus-group interviews and on some items on Questionnaire 1. I found some intriguing quotes, such as:

*"I didn't necessarily change; I just realized what I was doing."*

*"Well I thought about my habits, like how I write from a rough draft first."*

*"I could more quickly recognize what I was struggling with."*

*" I didn't really see my writing structure until I did the questionnaires."*

*"With the first questionnaire I began to realize how I process my thoughts."*

By early spring 2006, I began to reframe my thinking about the design of my action research. I started to view the activity of self-reflection itself as an innovative practice. I thought that the practice of students' reflecting on their writing and and how they go about writing could be an instructional intervention to improve writing. Rather than viewing the data collection in my action research as a period of diagnosis, why not see it, I thought, as a new practice initiated as an early action, the effects of which could be evaluated in the framework of proactive action research?

I returned to the focus-group protocols with new eyes and ears. I found that the students' abilities to self-regulate and to self-appraise had increased. Four students had begun to consider their personal learning styles in ways that were new to them. Two students said that because of the questionnaires they had adopted new strategies in writing. Three students described changes in their methods of planning an essay. One student commented about how Questionnaires 3 and 4 would remind them of areas they needed to change. One student reflected on how the questionnaires lead her to ask how writing an essay might be done better. Another student said that it was interesting to think about how I approached writing. Three students wrote on Questionnaire 4 that retrieving quotations from the text prior to writing a draft helped them focus their ideas.

The processes of self-reflection, self-regulation and metacognition taught me about my students as well as about myself doing action research. I learned about the importance of helping students assume authority over their own learning, and how I might use questionnaires and journal writing to facilitate that. I learned to accept the importance of my own continuous learning and development, both in relation to how I teach writing and how I deal with new information in general. Over the two years of this action research my self-perception as a teacher has changed. In the end, whether my action research answered exactly what I had set out to find mattered less than the fact that my students learned how to think about their learning. My action research succeeded, but not in the way I had envisioned at the start. My mission now is to take these new understandings about self-reflection to the next level of action. My action research has not ended; it will continue.

SOURCE: "Self Reflection in Essay Writing: An Action Research Project", by Ronald Bergez (2006) College of Education, Arizona State U. West.

# 11

## Initiating a Collaborative Action Research Project

### *From Choosing a School to Planning the Work on an Issue*

Eva Espido Bello

This article is centered on a preliminary phase of action research which the literature has not given much attention to. The initial stages are usually complex and the ideas on how to proceed are often unclear. Therefore, learning how different authors have dealt with them can serve as guidelines when initiating new research, which is why I have decided to dedicate the contents of this article to explaining how we developed the initial phase. Firstly, I begin mentioning my expectations in relation to the research, and I point out some of the problems I thought would appear at the beginning of the collaborative study. Later, I make reference to the criteria employed when choosing the school where the research was carried out and I describe the way we proceeded to negotiate the proposal and inform the school community of it. When describing the negotiation process, I give special importance to those matters which we dedicated more attention to, such as the discussion of the

SOURCE: "Initiating a Collaborative Action Research Project: From Choosing a School to Planning the Work on an Issue", by Eva Espido Bello (2006) *Educational Action Research*, Volume 14 (1), pp. 3–21. Taylor & Francis Ltd., http://www.tandf.co.uk/journals. Reprinted with permission of the publisher.

different issues, the selection of one and the initial planning directed towards its understanding and the introduction of orientative measures for its improvement. The description concludes with a reference to the elaboration, presentation and circulation of the written proposal, all of which closed the negotiation corresponding to this phase. Finally, I make an evaluation of the process and formulate a series of questions that can facilitate the development of the initial phase and subsequent studies. Nevertheless, the conditions that surround each piece of research are different and, therefore, the way it is carried out will depend, to a great extent, on those conditions.

# INTRODUCTION

Choosing a school and setting a collaborative action research project in motion are part of a very important preliminary phase of the research work, as has been mentioned by Adelman (1993) and Walker (1997). This requires negotiating the research proposal and discovering an issue to centre the inquiry on. At the beginning there is hardly any initial planning and the people taking part in the project have to construct their plan of action gradually as they go along. In this way, the foundations for all the subsequent work are laid.

In spite of its importance, I have encountered the paradox that very little attention has been given to these matters in the literature on action research. Perhaps this is due to the fact that it is a difficult and confusing stage, where hardly any 'results' are perceived and, in research, efficiency and tangible results have been given priority over the educational value of processes, as Pérez Gómez (1990, pp. 12–13) pointed out. Given that I consider the process important, I will describe this phase in detail, indicating the criteria on which I based the choice of school and the process followed to facilitate the negotiation of the research proposal, giving an account of how the issue was selected and alluding to the initial planning performed.

# THE STARTING POINT

The research project was initiated in March 2000. The initiative was taken by me, a lecturer at the Faculty of Education at the University of A Coruña. I wished to put a collaborative action research project into operation at a school, in order to know its impact on the professional development of the teachers involved.[1]

I was aware that the development of the research would pose a number of problems. The first was the little free time that the nursery school teachers had to dedicate to the research. The second was our lack of investigative experience in this line of work. Lastly, I should mention my difficulty in appreciating the praxis of nursery school teachers, due to my lack of teaching experience at that level. Woods (1989, p. 16) has referred to some of these problems. To make this collaboration possible, it would be essential to take advantage of the time and the knowledge we possessed and to try to obtain the greatest benefit from working in collaboration.

Contrasting points of view among the research participants would lead to the acquisition of further knowledge. The planning and development of the research would give us useful skills when initiating other studies, both in conjunction or separately. Reflecting on the process would help us to understand the possibilities that action research offers to promote learning, to narrow the gap between theory and practice and to create a collaborative culture between different institutions.

In short, putting this in motion required the commitment of both parts and this would limit, somewhat, the choice of a school, as teachers do not usually have much free time to dedicate to research (Hopkins, 1989, p. 59).

## THINKING IN A SCHOOL: CRITERIA AND GROUNDS FOR ITS CHOICE

When action research is undertaken, you need to ask yourself what characteristics the school must combine. Stake (1998, pp. 17–19) suggests some criteria that can help you to direct your choice. This author points out that we may choose a school because we know that the phase which the study wishes to focus on is taught there, because it has a long-standing tradition regarding activities of innovation, because of our belief that it will offer us the opportunity to acquire a great deal of new knowledge, or because different educational programmes are being implemented there. Furthermore, we might choose it for its geographical location, for the characteristics of the educational community, or because we believe that the inquiry will be well accepted.

In our case, I considered, like Stake did, that an important criterion for choosing a school ought to be that of offering a great many opportunities for us to acquire new knowledge. From the information I had, Andaina Municipal Nursery School (A Coruña, Galicia, Spain) fulfilled this criterion.[2] This school met certain important characteristics: it depended on the local administration; it was managed by a teaching cooperative that, when I established my first contact with them, was having a new nursery, primary and secondary education school built;[3] the teachers valued teamwork; participation of families in the life of the school was strongly encouraged; special care was taken with the selection of materials, which were adapted to the interests and needs of its pupils as well as to the context in which they learnt; and, finally special attention was given to the use of the Galician language and to transmitting its culture.

In order to understand this last point better, I should point out that Galicia is an autonomous region situated in the northwest of Spain and it has a language of its own called Galician. This language, rooted in the rural areas and mainly used by the older generation who received little or no school education and belonged to the lower classes, began to be spoken less during the 20th century and especially so from 1950 onwards. This was mainly due to the political rejection of the use of this language in the street, in the educational system and in the mass media during the Franco regime as well as to the impoverishment of the rural areas, which, from the mid-19th century, led to the emigration of these people (Bouzada Fernández *et al.*, 2002). With the approval of the Constitución Española in 1978, the Estatuto de Autonomía para Galicia in 1981 and the Lei 3/1983, de Normalización Lingüística of 1983, the bases of a series of measures to promote the use of the Galician language and its culture were established.

The sociolinguistic situation in Galician schools and the use of the Galician language by the teachers varies from one context to another. The use of the Galician language in the context surrounding the school is not especially favourable. Information received from parents indicates that 91 percent of the children understand the Galician language perfectly, and only 9 percent with difficulty. In relation to the use of the language, the information obtained is not very encouraging: only 12 percent express themselves in Galician, while 87.5 percent do so in Castillian and 0.2 percent in other languages (Colexio Andaina, 2004–05). This information gives us an approximate idea of the comprehension and use of the Galician language, although it should be said that it is taken at the moment of registration which, in most cases, is in the first cycle of nursery education, when oral expression is still a little limited. The scarce use of the Galician language by children is also related to the connection that their parents have between the language and poverty, the lack of school education and being ridiculed as country bumpkins.

Consequently, the teachers, conscious of this situation, have progressively increased the use of the language, up to its present level, where all the subjects except for Spanish language and English are taught in Galician.

All these characteristics, with special emphasis on the extension of the educational phases, proved to be very important for the development of this research as we will see further on.

Whereas the above-mentioned criterion was important, one of the requirements viewed as being indispensable was that of finding someone at a school who would be willing to cooperate actively with us on the research project. We needed to choose a school which would permit our presence there (Stake, 1998, p. 17) as well as allowing its staff to participate voluntarily (Grupo de Humanidades 109, Laboratorio para el Análisis del Cambio Educativo [Grupo LACE HUM 109], 1999, p. 8). The information which I had about the school was that its teaching team was open to interchanging ideas and experiences with other institutions, since they considered this to be a way of achieving mutual enrichment. This characteristic was very important at the moment of choosing the school, as their being so open guaranteed that they would let us in and collaborate in the study, which is not easy to achieve, as has been pointed out by authors such as Torres Santomé (1991) and Stake (1998). Torres Santomé, for example, states the reasons given by the teachers for not collaborating on the project as being insufficient time to dedicate to the research and no support given by the Department of Education of the regional Galician government.

These reasons did not deter the teachers from agreeing to participate in the research, although the lack of time due to the expansion of the school reduced the number of teachers able to participate. In spite of this, they considered it an opportunity to improve their professional skills and, consequently, their pupils' learning, without forgetting the prestige the school would receive.

These two examples are not sufficient to come to the conclusion that public school teachers are more willing to participate in action research than state school teachers. In both cases teachers can be found who will either collaborate or not and it can depend on many circumstances.

The likelihood of finding an issue that would interest not only the in-school researchers involved, but also the rest of the teachers and the external researcher, was yet another criterion which I took into consideration when making my choice. Choosing an issue which proves to be interesting to the professionals at the school is considered to be of vital importance.[4] If, moreover, the issue is also interesting to the external researcher, the motivation of all the members will be greater. Based on the information I had before visiting the school, some of the aspects which were given special attention there turned out to be issues of great interest to me too. Therefore, it was likely that if the interests of the school teachers converged and also theirs with mine, the motivation of all the members of the research team would be much greater.

At the moment of making my choice, I did not attach any importance at all to the criterion of geographical proximity between Andaina Municipal Nursery School and the Faculty of Education of the University of A Coruña, where the people who were going to be involved in the research project worked. However, on reviewing the process we had followed, with the benefit of hindsight, we realised that this type of research requires a lot of time to immerse oneself in the context in which the study is carried out, as well as time to work together and to reflect on that joint work. Therefore, proximity facilitates research work.

Once I had decided on this particular school, the next step was to get in touch with the teachers working there with the aim of submitting my research proposal to them and then waiting to see if they would agree to collaborate with me. The final decision was in their hands.

## THE NEGOTIATION OF THE PROPOSAL AND THE START OF THE STUDY IN COLLABORATION

The negotiation begins when the first contacts are established with the school. From that moment on, it is present during the entire investigative process, acquiring special relevance at certain stages.[5] One of them is the access to the school and the starting of the research, which I will now discuss. First, I will make reference to the actions carried out and, later,

I will describe the process in more detail. The main actions carried out during this period are described in Table 1.

## THE ORAL NEGOTIATION
## ON THE RESEARCH PROPOSAL

### The First Contacts With the School

The first contact I had with this school took place by means of a telephone conversation with its headmistress. This contact was provided to me by the head of my department. The backing given by him, together with the fact that the professionals at the school understood that the interaction between their place of work and its context was an opportunity to learn, made their acceptance to carry out the research project at the school a whole lot easier.[6] In fact, I perceived the headmistress's willingness to accept my project from the very first moment, even though she told me that she would need a few days to inform the people working at the school. During this telephone conversation she suggested having a meeting where we could specify the terms of the proposal in more detail. I dedicated the following days to drawing up a draft, although I finally decided not to take it the day of my first visit to the school so as not to condition the choice of issue. The headmistress informed the teaching staff of my request and they agreed that teacher researcher 1 should initially become involved in the research project. She was a teacher who had a lot of teaching experience in nursery education as she had been working in this school since it was created in 1987. At a later stage, when negotiating the research proposal with this teacher, we thought it would be convenient to have someone else cooperate with us so as to strengthen our research team and give it a somewhat more institutional nature.[7]

Teacher researcher 1 thought that the educational counsellor could cooperate with us and she asked me to give her some time to study whether it would be feasible for the educational counsellor to get involved in the project. To better understand the role of this professional, I would like to explain that the organisation and development of educational guidance has passed from being provided assistance by external services, attending the school only when necessary, to becoming an internal department in the school, helping in the development of the educational service. In Galicia, specifically, the law regulates professional and educational orientation and has created these departments in all secondary schools (see Decreto 120/1998). Primary and nursery schools, depending on the number of students, have their own or not but, in any case, they have connection to the secondary school corresponding to their geographical area. These departments offer psychopedagogical, educational and professional guidance. They evaluate the needs of the students, helping and advising them. They assist the teaching staff with respect to tutorial action and in the evaluation and promotion of the students. They also promote pedagogical training and school–family cooperation, etc. These departments are directed by educational counsellors who are professionals with degrees or with a doctorate in pedagogy, psychopedagogy or psychology.

**Table 1**

| Date | Action | Purpose | Description of the action | Participants |
|------|--------|---------|---------------------------|--------------|
| 6 April 2000 | First phone contact with the headmistress of Andaina Municipal Nursery School. | Inform the school of my wish to carry out an action research project there and sound out their acceptance. | I contacted the school headmistress and explained the reason for my call. We spoke briefly of the investigative proposal and of possible issues. We fixed a date to discuss the proposal in more detail. | The headmistress and the university researcher |
| Between 6 and 12 April 2000 | The elaboration of a first research proposal draft. | Organise my ideas in order to present the research proposal. | I made some enquiries about the school's educational project,[a] and selected some strategies for the collection and analysis of information. | The university researcher |
| 12 April 2000 | First visit to the school: an interview with the headmistress. | To discuss my research proposal. | The headmistress informed me of the school's educational project and handed me a document to complete the information. I informed her of the research proposal and she invited me to see the classrooms and other areas, helping me in my immersion into the culture of the school. | The headmistress and the university researcher |
| 12 April 2000 | Submitting the documentation. | To facilitate my knowledge of the school. | The headmistress gave me a document called Andaina: a nosa escola [Our school],[b] containing information about the school's educational project. | The headmistress and the university researcher |
| 12 April 2000 | Observation in classroom number 1. | To facilitate my knowledge of the school. | To help me get into the culture of the school and to understand how the educational activities in a nursery education classroom at this school are carried out. | Teacher researcher1,[c] the students and the university researcher |
| 12 April 2000 | Meeting. | To discuss the research proposal | We discussed the research proposal. We saw that it was necessary to involve someone else apart from teacher researcher 1, who would undertake to contact the school's educational counsellor and later inform me of the outcome. We also decided which days of the week and what hours were more convenient for our meetings. | Teacher researcher 1 and the university researcher |
| 28 April 2000 | Phone contact (message). | To propose a date and a time for the next meeting where our aim would be to choose a research issue. | Teacher researcher 1 set a date and time to choose the issue of investigation. | Teacher researcher 1 and the university researcher |

| Date | Action | Purpose | Description of the action | Participants |
|---|---|---|---|---|
| 1 May 2000 | Phone contact (conversation). | To confirm the date and the time of the meeting. | I called teacher researcher 1 to confirm my attendance at the meeting on the date and at the time proposed. | Teacher researcher 1 and the university researcher |
| 2 May 2000 | Meeting. | To choose the research issue. | We discussed different issues that could be an object of study. We chose one. The lines of inquiry were defined. | Teacher researcher 1, the educational counsellor and the university researcher |
| 7 June 2000 | Phone contact (message). | Set a date for a meeting. They formulated a request. | Teacher researcher 1 left me a message setting a date to discuss the work done and asked me to prepare an access application form together with a written research proposal, which would be discussed in a staff meeting and, if approved, would be presented to the school board so as to inform the entire school community. | Teacher researcher 1 |
| 8 June 2000 | Phone contact (conversation). | To inform her of my progress with the inquiry. To confirm the date and the time of the meeting. To request information on how they would like that document to be worded. | I contacted teacher researcher 1 to inform her that I had not finished my task. We decided to meet anyway on the proposed date and I asked her to express in more concrete terms her request. | Teacher researcher 1 and the university researcher |
| 13 June 2000 | Meeting. | Interchange the documentation individually prepared and discuss the work carried out to date. | Teacher researcher 1 and I exchanged documentation,[d] read and discussed the contents with the purpose of sharing the information about the work that each of us was doing. | Teacher researcher 1 and the university researcher |
| 15 June 2000 | Meeting. | To submit the research proposal for approval at a staff meeting. | | All the teachers at the school |

(Continued)

**Table 1** (Continued)

a. The idea for the schools to elaborate their educational project appears in the 1980s, with the intention of providing them with autonomy to adapt the curriculum proposed by the educational administration to the context of the school (Rey & Santamaria, 1992, pp. 153–163). Subsequently, the legal regulations prescribed that schools elaborate their educational project. They specifically point out that the teaching staff must define the proposals, the school board must establish the criteria for its elaboration, approval and evaluation and, finally, the governing body must draw it up, taking into account the analysis of the students' specific educational needs, the characteristics of the school and its geographical area. With all this information, objectives, priorities and procedures are determined. The school's educational project must include the school's organisation, the educational objectives, the objectives designed to achieve the normalisation of the Galician language, the preparation of the school to reach the educational objectives of each phase, the school's own regulations, the activities and services provided by the school, the channels of collaboration and participation between the different sectors of the educational community as well as the collaboration and cultural interchange with the town hall's social and educational services and those of other institutions (for a more detailed description see Decreto 374/1996).

b. This is a document which is handed to families when a boy or girl is enrolled at the school.

c. The teachers who have became progressively involved in the project will be identified in the research report and in any future publications as teacher researcher 1, teacher researcher 2, etc. This decision was taken after discussion with the internal researchers. This way of identifying the participants is due, on the one hand, to the interest in mentioning the roles carried out by those involved in the research and, on the other hand, to finding an identification compatible with the idea that the participation of a teacher is done in representation of a team which is the result of a decision taken by the cooperative. For this reason they do not consider it correct to use real names.

d. We interchanged the following documents: a report prepared by teacher researcher 1 and the access application form and the research proposal draft prepared by me. The report contained information on the commitment made by the teaching staff in relation to the Galician culture and language from the moment the school was opened in 1987 to the school year 1999–2000. By preparing this report we wanted to go over the steps taken by the school in relation to the subject of study chosen, so as to continue advancing in its understanding and improvement of its educational action.

176

## Participants and Roles in This Phase of the Research

During this phase, there were four people who began to familiarise themselves with the research project: the headmistress, teacher researcher 1, the educational counsellor and myself. My role consisted in keeping the school informed of the type of research work I wished to perform and sounding out the possibilities of having my proposal accepted. At the same time I obtained data on the school by engaging in dialogue with different professionals, by observing and by going through the documentation in order to view and submit various issues with the aim of knowing which of them might interest the school most. Furthermore, I tried to have more than just one person at the school become involved in the study so as to strengthen the team, as I considered, the same as Elliott (1990, p. 79), that if there was no process of collective reflection, the opportunities for developing the teaching practices of a specific teacher would be very limited.

The role of the school teachers involved in this phase of the research consisted in providing me with information on their school's educational project, facilitating my access to obtain information first hand, finding time to discuss the proposal and informing the other members of the school community of it. Their queries and requests helped me to define the proposal and later formulate it in writing.

The interchange of information during this time was fundamental to begin the study in collaboration. Different issues emerged, were discussed and finally we decided to centre the study on promoting the use of the Galician language and transmitting its culture in the school. Once the issue was chosen, we decided that on behalf of the school teacher researcher 1[8] and teacher researcher 2 would participate, as both were part of the school's Linguistic Normalisation Team.[9] This team is in charge of activities related to promoting the use of the Galician language in schools and its coordinator is also part of the Committee of Pedagogical Coordination.[10] Therefore, the research would acquire an institutional nature and the communication between the research team and the other members of the school's teaching staff would become easier. The participation of teacher researcher 2 was no impediment to the involvement of that of the educational counsellor, but the fact that the teaching team were extending and expanding their educational project to new stages reduced their possibilities of participating.

## Emergence and Relevance of Different Issues

The subject related to the issues was present during the phase of the research described in this article and was the centre of our conversations from the moment of my first contact with the school's headmistress. Before this, I had information that there were some issues that constituted elements of identity of the school's educational project and I used it to see if any of them could become our issue.

In my first conversation with the headmistress, I alluded to subjects such as the promotion and use of the Galician language and the transmission of its culture in the school, the interest in the participation of families in school life and the process of expanding the school's educational project to include primary and secondary education. The dialogue with the headmistress, with teacher researcher 1 and with the educational counsellor; the observation of the activities taking place in classroom number 1; and the information on view in the different parts of the school, as well as the analysis of the contents of the document handed to me by the headmistress, all contributed to the appearance of other issues, such as the selection and elaboration of didactic materials and resources suitable to the context interests and needs of the students, the transversal subjects, pupil self-evaluation, etc.

The two which were the subject of discussion at all the conversations were, first, that of the participation of families in school life and the communication between family and school, and second, the promotion and use of the Galician language and the transmission of its culture in the school. The first was already well established. In the second they were introducing measures for the advancement of its understanding and improvement, but they considered that there was still a lot to do.

Evaluating the process of putting the new nursery, primary and secondary education school into motion was an interesting matter; nevertheless, it was still nothing but a project and the teachers would not feel as confident and comfortable about these new stages as they would about nursery education.

The issue of the selection and elaboration of didactic materials and resources was also interesting for the school, although, on the day we made our definite choice, it was not included in the debate.

They were already working on some transversal issues such as environmental education, consumer education, traffic code education, etc. In the in-school researchers' opinion, environmental education was the one where they had advanced the most, but viewed as a whole, they believed that they still had a lot of work to do. They preferred to develop them more before making them the focus of our project.

At the time of making our choice, the issues of pupil self-evaluation and the promotion and use of the Galician language and the transmission of its culture had become the most interesting to the teachers at the school. The former was worked on mainly in the groups of four- and five-year-olds, and the latter in all the groups.

All during this period, other issues such as making the most use of the space, the students taking on some responsibilities or the analysis of the didactic strategies employed by the teachers gradually appeared. However, they never constituted key issues of debate during this phase.

### Criteria for Our Choice of Research Issue

In this section I shall mention the criteria employed in choosing the research issue. They emerged gradually during our discussions on the research proposal and on possible subjects of study.

One of the principal criteria which we took into account when choosing our research issue was that it ought to be of interest to the teachers at the school.[11] This way, they would feel more motivated to conduct research and to take gradual steps aimed at improving the situation in connection with the issue.

On the day we made our choice, other criteria gradually emerged as we discussed different issues. One of them was the significance of the issue at the school, i.e. the sphere where the issue became important. Whenever it is possible to do so, it is more appropriate to choose an issue which affects a school as a whole rather than only a part. This way, it will be easier to get people to gradually become involved in the research project or to get them to take an interest in its progress.

Another criterion that surfaced was the degree of development of each one of the issues at the school. It does not appear to be highly advisable to choose an issue which has already been developed extensively nor one on which little work has been performed. If it has been developed extensively, the advances will hardly be perceived and people will not feel very motivated to take part in such a study, and on the contrary, if it has not been developed as much as it should have been, it is possible that the people responsible for its development may feel threatened by the research project.

The issue that fulfilled all the criteria was the promotion and use of the Galician language and the transmission of its culture in the Andaina Municipal Nursery School.

## From Choosing the Research Issue to the Initial Planning of the Work

At the moment of making the choice, we were conscious that the issue we had chosen was complex. In spite of that, we considered it was worthwhile getting involved in its study. On the one hand, it met all the criteria previously mentioned. On the other hand, it had especial interest for the school at that time, given that, in precisely that school year, the teaching staff had taken the decision of carrying out an immersion model of the Galician language. The research could contribute to an understanding of the impact the decision taken would have on the students and to introducing measures oriented to improving the situation in relation to the chosen issue. Besides, the analysis of the issue required taking into consideration other subjects which we have already mentioned such as the didactic and organisational strategies, the subject of the materials and resources employed, the family–school relationship, etc., making it more interesting and educational.

At the same time, the monitoring of this issue in the classrooms and at the school required gathering a lot of information on communication processes, as well as on the contextual situations where those processes took place. This information could also be useful for other issues.

Once the issue was chosen we modified the composition of the research team, we defined the lines of work oriented to favour its understanding, we selected those on which to start working, and we distributed tasks. These lines were as follows.

(1) Review of the chosen school subjects for nursery education and analysis of the materials and didactic resources used.

(2) Analysing the methodology employed to expose students to the use of the Galician language and to encourage its use.

(3) Studying the coherence between the educational line of the school and that of the families in connection with this issue.

(4) Monitoring and following up on the attitude of the teachers, of the families, and the pupils, as well as the administration, with regard to the promotion of the Galician language.

(5) Monitoring and following up on the introduction and the fostering of the use of the Galician language at this school starting from its creation up to the present.

(6) Analysing the evolution of the rules drawn up by the Ministry of Education of the regional government of Galicia in order to promote and strengthen the Galician language and the Galician culture in our autonomous region, in particular the one which makes reference to schools.

(7) Providing a context for the research issue within the sociopolitical and cultural framework of the municipality of A Coruña.

In this initial planning, we did not determine the amount of time we intended to dedicate to each of these aspects. Some months passed before we managed to make our planning somewhat more precise and well-adjusted to our real possibilities of action.

## SUBMITTING THE PROPOSAL IN WRITING AND ITS ACCEPTANCE

Once some of the main aspects of the research project had been discussed orally, the researchers at the school asked me to submit a proposal in writing, with the objective of requesting permission from the teaching staff and the school board to carry out our research project at their school. I resumed work on the drafts I had first drawn up, to submit an oral presentation of my proposal, and I complemented the information following the guidelines provided by authors such as Elliott (1993) and Kemmis and McTaggart (1992). In my understanding, this was a provisional document, a draft, on which we would base our joint elaboration of a proposal. The document contained information about the following aspects: the diagram which is normally employed to reproduce action research graphically,[12] the phases of a cycle of that diagram, the approximate amount of time it would take to carry out the study, the data collection and analysis methodology, the aspects which should be submitted for negotiation, the information that the research report should contain, the principles of procedure and those issues which are of an ethical nature.[13]

In a meeting we had in June 2000 I submitted the proposal to teacher researcher 1 but, at that moment, we hardly discussed it. Later, this in-centre researcher informed the teaching staff and the school board about the pro-posal in their respective end-of-year meetings.[14] At the beginning of the next school year she resumed contact with me to invite me to the inaugu-ration of their new school and to continue our study. At that moment, I did not ask whether the proposal had been accepted or not, although I took for granted that it had, since she had contacted me. Their wish to open the new school in September had kept the teaching team busy during the summer months, and that was the reason for their informative slip, which teacher researcher 1 made reference to in one of the emails she sent me with regard to the report I elaborated corresponding to that phase of the research:

> I regret the informative slip on the decision taken by the teaching staff in relation to the research. (Email, 21 December 2004)

In short, my written proposal was accepted by the school without there having been a real debate about it among the members of the research team, in spite of pointing out in it that it was merely a draft. I consider that the debate of the proposal would have helped us to have a clearer general idea and make the planning more concrete, which would permit us to advance more rapidly later. However, this debate did not occur. There could have been several reasons for that. First, I think that I did not place special emphasis on this matter verbally. Second, I consider that we, at that moment in time, were not sufficiently aware of what putting the principles which the proposal was founded on into practice. Third, we wished to progress. Finally, there were many questions and problems that the school had to find answers for at that moment, as they were expanding and extending their educational project to new stages.

## BY WAY OF REFLECTION

The contents of this article are centred on a preliminary phase of action research initiated in a municipal nursery school. Consequently, I consider it more appropriate to include in this section a few reflections raised by the review of our performance during that period than to draw conclusions, making a balance of our strong and weak points, and giving reasons for having acted in the way we did. From that balance, I provide alternative ways of action.

Judging by the description of the process which has been followed, one might think that our actions were carried out in a clear and orderly man-ner. However, from my point of view, this was rather a messy phase but, at the same time, it constituted an educational and enriching experience.

On the one hand, none of the other people belonging to the research team had ever participated in carrying out this sort of study before. I, personally, hardly had any knowledge of the syllabus corresponding to the nursery education phase and its development in concrete contexts. Besides, at the moment of beginning the study, the cooperative which managed the school was expanding its educational project to new stages, and this did not leave much time for the research.

On the other hand, this collaborative study enabled us to live the experience of putting an action research project into motion and learning from the process. Moreover, it made it possible for us to start a relationship between teachers working at different educational institutions, and to learn not only from our own way of thinking, acting and behaving, but also from that of the other members of the team. The requests and demands which were made by each one of the members of the group caused individual and group reflection, promoted learning and contributed to the advancement of the project. The fact that the cooperative was extending its educational plan to new stages gave continuity to the research of the issue, and although it was not the most appropriate moment, motivated people to be involved in it.

Among the strong points of our performance, the most outstanding in my opinion are the following. First, I believe that the way in which we proceeded to negotiate the research proposal, by establishing an oral debate before drawing up a written proposal, was appropriate. Second, the way the school's teachers facilitated the debate of the research proposal and helped me to get to know how their school's educational project was developing was also appropriate. All of this contributed to make the collaboration possible. Third, I understand that the moment of the school year chosen to initiate contact with the school was fortunate. It took place at the beginning of April, and this gave us time to discuss and choose the issue before the end of the school year, allowing us to take advantage of the existing school end-of-year meetings with the objective of providing information to the teaching staff and the school board about the research project.

Summarising, in my opinion, the balance of our performance was positive. However, I think that it would have been advisable to have created favourable conditions for a more comprehensive debate at the beginning, given that it would have helped us to advance more quickly and with more confidence later. This idea was also shared by teacher researcher 1, who, after reading the draft of my report corresponding to this phase, wrote:

> I completely agree on the need to study the research proposal more in-depth. (Email, 21 December 2004)

In my opinion, to create those conditions and to study the proposal in-depth we could begin mentioning some of the basic characteristics and objectives of action research, and promoting the initial debate, by way of a series of questions of the type set out below.

> What research issue could we choose? Why? On what criteria could we base our choice of research issue? What lines of action can we implement with a view to understanding and trying to improve the situation in connection with the issue?

What information do we need to advance the understanding of each of those lines of action? Which are the sources to obtain this information?

What data collection and analysis strategies and techniques can we employ?

Who is going to take part in the research project? Why?

How much time are the people taking part in the research project able to devote to it?

How long do we expect the study to take?

How much work do we think that getting involved in the project is going to entail for the parties concerned?

What roles can each member of the team take on?

How much time are we going to dedicate to the planning, the collection of information and the individual and joint analysis?

On which groups will we centre the observation? Why?

How are we going to proceed to exchange information?

Who is going to have access to that information?

When should we draw up partial reports of the research? Who will be responsible for their editing and what circulation will they have?

How are we going to inform the other members of the school community about our research work and how are we going to collect and reflect on their suggestions?

The questions I have posed to promote a greater debate arose from the reflection on the process followed in this phase and from the knowledge obtained from reading the literature of qualitative research and evaluation. In fact, most of them have already been proposed by other authors.

The dialogue on these and other possible questions could have led us to contrast our ideas with those of other professionals who have previously carried out similar studies.[15] This would help us to have a clearer idea on how to proceed and the reasons for doing it in a particular way. We would then have been in a better condition to draw up a document to include all the agreements reached.

However, we cannot forget that while the members of the research team are getting to know each other, it will be difficult for them to freely express their points of view. Moreover, the conditions that surround an action research project give it its own particular character. Therefore, training and experience in relation to projects of this type should help us to act in a more reflexive manner and confront better the uncertainty that characterises each project. Consequently, progress without much specification has its advantages, gaining in creativity and autonomy.

Finally, I would point out that part of these reflections appeared when writing the report corresponding to this phase of the study, which took place quite some time after finishing it. The act of putting it in writing made me revise the process followed, helping me to understand it better and proposing alternative forms of action. The educative potential of writing has made me appreciate the convenience of having the research team members elaborate partial reports during the whole process—a measure which should be taken into account in the research schedule and undertaken by each and every participant. In turn, it would be important to establish channels for their circulation outside of the research context. In this way, knowledge would be generated and made public, and it could serve as a base for subsequent debates and orientation for subsequent studies. The convenience of elaborating these reports and using them to reflect on one's own performance is alluded to by several authors. However, some of them do not give priority to the elaboration and circulation of knowledge beyond the limits of the school context of those participating in the research.

## ACKNOWLEDGMENTS

The author would like to express her gratitude to the educational community at Andaina Municipal Nursery School for agreeing to have the research project carried out there, and she would especially like to thank its team of professionals for volunteering to collaborate in this study. It could not have been carried out without their collaboration. The author would, likewise, like to thank the Department of Pedagogy and Didactics at the Faculty of Education of the University of A Coruña, and, indeed, the University of A Coruña, for having provided her with every facility to participate in a project of this type. Professor Jurjo Torres Santomé, the author's thesis supervisor, deserves a special mention for suggesting the school where the research project was eventually carried out, as well as for all the help and guidance he has given the author all through the research process. Finally, the author would also like to extend her gratitude to Professor Narciso de Gabriel Fernández for helping her contact the school. To all of those who have helped, assisted and guided the author—thank you.

## NOTES

1. A lot of authors refer to the relationship between action research and professional development. See, for example, Carr and Kemmis (1988); Kemmis and McTaggart (1992); Elliott (1993); Walker (1997); McKernan (1999).

2. In this article, I have decided to use the real name of the school instead of an anonymous one for several reasons. First, I consider that it is a way of acknowledging the agreement of the teachers to the collaboration and their involvement in the development of this action research. Second, I understand it as a gesture directed towards the construction of the identity of the institutions who become involved in research

projects of this type with little incentive for them. Third, the first results of this experience were presented together with one of the school teachers, and by the author, in the forum of the Collaborative Action Research Network Annual Conference held in November 2004 in Malaga (Spain), where we identified the school by its real name. The debate on this subject emerged at the time the presentation was being prepared. At that moment, we assessed the consequences that could result from using real names and it was finally decided that from that moment on, we would use the real names both in joint publications as well as in those produced individually. Authors such as Kushner (2002), Simons (1999), Walker (1997), Richardson (1973) and Stake (1998) have argued for and against using real names.

3. To understand the context better, it should be pointed out that with the approval of the Ley Orgánica 1/1990, de 3 de octubre, de Ordenación General del Sistema Educativo there was a general restructuring of the system. The legal text states that in nursery school, education is voluntary; it has been conferred an educational character and not only of attendance. The age of the students ranges up to six years old and, for organisational and curricular effects, this phase is divided into two three-year cycles. The age of students in compulsory education ranges from six to 16. This period is divided into two phases: primary education from six to 12 and secondary education from 12 to 16.

4. Numerous authors coincide with this idea. See, for example, Elliott (1990, p. 80).

5. Looking through the literature on qualitative research methodology we see that there always appears a section dedicated to the negotiation wherein the authors provide a useful orientation to carry it out. By way of example, please refer to Goetz and LeCompte (1988, chapter 3), Woods (1989, chapter 2), Walker (1997, pp. 35–36), Stake (1998, pp. 58–60), Grupo LACE HUM 109 (1999, pp. 11–13) and Flick (2004, chapter 6).

6. As Simons (1999, p. 205) points out, when a school is used to receiving frequent visits by researchers or other people, it is usually much easier to gain access to it.

7. To be able to introduce significant changes in a school through action research, it seems necessary to choose general subjects that affect a greater number of the teachers. This has already been stressed by Elliott (1990, p. 40).

8. When we began the research this teacher was the coordinator of the school's Linguistic Normalisation Team.

9. Specifically, this team is responsible for the following.

- Presenting proposals to the school's governing body to define the linguistic normalisation (linguistic normalisation consists in a social and cultural process that permits the expansion of a language to all possible areas of use) objectives to be included in the school's educational project. These will be presented through the teaching staff.
- Proposing to the Committee of Pedagogical Coordination the general plan for the use of the language with the objective of including it in the syllabus. Therein, the measures oriented to promoting the use of the Galician language in the school's activities and the projects aimed at improving the attitude towards the language and the linguistic skills of the members of the educational community are specified.
- Proposing to the Committee of Pedagogical Coordination the specific plan to promote the presence of the reality of Galicia, its culture, history, geography, economy, ethnography, language, literature, art, folklore, etc. in education. This plan should be included in the syllabus.

- Elaborating a yearly plan of activities oriented to the attainment of the objectives included in the aforementioned plans.
- Presenting to the school board an economical budget to be dedicated to these objectives for its approval.
- Other duties that the Departament of Education of the regional Galician government plans in its specific regulations.

10. This body is in charge of coordinating the teachers' work and its functions are to support the planning and development of the school syllabus and to guarantee the coherence between the school's educational project, the syllabus projects and the annual general plan, making sure that the planning is carried out and evaluated. Please refer to chapter II of Decreto 374/1996, wherein reference is made to the composition and responsibilities of the Committee of Pedagogical Coordination.

11. This is one of the three criteria suggested by Hopkins (1989, pp. 64–65) when choosing an issue. He also suggests that the chosen issue is concrete and its study viable.

12. We may find references to some of the graphical representations in Hopkins (1989), Kemmis and McTaggart (1992), Elliott (1993), Walker (1997) and McKernan (1999), among others.

13. In my opinion, the ethical issues occupy a central point in this type of study. I completely agree with Elliott (1990, p. 26) that action research cannot be carried out if there is no trust based on loyalty to a mutually accepted ethical framework that governs data collection and communication. Consequently, I have taken the time to analyse how these issues are dealt with by other authors such McKernan (1999), Grupo LACE HUM 109 (1999), Walker (1997), Gimeno Sacristán (1992), Kemmis and McTaggart (1992), Hopkins (1989), Law (1984) or Richardson (1973).

14. When wishing to carry out a case study at a school, the dates that are close to the beginning and the end of the school year may be appropriate for establishing the first contacts. That way, the meetings which are usually held by the teaching staff and the school board can be very useful for submitting the research proposal to the school community.

15. In this sense, it would be helpful to examine some case studies. We can find some examples by Elliott (1993), Atweh *et al.* (1998), Cochran-Smith and Lytle (2002) and Reason and Bradbury (2002). Reviewing them is of great assistance as they provide us with varied information on ways of proceeding in context and under different conditions. It is often interesting to know what has motivated a project, the support that one counted on, the role of internal and external researchers, etc. Consulting literature on the characteristics and objectives of action research and the guidelines provided by several authors to begin a project of this type are very useful at the beginning. We can find information on these aspects in Oja and Smulyan (1989), Elliott (1993), Bárcena (2005), Altrichter *et al.* (1993) and Hopkins (1989).

# REFERENCES

Adelman, C. (1993) Kurt Lewin and the origins of action research, *Educational Action Research*, 1, 7–24.

Altrichter, H., Posch, P. & Somekh, B. (1993) *Teachers investigate their work. An introduction to the methods of action research* (London, Routledge).

Atweh, B., Kemmis, S. & Weeks (Eds) (1998) *Action research in practice. Partmerships for social justice in education* (London, Routledge).

Bárcena, F. (2005) *La experiencia reflexiva en educación* (Barcelona, Paidós).

Bouzada Fernández, X. M., Fernández Paz, A. & Lorenzo Suárez, A. M. (2002) *O proceso de normalización do idioma galego 1980–2000. Vol. II. Educación.* (Santiago de Compostela, Consello da Cultura Galega).

Carr, W. & Kemmis, S. (1988) *Teoría crítica de la enseñanza. La investigación-acción en la formación del profesorado* (Barcelona, Martínez Roca).

Cochran-Smith, M. & Lytle, S. L. (2002) *Dentro/fuera. Enseñantes que investigan* (Madrid, Akal).

Colexio Andaina (2004–05) *Datos do estudo sociolingüístico do centro e de cada unha das aulas correspondentes ao curso 2004–2005.*

Elliott, J. (1990) *La investigación-acción en educación* (Madrid, Morata).

Elliott, J. (1993) *El cambio educativo desde la investigación-acción* (Madrid, Morata).

Flick, U. (2004) *Introducción a la investigación cualitativa* (Madrid, Morata).

Gimeno Sacristán, J. (1992) La evaluación en la enseñanza, in: J. Gimeno Sacristán & A. I. Pérez Gómez (Eds) *Comprender y transformar la enseñanza* (Madrid, Morata), 334–397.

Goetz, J. L. & LeCompte, M. D. (1988) *Etnografía y diseño cualitativo en investigación educativa* (Madrid, Morata).

Grupo LACE HUM 109 (1999) *Introducción al estudio de caso en educación* (Cádiz, Facultad de Ciencias de la Educación de la Universidad de Cádiz).

Hopkins, D. (1989) *Investigación en el aula: guía del profesor* (Barcelona, Promociones y Publicaciones Universitarias [PPU]).

Kemmis, S. & McTaggart, R. (1992) *Cómo planificar la investigación-acción* (Barcelona, Laertes).

Kushner, S. (2002) *Personalizar la evaluación* (Madrid, Morata).

Law, B. (1984) *Uses and abuses of profiling* (London, Harper & Row).

McKernan, J. (1999) *Investigación-acción y curriculum* (Madrid, Morata).

Oja, S. N. & Smulyan, L. (1989) *Collaborative action research. A developmental approach* (London, Falmer Press).

Pérez Gómez, A. I. (1990) Comprender y enseñar a comprender. Reflexiones en torno al pensamiento de J. Elliott, in: J. Elliott (Ed.) *La investigación-acción en educación* (Madrid, Morata).

Reason, P. & Bradbury, H. (Eds) (2002) *Handbook of action research. Participative inquiry & practice* (London, Sage).

Rey, R. & Santamaría, J. M. (1992) *El proyecto educativo de centro: de la teoría a la acción educativa* (Madrid, Escuela Española).

Richardson, E. (1973) *The teacher, the school and the task of management* (London, Heinemann).

Simons, H. (1999) *Evaluación democrática de instituciones escolares* (Madrid, Morata).

Stake, R. E. (1998) *Investigación con estudio de casos* (Madrid, Morata).

Torres Santomé, J. (1991) La construcción del género en las aulas. Proyecto de investigación presentado al ejercicio para la obtención de una cátedra de universidad en la Universidad de A Coruña.

Walker, R. (1997) *Métodos de investigación para el profesorado* (Madrid, Morata).

Woods, P. (1989) *La escuela por dentro. La etnografía en la investigación educativa* (Barcelona, Paidós–MEC [Ministerio de Educación y Ciencia]).

# 12

## Promoting Quality for Teacher Action Research

### *Lessons Learned From Science Teachers' Action Research*

Brenda M. Capobianco and Allan Feldman

## INTRODUCTION

During the past 10 years teachers in the United States have been under increasing pressure to implement 'research-based' practices in their classrooms. Reform efforts, such as the 'Leave No Child Behind Act,' have fueled debates over how researchers and policy-makers conceptualize links between research, policy and practice, and what qualifies as sound practice-based or applied research (US Department of Education, 2001; Shavelson & Towne, 2002). As a result, there has been very little attempt not only to clarify these variations, but also to address the issue of quality in practice-based research. While we believe that these demands from federal and state agencies are ideologically driven, they do raise questions about how one evaluates the quality of educational research, who evaluates it and for what purpose. Therefore, in this paper we ask 'What does

SOURCE: "Promoting Quality for Teacher Action Research: Lessons Learned from Science Teachers' Action Research", by Brenda M. Capobianco and Allan Feldman (2006), Educational Action Research, Volume 14 (4) pp. 497–512. Taylor & Francis Ltd., http://www.tandf.co.uk/journals. Reprinted with permission of the publisher.

quality in teacher action research look like?' and 'What steps can be taken to promote quality in teacher action research?'

To address these questions, we re-examined our participation with science teachers during the past 15 years in several different collaborative action research projects (Feldman, 1994; Capobianco & Feldman, 2002; Feldman & Capobianco, 2003; Capobianco, 2006) and explore key conditions that help establish high-quality action research. In this essay we present an argument based on our theoretical perspective and our experiences with science teachers engaged in action research for a set of reflexive conditions to promote and sustain quality teacher action research. The primary purpose of this article is to provide a flexible framework for other researchers, teacher educators and practitioners to draw from when establishing and facilitating their own action research projects. Furthermore, we seek to stimulate discussion about potential ways we can not only ensure, but also sustain, quality action research.

## DEFINING 'QUALITY' IN ACTION RESEARCH

Before we turn to our examination of the conditions for promoting quality action research, we want to acknowledge that we find problematic the whole notion of categorizing forms of research as having or not having varying degrees of quality. Rather, we believe that it is important to be able to evaluate the quality of research efforts and products within the domain of a particular methodology, in this case collaborative action research, to help researchers improve their practice. Therefore, we begin by defining what quality means to us and help locate our working conception in a wider context.

In Peter Reason's (2003) quest for quality action research, he contends that:

> quality in inquiry comes from awareness of and transparency about the choices open to you and that you make at each stage of the inquiry ... Quality comes from asking, with others, what is important in this situation? How well are we doing? How can we show others how well we have done? (p. 32)

According to Bridget Somekh (1993), high quality in educational research 'resides in its ability to explore, resonate with, explicate and improve practice. Insofar as it has the ability to do this well, action research is high quality educational research' (p. 31). Reason's and Somekh's explorations of quality suggest that there are at least two ways in which we can talk about the quality of action research. Reason points toward the ways in which action research is done, while Somekh points us in the direction of the action research product.

Following Reason, we interpret quality as a coherent body of goals, objectives and methods aimed at recognizing a level of competence associated with reflection and understanding of the methods and conceptions related to conducting action research. Quality originates from inquiring, testing out and reflecting upon practical, personal or political issues within various educational situations. Accompanying this disposition for inquiry is the ability and interest on the part of teachers to stimulate open discussions, or what Feldman (1999) refers to as 'long and serious conversations,' whereby teachers question, explore different ideas and consult with one another with the intention to exchange new knowledge and/or gain new understandings.

But attention to how the action research is done is not enough. Action research has as its purposes to improve one's practice and to develop knowledge and understanding of one's practice that can be shared with others. An impact on practice is the first marker of quality in action research, but the value of this impact is, of course, grounded in the knowledge and understanding the research generates. The nature of the impact is important: it is possible to change for the worse, if the knowledge is not trustworthy (Somekh, 1993). In addition, research needs to be grounded in what is already known. Teachers should ask themselves: 'What do I know already about this particular phenomenon? How do I understand what is happening?' and 'Is the knowledge already available and could I acquire it in any other way?' The construction of knowledge and understanding is important to building quality action research. It is important to note that we refer to knowledge *and* understanding because what is constructed through action research is more than information. It is personally and socially constructed by the knower and the social context in which the knower lives and learns (Wenger, 1998). Furthermore, the knowledge and understanding generated by action research is put into use as an integral part of the action research process. It is knowledge and understanding of the particular, rather than generalized knowledge, and is rooted in the ability of teachers to change what they do and how they think (Somekh, 1993). This power of action research to bring about change and development in knowledge and understanding among and by teachers is critical in laying the foundation for quality in action research.

## CONTEXT

This article represents an effort on the part of both authors to seek new understandings from our own individual and joint collaborative science teacher action research projects. Unique to our quest for quality action research is the dynamic nature of our relationship. We represent two generations of researchers of action research. Allan Feldman represents a first generation. He has conducted research on teachers engaged in action research, developed his own theories for action research in science education (Feldman, *1996, 1999, 2002*) and studied the dimensions of action research (Rearick & Feldman, *1999*). Brenda Capobianco represents a second generation. She completed graduate work in action research under the direction of Allan Feldman, conducted action research as a practicing middle-school science teacher and as a university instructional consultant, and co-facilitated collaborative action research groups with him (Capobianco & Feldman, *2002).* We collectively shared the same ultimate goals: to improve our own practice by studying and conducting action research; and to learn more about how we can build and sustain quality action research among teachers, teacher educators and educational researchers.

The context of our work falls in the arena of science teacher education. Each researcher has facilitated collaborative science teacher action research groups with a focus on several different issues related to science teaching including physics teaching, feminist pedagogy in science education, and formative assessment using technology in the science classroom. A distinct feature to our approach to collaborative action research is that we strive to ensure that our groups are non-hierarchical in nature and assume a more enhanced, active and involved role of the practitioners (Feldman, 1993; Capobianco, 2003). Members of each collaborative action research group and the processes associated with facilitating the group remained separate from outside institutions and the power structures associated with those institutions. Thus the framework and operations of our collaboratives were not dictated by district-based guidelines nor were they facilitated by administrators, educational consultants or science curriculum experts who dictated what teachers must do in order to comply with standards for professional development. Our conception of collaborative action research is one that is driven and directed by and for teachers. The actions taken by the teachers in the group were for the purpose of heightening their own awareness of the issues associated with improving their science teaching. Underpinning each of our studies is the goal to help teachers develop understanding of their own development of practical knowledge, improve their own practice in science education and understand the context or landscape from where teachers work.

## FIRST-ORDER AND SECOND-ORDER ACTION RESEARCH

We elected to use first-order and second-order action research in two ways. The first way was as a means of distinguishing the roles of the participants involved in collaborative action research (i.e. the teachers and university researcher) (Feldman, 1993; Losito *et al.,* 1998). The second way was as means of analysis of our role in the collaborative inquiry process and our influence on the development of quality action research. Throughout our work with teachers, we maintained individual research notebooks, reporting and reflecting on what we were doing, how and why the research process developed, and which collective processes were established and sustained by the group (Capobianco, 2003). The second-order inquiry aimed at improving our facilitation of the first-order inquiry done by the teachers, and at generating knowledge and understanding of collaborative action research. More specifically, our inquiry was focused on the actions we took to facilitate teachers' reflective capacities. What this article represents are the implications of our second-order action research rather than a set of empirically based findings.

In this paper we draw upon our second-order action research on three different collaborative action research projects conducted during the past 15 years; two of which we facilitated independently and one of which we facilitated together. In the early 1990s, Feldman facilitated a group of high-school physics teachers, the Physics Teachers Action Research Group. These teachers were concerned that the way that they taught physics did not engage all the students in their classes. They talked about new methods, tried them out in their classes, and collected and analyzed data about their practice, which led them to improve their teaching and develop new knowledge and understanding of their practice (Erzberger et al., 1996). Feldman and Capobianco co-facilitated a second group of physics teachers engaged in collaborative action research. The focus of this group was to improve their use of an electronic personal response system to incorporate formative assessment into their practice (Capobianco & Feldman, 2002). Capobianco facilitated a group of high school science teachers engaged in a collaborative action research project in which they attempted to make science more inclusive of all students, including students traditionally marginalized in science (i.e. women and minorities) (Capobianco, 2006). Over the course of six months, Capobianco and the science teachers joined together to explore and reflect on their own interpretation and integration of feminist pedagogies as a way of making science more accessible to all students. The data from these projects included semistructured interviews, audio-taped group discussions, classroom observations and supporting documents (i.e. lesson plans, curriculum activities, rubrics, student work and action research reports) (Feldman, 1993, 1994, 1999; Capobianco, 2003, 2006; Feldman & Capobianco, 2003).

Teacher participation within our respective collaborative action research groups ranged from six months to three years. During this time the teachers and university researchers met every three weeks to eat dinner and engage in collaborative conversations about learning how to improve science instruction. The rationale for our reflective conversations and practical inquiries was to examine closely the pedagogical and curricular changes the science teachers made and the decisions associated with making those changes while attempting to transform their practice. In addition, we examined the struggles the teachers experienced as a result not only of trying to change their practice, but of trying to learn how to conduct collaborative action research while simultaneously gaining knowledge and understanding about new pedagogical tools and curricular strategies in science education.

Before we proceed to make our assertions about the conditions that promote quality collaborative action research, it is important for us to make clear that we believe the three projects we facilitated and studied were examples of quality collaborative action research. That is, in each of the three projects, the teachers had a coherent body of goals, objectives and methods. They inquired into their practice and tested out and reflected upon practical, personal and/or political issues within their educational situations. During their meetings they engaged in long and serious conversations in which they shared anecdotes of practice, reported on ideas that they tested in their classrooms and developed systematic research projects. In addition, they improved their practice and generated knowledge and understanding that they shared with their colleagues (Erzberger *et al.*, 1996; Kropf *et al.*, 2001; Trimarchi 2004; Trimarchi & Capobianco 2005; Capobianco *et al.*, 2006). However, we also note that while these are examples of quality collaborative action research, the teachers' individual projects and reports varied greatly in quality. We return to this later in this article.

# CONDITIONS FOR QUALITY COLLABORATIVE ACTION RESEARCH

We now present four assertions about the conditions that we believe promote quality collaborative action research, which emerged from our reading and re-reading the reports of our second-order action research, revisiting our data and reviewing the research literature. They are that (condition 1) the collaborative action research group must function as a community of practice (Wenger, 1998) and (condition 2) as a knowledge-producing, epistemic community (Creplet *et al.*, 2003). For the first two conditions to be met, the teachers need to have (condition 3) a thorough grounding in the nature of action research and (condition 4) a knowledge of appropriate research methods. Each condition is now presented with a brief discussion of its value and importance. Additionally, we support each condition with purposeful examples from our work with various collaborative action research groups. It is important to note that the conditions are closely interrelated.

## A community of practice

According to Wenger (1998), a community of practice defines itself along three dimensions: mutual engagement; a joint enterprise; and a shared repertoire. A community of practice involves more than the technical knowledge or skill associated with undertaking some task. Members are involved in a set of relationships over time (Lave & Wenger, 1991; Wenger, 1998) and communities develop around things that matter to people (Wenger, 1998). The fact that they are organizing around some particular area of knowledge and activity gives members a sense of joint enterprise and identity. For a community of practice to function it needs to generate and appropriate a shared repertoire of ideas, commitments and memories. It also needs to develop various resources such as tools, documents, routines, vocabulary and symbols that in some way carry the knowledge of the community. In other words, it involves practice: ways of doing and approaching things that are shared to some significant extent among members.

In the context of our work with practicing science teachers, we define a community of practice as a collective forum of teacher researchers who serve as critical friends with similar, shared goals, expectations and intentions (Capobianco, 2003). What follows is our description of the different ways our interactions with science teachers engaged in collaborative action research exemplify Wenger's three dimensions: mutual engagement; a joint enterprise; and a shared repertoire.

Membership in a collaborative action research group is a matter of mutual engagement. The science teachers in our respective projects represented a cadre of professionals from an array of diverse school settings and educational situations. Some are young, some old; some conservative, some liberal; some outgoing, some introverted. They are different from one another and have different professional and personal aspirations and problems. While the majority of the teachers' reasons for joining any one of the collaborative action research projects were influenced by professional obligations and/or requirements, the teachers themselves showed an overwhelming interest in examining their own practical inquiries. Unlike more traditional, school-based and university-based models for teacher action research (Sagor, 1991; Calhoun, 1994; Burnaford, 1996; Saurino, 1996), our approach to collaborative action research positioned the teachers in the roles of collaborators and researchers of their own work, with emphasis on their own lived experiences with science and science teaching.

To develop and facilitate a community of teacher researchers requires attention to both the procedural techniques for programming and convening meetings as well as equitable practices for establishing a safe, participatory environment. Practices such as negotiating guidelines for safe, collaborative discourse are important structural features to consider when working with the teachers (Lieberman, 1988; Catelli, 1995). Common to all these practices is the goal to develop a community that takes positive steps toward trust and confidentiality; values others' experiences, needs and emotions as knowledge; and establishes respect for and recognition of others. Capobianco examined carefully the collective processes she and the science teachers established as a way of meeting the needs of all the teachers, developing a collaborative community of teacher researchers, and maintaining respect for and recognition of others' ideas, concerns and issues related to transforming his/her own practice (Capobianco, 2003). When using the term collective processes, Capobianco is referring to the significant structures the teachers and university researcher put into place to allow for productive and meaningful conversations that enabled all of them to gain new knowledge about different aspects of inclusive science teaching and learning. Establishing guidelines for their collaborative conversations included 'checking in with one another' (Capobianco, 2003) through anecdote-telling (Feldman, 1996) and sharing personal cover stories (Clandinin & Connelly, 1999). The teachers discussed their personal goals and expectations as a means of taking the first steps toward developing a group theme for their action research. Through extended conversations, the teachers mutually agreed upon and began formulating their own start-ing points for action research.

The last characteristic of practice as a source of community coherence is the development of a shared repertoire. Over time, the joint pursuit of an enterprise creates resources for negotiating meaning. This includes knowl-edge and competence, which has been learned through mutual engagement in a specific practice and has been deposited in a partially shared repertoire of expertise (Wenger, 1998). This may also include material results (e.g. tech-nical reports, documents or conference presentations). In our collaborative action research projects, these artifacts ranged from action research reports to paper presentations at state and national conferences, from entries in a reflec-tive journal to publications in practitioner-oriented journals (Erzberger *et al.*, 1996; Kropf *et al.*, 2001; Capobianco *et al.*, *2003, 2006;* Trimarchi, *2004;* Trimarchi & Capobianco, *2005)*. This repertoire also includes routines, stories and ways of doing things that were unique to our respective research proj-ects. In Capobianco's collaborative action research project, science teachers often vocalized strong political agendas, favoring feminist science teaching as an alternative approach to addressing issues of equity and diversity in science education. However, not all of the science teachers accepted this line of thinking. Over time, members of the group collectively negotiated and developed a discourse less politically charged and more pedagogically invit-ing to all the teachers. Terms such as feminist, feminist pedagogy and libera-tory practices were replaced with gender-inclusive, female-friendly and accessibility. By broadening and mutually agreeing upon a new agenda, the science teachers adopted a discourse that later became an integral part of their own practice as teacher researchers. Reflections on quality in action research must include careful exploration of the quality of discourse and par-ticipation that is needed in a particular situation along with careful and in-depth exploration of how such discourse can be established and developed.

## An epistemic community

According to Altrichter *(2005)*, the concept of 'community of practice' resonates well within the field of action research. The processes of knowl-edge development go hand in hand with processes of practice develop-ment. In addition, this development takes place in the context of a professional community that is characterized by the fact that its members participate in the construction of knowledge, practice and identity (Altrichter, 2005). However, the knowledge that is generated and shared in a community of practice is typically the 'know-how' of the practice because these communities have as their immediate concern the achievement of an activity. Knowledge creation occurs then as a side effect of the process of achieving the activity (Lave & Wenger, 1991). Even though the knowledge creation is a side effect or 'unintended spillover' (Creplet *et at.*, 2003, p. 45) of communities of practice, they can be considered cognitive communities because they are engaged in knowledge creation (Creplet *et al.*, 2003).

In their book chapter 'Episteme or Practice,' Creplet *et al.*, (2003) develop the idea of another type of cognitive community, an 'epistemic community,' which they based on the concept of epistemic culture introduced by Karin Knorr Cetina (1999). For Knorr Cetina, 'Epistemic cultures are cultures that create and warrant knowledge' (1999, p. 1). When combined with the characteristics of community that we described in the preceding section, and a definition of culture such as 'A historically transmitted pattern of meanings embodied in symbols, a system of inherited conceptions expressed in symbolic form by means of which men communicate, perpetuate, and develop their knowledge about and attitudes toward life' (Geertz, 1973, p. 89), it follows that an epistemic community is a group of people, with a shared repertoire, mutually engaged in a shared repertoire that has as its primary goal the creation and warranting of knowledge.

The epistemic community's explicit goal is to create and warrant knowledge. This distinguishes it from a community of practice, which has as its primary goal to improve practice. Because the community of practice focuses on the improvement of practice of its members, questions about the quality of the research of its members can be answered by examining how useful it is for improving the practice of that community member. This still remains problematic because it is necessary to define what constitutes improvement and the ways in which one determines whether or not the practice has been improved toward the desired end.

Because epistemic communities have as their goal the creation of knowledge for the use by people who are not necessarily members of the local community (i.e. the collaborative action research group), there is the need to convince the others that the members of the epistemic community are correct; that is, the knowledge must be warranted in some way. Therefore, epistemic communities must rely on some type of implicit or explicit procedural authority that plays a role in how the knowledge is warranted. In academia, procedural authority explicitly resides in guidelines for research and publication, and more implicitly in the review process for journal articles, conference papers and funding proposals.

The question arises as to why we believe that a condition for quality action research is that a collaborative action research group has the characteristics of an epistemic community. Before answering this question, it is important for us to underscore that we are not proposing that there ought to be two different types of collaborative action research groups. Rather, a single group can have characteristics of both types of cognitive communities, and that different members of the group can participate in ways that focus on improvement of practice, the creation of warranted knowledge, or both. This is in fact what Creplet *et al.*, (2003) observed in their study of participants in a biology research group, and what Feldman found in his study of participation in an interdisciplinary science research study (Feldman, 2006)-individuals within a group can be seen as participating in a community of practice, an epistemic community, or as movers or crossing bonders between the two types of cognitive communities.

We have two main reasons for the condition that, for teachers to do quality collaborative action research, the group functions as an epistemic community. The first is that, following Stenhouse, we see action research as systematic, critical inquiry made public (Stenhouse, 1975). Once the research is made public outside of the domain of the local group, the results of the research, to be useful to others, has to be presented in such a way that it can be seen to transcend the local conditions. That is, there needs to be at least some form of implicit procedural authority to convince others that the new knowledge is of use.

The second reason is that teacher research is moral and political work. Because teachers' practice affects other people, there is a moral obligation that any change in practice is good for the others. Teacher action research is also political work because it has a normative, teleological component. Not only must the change be good for those who are affected by the changes in practice, the knowledge embedded in the nature of the change and why it is good should be presented in ways that affect the political context of schooling. If that knowledge is to be trusted and put to use in these larger contexts, then there must be reason for other teachers, administrators, policymakers and parents to believe and trust that knowledge. According to our analysis, it is epistemic communities that are capable of creating and warranting knowledge that is believable and trustworthy to others outside of the local group.

The knowledge constructed by the teachers within the community is a result of recognizing, negotiating and understanding one another's responsibilities, experiences and contributions to their respective classrooms and the community itself. Essentially, teachers and students negotiate what counts as knowledge in the classroom, who can have knowledge and how knowledge can be generated, challenged and evaluated. As a community, teachers come together to understand how this happens in their own classrooms and how their own interpretations of classroom events are shaped. By consulting with other teachers, they begin to recognize the significance of their actions, negotiate their responsibilities at teachers, teacher researchers and learners within the group, and co-construct new meaning of their educational situations, ultimately leading to the generation of new knowledge and understanding. It is when teacher researchers make their research public and open to the review and critique of a procedural authority, either implicitly or explicitly, that they become participants in an epistemic community.

Up until now we have discussed how a collaborative action research group functions both as a community of practice and an epistemic community. In order for these two types of communities within one collaborative action research group to conduct quality action research, we assert that teachers need to have a thorough grounding in the nature of action research and a fundamental knowledge of appropriate research methods. In the following section, we elaborate on these characteristics and attempt to describe how these characteristics function in the community of practice and epistemic community framework.

## A thorough grounding in the nature of action research

Our views of the nature of action research align with the work of Altrichter *et al.* (1993), Carr and Kemmis (1986), Elliott (1991) and Somekh (1993). Inherently, we believe action research to be a flexible methodology, not merely in terms of being diverse in research methods, but more fundamentally in needing to adapt to the personal, professional and political aspects of teachers' daily practice. Our conceptualization of action research as a flexible research methodology builds upon Sandra Harding's distinction between method and methodology (Harding, 1989, p. 420), in which methodology denotes an orientation towards research, rather than a particular set of research methods (Feldman, 1999). According to Feldman and Minstrel] (2000), 'it is characterized by the focus of the research-the teaching done by the researcher-and the goals of that research the improvement of teaching and learning and a better understanding of the researcher's educational situation' (p. 3).

Seeing action research as a methodology rather than a set of methods allows us to make problematic its focus-practice-and as such how its choice of questions to be investigated and the methods one chooses to use to answer those questions is shaped by that practice. For teachers that means understanding how the structure and context of their work affects the nature of their action research. Feldman explored this in his work with the Physics Teachers Action Research Group (PTARG). The PTARG teachers were embracing new forms of pedagogy and were concerned that these new methods were not serving their students well. They felt a 'need to know' that what they were doing new in the classroom was more effective than what they had done previously. But most of the PTARG teachers were trained in the physical sciences and saw research as carefully controlled laboratory experiments (Feldman,1994). Their need to know coupled with their conceptions of research made it difficult for them to proceed with action research. Feldman (1994) explored this in a case study of Andria Erzberger, one of the PTARG teachers. To Erzberger, with her training in physics, the way to answer her question 'How do I know if my students are learning any better?':

> ... would be through careful collection and analysis of data. However, her training in the physical sciences has led her to conclude that there is no way that she could have the faith in the data that she could collect in her classes that she would have in data from a physics experiment. She is aware that there are too many variables in her teaching, classes, and students to do the sort of controlled experiment, or even a statistical analysis, that would satisfy her demands. (Feldman, 1994, p. 96)

The dilemma that she found herself in was that she wanted to base her decisions about what and how to teach on more than reflection on her practice, but she felt that the methods of teacher research would not satisfy her need to know because these methods did not pass her test for what could count as 'real' research. In order for Erzberger to do quality action research, she needed to change her conception of what counts as research, and, more importantly, she needed to abandon her need to know that her new teaching methods were more effective and instead seek to answer questions such as 'What is happening in my class?' 'What is important here?' and 'How can I understand what is happening?' Questions such as these can lead to inquiring, testing out and reflecting upon practical, personal or political issues within educational situations. This grounding in the nature of action research developed in the PTARG collaborative action research group as the community of practice that focused on the generation and sharing of pedagogical content knowledge also became an epistemic community that sought to generate knowledge and understanding about the significance of their actions, their responsibilities as teachers and teacher researchers, and their educational situations.

## Knowledge of appropriate research methods

According to Reason (2003), 'Quality action research does not arrive fully-fledged in a clear research design separate from the stream of life, but evolves over time as communities of inquiry develop within communities of practice' (p. 5). This means that the action research (inquiry) process begins at the initial moment of inception, however tacit it may be-and continues after formal research is complete. This also means that decisions teachers make about which research methods to employ during the process may be quite different from those in a more established process (Reason, 2003). The practice of quality action research within a community of practice demands that teachers as researchers need to know which methods to employ and, more importantly, which research methods are most appropriate for promoting quality action research.

It should be clear from our discussion so far that, because we see action research as a methodology in which practice is made problematic, the decision about what methods to use in response to a particular question or problem is dependent not just on what produces the best research results, but also on how they ultimately affect one's practice and understanding of it. And because teachers' practice affects children's lives, teachers who engage in action research have a moral obligation to ensure its trustworthiness. When teachers engage in quality collaborative action research they seek trustworthiness through explicitness in designing and reporting research, triangulation and by providing evidence of the value of the changes in their practice and their understanding of it.

Explicitness implies that a great deal of care, reflexivity and systematic attention to detail need to be involved in the design and the reporting of research, together with an effort to make it as clear and communicable to others (Marshall & Rossman, 1999). Explicitness is essential in that it is the feature that makes research worthy of being reviewed and critiqued by peers. By encouraging teachers as researchers to explicate the design and methods in detail, other interested researchers, including critical friends with the community of practice, can judge whether they are adequate and make sense. This includes, but is not limited to, a rationale for action research and the specific genre in which the study is situated. The methods for data collection, recording, analysis and ethics are described. Most importantly, data collection and analysis procedures are made public. Explicitness not only promotes quality action research, but also enhances the validity of teachers' interpretations and representations of their action research.

Finally, triangulation must be considered as an instrumental method in building quality action research. The aim of triangulation is to gather multiple perspectives on the educational situation being studied. It is a term that is used in different ways by qualitative researchers. Denzin (1978) states that triangulation is a way of arguing that if different methods of investigation produce the same result then the data are likely to be valid. Silverman defines triangulation as:

> Comparing different kinds of data (e.g. quantitative and qualitative) and different methods (e.g. observation and interviews) to see whether they corroborate one another . . . This form of comparison, called triangulation, derives from navigation, where different bearings give the correct position of an object. (1993, p. 156)

These interpretations differ from the way triangulation has been described by some scholars of action research. Elliott (1991), for example, defines triangulation in action research as follows:

> Triangulation is not so much a technique for monitoring, as a more general method for bringing different kinds of evidence into some relationship with each other so that they can be compared and contrasted. The basic principle underlying the idea of triangulation is that of collecting observations/accounts of a situation (or some aspects of it) from a variety of angles or perspectives, and then comparing and contrasting them. (p. 82)

Elliott further suggests that triangulation involve three different points of view; namely those of the teacher, the students and a participant observer. Teacher researchers use multiple methods and the perspectives of different participants in order to gain a richer and less subjective picture than they obtain by relying on a single data gathering technique. Cohen and Manion (1994) point out that using a single method gives us only a partial view of a complex situation, such as a classroom, where people interact. Any one data gathering technique is not in itself neutral, but a filter through which experiences are sampled.

Accompanying triangulation is the method of peer debriefing. In short, peer review and debriefing involve external reflection and input on a researcher's work (Glesne, 1998). In the context of a community of practice, peer debriefing plays an integral role in how teachers mutually engage in the practice of collaborative action research. As teachers join together, they share detailed accounts of their classroom experiences while others are hearing and listening and responding by asking questions. It is through this exchange of anecdotes that teachers reveal preliminary findings from their research, begin to make meaning of their data and seek alternative perspectives from their critical friends. By having different people look at the data, it provides an opportunity for all teachers in the group, not just the individual researcher, to critically reflect on, talk about and make meaning of what is happening. According to Feldman (1999, p. 131), 'it is through this recounting and questioning of some teaching event or explanation of one's understanding to others that critical reflection takes place and eventually leads to the construction of new knowledge.' This form of debriefing validates not only the significance of the changes teachers make within their own practice, but, more importantly, it highlights the capacity for and evidence of the knowledge and understanding they gain as a result of the changes they make. Hence, triangulation accompanied by peer debriefing are invaluable in enhancing the validity and quality of collaborative action research as well as promoting dialog and the construction of new knowledge and understanding.

## CONCLUSION

The purpose of this theoretical essay was to explore the concept of quality in teacher action research from the perspective of researchers facilitating collaborative action research. Although we grapple with the notion of categorizing action research as having or not having varying degrees of quality, we believe it is important to be able to assess the quality of research efforts and products by teachers under the umbrella of action research as a *methodology* that helps teachers as researchers improve their practice and understanding of their practice. By taking a methodological stance, we place focus on teachers' orientation towards research, rather than a particular set of research methods. Emphasis, therefore, is placed on both the improvement of practice and the teachers' generation of new knowledge and understanding about the significance of their actions and responsibilities as teachers and researchers.

Using our experiences of conducting second-order action research on various collaborative science teacher action research projects, and our theoretical perspective, we proposed a framework for others to consider when promoting quality action research. For quality action research, we assert that a collaborative action research group must function as both a community of practice and an epistemic community if both practice is to be improved and knowledge and understanding is to be generated.

For the collaborative action research group to function effectively and productively as a community of practice and an epistemic community, the teachers must have a thorough grounding of the nature of action research and knowledge of appropriate research methods. The framework we have outlined only goes as far as suggesting a possible set of guidelines or conditions, and is not intended to be prescriptive. We suggest using the framework as a starting point and letting the framework either guide or transform you and your partners in collaborative action research.

Central to our thinking is the idea that (over time) any one collaborative action research project is likely to favor some aspects of the framework over others. That is because we believe that the ways in which this framework for quality action research is used needs to be based on a clear description of the situation or context for collaborative action research, the goals and intentions of that effort, and a commitment as a part of the community of practice to enhance knowledge and understanding of practice.

We end by raising the question that has been lurking in the shadows. In our explication of the nature of epistemic communities we noted that these communities are associated with procedural authorities. The question is 'What is, or should be, the procedural authority for the warranting of knowledge created as a result of teachers' collaborative action research?' We want to make clear that we are not advocating for the creation of an authoritative body or even a set of specific guidelines or standards to warrant the products of action research. We believe that would put unnecessary restrictions on what counts as action research and could concentrate power in an undemocratic fashion. In addition, we believe that there may already exist sufficient explicit and implicit procedural authorities, such as practitioner, professional and research peer-reviewed journals, and criteria for the awarding of advanced degrees. While action research as a methodology may not be recognized as legitimate by some of those authorities, we believe that when teacher action researchers participate as members in epistemic communities and have a thorough grounding in the nature of action research and of appropriate research methods, they can and will convince those procedural authorities of the legitimacy of action research.

## REFERENCES

Altrichter, H. (2005) The role of 'professional community' in action research, *Educational Action Research*, 13(1), 11–26.

Altrichter, H., Posch, P. & Somekh, B. (1993) *Teachers investigate their work: an introduction to the methods of action research* (London, Routledge).

Burnaford, G. (1996) Supporting teacher research: professional development and the reality of schools, in: G. Burnaford, J. Fischer & D. Hobson (Eds) *Teachers doing research: practical possibilities* (Mahwah, NJ, Lawrence Erlbaum Associates, Inc.).

Calhoun, E. (1994) *How to use action research in the self-renewing school* (Alexandria, VA, Association for Supervision and Curriculum Development).

Capobianco, B. *(2003)* Facilitating collaborative science teacher action through collective processes, paper presented at the *Association of Science Teacher Educators*, St Louis, MI, January.

Capobianco, B. (2006) Science teachers' attempts at integrating feminist pedagogy through collaborative action research, *Journal of Research in Science Teaching*, 44(1), 1–32.

Capobianco, B. & Feldman, A. (2002) Formative assessment action research: A study of teacher learning by using technology, paper presented at the *National Association for Research in Science Teaching International Conference,* New Orleans, LA, April.

Capobianco, B., Canuel-Browne, D., Lincoln, S. & Trimarchi, R. (2003) *Disseminating and sustaining 'action' in teacher action research,* poster presented at the *Annual Convention for the National Science Teachers Association,* Philadelphia, PA, April.

Capobianco, B., Lincoln, S., Canuel-Browne, D. & Trimarchi, R. (2006) Examining the experiences of three generations of teacher researchers through collaborative science teacher inquiry, *Teacher Education Quarterly,* summer, 33(7), 61–78.

Carr, W. & Kemmis, S. (1986) *Becoming critical: education, knowledge, and action research* (London, Falmer Press).

Catelli, L. A. (1995) Action research and collaborative inquiry in school-university partnership, *Action in Teacher Education,* 26, 25–38.

Clandinin, D. J. & Connelly, F. M. (1999) *Shaping a professional identity: stories of educational practice* (New York, Teachers College Press).

Cohen, L. & Manion, L. (1994) *Research methods in education* (4th edn) (London, Croom Helm). Creplet, F., Dupouet, O. & Vaast, E. (2003) Episteme or practice? Differentiated communitarian structures in a biology laboratory, in: M. Huysman, E. Wenger & V. Wulf (Eds) *Communities and technologies* (Dordrecht, Kluwer Academic Publishers), 43–63.

Denzin, N. K. (1978) *The research act: a theoretical introduction to sociological methods* (2nd edn) (New York, McGraw-Hill).

Elliott, J. (1991) *Action research for educational change* (Philadelphia, PA, Milton Keynes/Open University Press).

Erzberger, A., Fottrell, S., Hiebart, L., Merrill, T., Rappleyea, A., Weinmann, L., *et al.* (1996) A framework for physics projects, *The Physics Teacher,* 34(1), 26–28.

Feldman A. (1993) Promoting equitable collaboration between university researchers and school teachers, *International journal of qualitative studies in education,* 6(4), 341–357.

Feldman, A. (1994) Erzberger's dilemma: validity in action research and science teachers' need to know, *Science education,* 78(1), 83–101.

Feldman, A. (1996) Enhancing the practice of physics teachers: mechanisms for the generation and sharing of knowledge and understanding in collaborative action research, *journal of Research in Science Teaching,* 33(5), 513–540.

Feldman, A. (1999) The role of conversation in collaborative action research, *Educational Action Research,* 7(1), 125–144.

Feldman. A. (2002) Existential approaches to action research, *Educational Action Research,* 10(2), 233–252.

Feldman, A. (2006) Learning to be a scientist: implications for science teacher education, paper presented at the *Annual Meeting of the American Educational Research Association,* San Francisco, CA, April.

Feldman, A. & Capobianco, B. (2003) Real-time formative assessment: a study of teachers' use of an electronic response system to facilitate serious discussions about physics concepts, paper presented at the *Annual Meeting of the American Educational Research Association,* Chicago, IL, 21–25 April.

Feldman, A. & Viinstrell, J. (2000) Action research as a research methodology for the study of the teaching and learning of science, in: E. Kelly & R. Lesh (Eds) *Handbook of research design in mathematics and science education* (Mahwah, NJ, Lawrence Erlbaum Associates).

Geertz, C. (1973) *The interpretation of cultures* (New York, Basic Books).

Glesne, C. (1998) *Becoming qualitative researchers: an introduction* (2nd edn) (New York, Longman).

Harding, S. (1989) *Is there a feminist method?*, in: N. Tuana (Ed.) *Feminism and science* (Bloomington, IN, Indiana University Press), 18–32.

Knorr Cetina, K. (1999) *Episternic cultures: how the sciences make knowledge* (Cambridge, MA, Harvard University Press).

Kropf, A., Cunha, M., Hugenin, E., Emery, C., Venemen, V. & Rappold, A. (2001) A FAAR look at improving physics education: formative assessment action research, paper presented at the *Summer Meeting of the American Association of Physics Teachers*, Rochester, NY, 23 July.

Lave, J. & Wenger, E. (1991) *Situated learning: legitimate peripheral participation* (Cambridge, Cambridge University Press).

Lieberman, A. (Ed.) (1988) *Building a professional culture in schools* (New York, Teachers College Press).

Losito, B., Pozzo, G. & Somekh, B. (1998) Exploring the labyrinth of first and second order action research, *Educational Action Research, 6(2)*, 219–240.

Marshall, C. & Rossman, G. (1999) *Designing qualitative research* (3rd edn) (Thousand Oaks, CA, Sage).

Rearick, M. & Feldman. (1999) Orientations, purposes and reflection: a framework for understanding action research, *Teaching and Teacher Education*, 15, 333–349.

Reason, P. (2003) Choice and quality in action research practice, paper presented at the *World Congress of Participatory Action Research*, Pretoria, South Africa, September.

Sagor, R. (1991) What project LEARN reveals about collaborative action research, *Educational Leadership*, 48(6), 6–10.

Saurino, D. (1996) Teacher team collaborative action research, paper presented at the *Annual Meeting of the American Educational Research Association*, New York, April.

Shavelson, R. J. & Towne, L. (Eds) (2002) *Scientific research in education* (Washington, DC, National Association Press).

Silverman, D. (1993) *Interpreting qualitative data: methods for analyzing talk, text, and interaction* (London, Sage).

Somekh, B. (1993) Quality in educational research: the contribution of classroom teachers, in: J. Edge & K. Richards (Eds) *Teachers develop teachers research: papers on classroom research and teacher development* (Oxford, Heinemann).

Stenhouse, L. (1975) *An introduction to curriculum research and development* (London, Heinemann).

Trimarchi, R. (2004) Drawing out the quiet voices: making science lectures accessible to all science learners, *The Science Teacher*, 69(1), 30–34.

Trimarchi, R. & Capobianco. (2005) Action research on interactive lectures: engaging 'all' students in verbal give-and-take, in: R. Yager (Ed.) *Evemplary science in grades 9–12: standards based success stories* (Washington, DC, National Science Teachers Association).

US Department of Education (2001) *No child left behind.* Available online from: http://www.ed.govl nclb/landing.jhtml?src=pb (accessed 12 June 2005).

Wenger, E. (1998) *Communities of practice: learning, meaning, and identity* (Cambridge, UK, Cambridge University Press).

# 13

# Schoolwide Action Research

## *Findings From Six Years of Study*

### Lew Allen and Emily F. Calhoun

From 1990 through 1996, a collaborative research team consisting of university and school-based staff members conducted an ongoing inquiry with two groups of schools that made a commitment to conducting schoolwide action research. The schools were members of the University of Georgia's League of Professional Schools or part of the Ames (Iowa) Community Schools. By 1996, 100 schools in the Georgia network and 11 schools in the Iowa network were participating.

The League of Professional Schools is a school/university collaboration designed to support democratic school improvement. Its school renewal efforts are based on three ideas: 1) shared governance for schoolwide decisions, 2) a focus on instruction and curriculum to enhance education, and 3) the use of schoolwide action research to study the health of the school and the results of its collective action. School faculties seek membership in the League and must have at least 80% of the faculty voting in favor of affiliating if they are to join.

The League offers its members various support services. Three meetings each year for school teams provide a forum for schools to share best practices and to reflect on their common work, summer institutes are offered on topics of common interest, site visits allow practitioners to

SOURCE: Schoolwide Action Research: Findings From Six Years of Study", by Lew Allen and Emily F. Calhoun (1998) PHI DELTA KAPPAN 79 (9): 706-710. Used with permission.

observe firsthand the work of their colleagues in other League schools, and newsletters describe initiatives being pursued in League schools. The League also provides access to information from the larger education community through an information retrieval system.

In Iowa, a bargained agreement between the Ames Community School District and the Ames Education Association led to the creation of the schoolwide action research initiative. The agreement provided for a district instructional leadership team (ILT), to be composed of representatives appointed in equal numbers by the district and the teacher union. A per-teacher funding allocation was granted to each school to support its action research activities. The ILT arranged professional development workshops and seminars, provided out-of-district and within-district consultation services, and supplied a local teacher as a part time coordinator of action research. To allow time for faculties to work together, another negotiated agreement arranged for early dismissal of students every Wednesday.

*In schoolwide action research, participants live the problem-solving process . . . and model it for their students.*

## HISTORY AND PROMISE OF ACTION RESEARCH

Why are these schools trying to implement schoolwide action research? Like many other good ideas, such as nongraded schools and interrelated curriculum units, action research has been around for some time as a popular initiative in some school districts. It was a topic of interest in the 1940s and 1950s, drawing largely on the work of Kurt Lewin and his colleagues and their development of a collective problem-solving cycle for improving life in organizations.[1] Today, action research is promoted as a process of individual reflection on practice, as a process to support staff development in schools, as a collaborative process to support teachers' professional development, and as a strategy to guide site-based school improvement.[2]

Whether action research is undertaken by an individual, a small group, or a school faculty, part of its promise is the ability to build the capacity of individuals and organizations to move beyond current understandings and practices. In the past, action research was recognized as a tool to improve the health of a school, and the appeal remains just as powerful today. In schoolwide action research, participants live the problem-solving process themselves and model it for their students. They focus on the collection of data to diagnose problems, they conduct a disciplined search for alternative solutions, they take collective action, and they conscientiously monitor whether and how well a "solution" works.

For those seeking whole-school improvement—both in terms of student learning and in terms of the conditions of the professional workplace—action research places disciplined inquiry (i.e., research) in the context of focused efforts to improve the quality of the school and its performance (i.e., action). The integrity of the process for site-based school improvement lies in the union of the "researchers" and "action takers," for action research is conducted by those persons responsible for bringing about changes. Its ultimate aim is to have all faculty members and, eventually, students and parents involved in the research on student learning.

*Most teachers perceived a conflict between focusing on the needs of the students in their classrooms and focusing on schoolwide issues*

## THE STUDIES

The studies consolidated here—some conducted by League staff and associates and others by a collaboration of staff, associates, and teachers in the schools—analyzed 1) the schools' yearly action plans that involved action research, 2) reports from annual site visits to each school, 3) transcripts of in-depth interviews with practitioners, 4) questionnaires completed by school-based facilitators, and 5) reports prepared by faculties about their progress with action research.[3]

Together, all of us—practitioners in schools, League staff members, and out-of-district consultants—have increased our understanding of best practices and of the obstacles to using action research for school improvement. In this article we focus on what we think are the most significant findings that relate to schools' building their capacity to be responsive organizations and to make desired changes.

## FINDINGS

**Finding 1.** While teachers generally valued working with their grade-level or subject-area peers, most schools found it difficult to convince people of the importance of a schoolwide focus. Most teachers perceived a conflict between focusing on the needs of the students in their classrooms and focusing on schoolwide instructional and curricular issues that cut across all grades and subjects. People in League schools expressed concern over the difficulty of getting teachers to appreciate the importance of collaborations outside of their immediate grade or subject area. For instance, most League schools created interdisciplinary groups whose function was to provide opportunities for people to interact with a wide range of colleagues across varied job descriptions. But these groups often had low levels of participation. Furthermore, schools that were successful in involving people in schoolwide issues reported that they had to work continually to keep participation levels high. In other words, the basic notion of the importance and usefulness of working together as a faculty was problematic.

**Finding 2.** Faculties had difficulty conducting schoolwide action research on teaching and learning because the public study of the effects of instruction collided with norms of privacy and isolation. Each of the studies conducted in the first four years of our inquiry noted that many school faculties were not focusing their action research efforts on classroom instructional practices. Consequently, each year facilitators increased their efforts to provide schools with information about how to study teaching and learning. Studies completed in the fifth and sixth years revealed that it was not simply a lack of information that was holding schools back, but a reluctance on the part of many teachers to open up their classrooms. Schools failed to focus on instructional issues not because they didn't know how, but because many people in the school felt threatened by the very idea. To teachers accustomed to closing their classroom doors and teaching in private, it was much less threatening to gather information about student behavior in the lunchroom than to study individual classroom instructional practices for their effects on student achievement. Moreover, in most schools there was no sustained assistance to support such efforts.

**Finding 3.** Trust in the ability to "look on" and know if something is "working" competed with the conducting of formal schoolwide action research. Many school-people demonstrated confidence in and reliance upon their own abilities, both individually and collectively, to observe whether a particular lesson was effective, whether a program was producing the desired results, or whether the school as a whole was successfully addressing its students' needs. Teachers relied on and felt confident in using an intuitive approach to determine the effectiveness of their practices. Although the schools administered standardized tests, the scores were not used to identify, plan, guide, or evaluate schoolwide initiatives. Before joining the League, very few schools used anything other than a yearly review of standardized test results and perceptual information to guide their schoolwide efforts.

**Finding 4.** Schoolwide action research was defined, operationally and literally, in various ways within and across schools. People within schools and across schools often held different understandings of "action research" and stated different reasons for doing it. The differences between these understandings are subtle but crucial.

*Action research can provide information that assists schools as they set annual schoolwide goals.*

First, action research can help form a clearer picture of what an innovation will be like when it is implemented. It provides background information and so can enhance people's understanding. For example, one school that was considering changing its report cards visited a school that had already done so in order to discover what problems had to be overcome and whether the new system was satisfactory.

Second, action research can be used as a tool to generate support for beliefs. For example, faculty members teaching in multi-age classrooms saw action research as a way to document that their approach had greater benefits for students than did the traditional approach. Meanwhile, those who did not wish to teach in multi-age classrooms saw action research as a tool in a propaganda campaign to pressure them into making an unwarranted change.

Third, action research can document support for a proposed initiative. In one case, surveys of parents, students, and teachers were used as evidence of support for a proposal to the school board to change a school's daily schedule.

Fourth, action research can provide information that assists schools as they set annual schoolwide goals. For instance, at the end of each school year, faculty members can examine their action research data to assess their progress on reaching the current year's goals and to set goals for the following year.

Fifth, action research can help faculty members study student learning and refine their instructional practices. The action research process can focus conversations and collective work on designing lessons and on specific teacher behaviors that can bring about measurable learning gains for students. For example, teachers can create or adopt a new approach to teaching writing and use action research to monitor its effects and to refine their classroom practice. This last understanding most closely matches the full promise of schoolwide action research.

**Finding 5.** The schools that made the most progress had the most technical assistance and staff development. Schools that made a great deal of progress both sought and received more support for their efforts. People in schools that successfully conducted action research had an attitude toward technical assistance and staff development that was different in breadth and intensity from the attitudes at other sites. Core team members and others at successful schools were determined to get technical assistance with anything from data collection to reconceptualizing their mathematics curriculum. The faculties of successful schools had some knowledge of the change process and of the nature of staff development required to transform curriculum changes into instructional changes in the classroom. Not only did they want technical assistance and staff development, but they were also disciplined in allocating resources to provide this support for themselves.

*Schools that made a great deal of progress both sought and received more support for their efforts.*

These successful schools often turned to their district office for support. They used members of the district staff and any other connections they might have. They asked for help to solve problems, to locate additional technical assistance, to arrange for staff development, to plan projects, and to obtain additional information for the faculty to study.

**Finding 6.** Effective action research leadership teams generally consisted of teacher leaders who worked closely with school administrators. In schools in which action research played an important role, at least one administrator, generally the principal, took an active part in the effort. These administrators steadfastly pushed and supported the action research efforts. They used their access to information and their mobility within the school and the district to provide support (e.g., encouragement, professional development, time, and information). Their active participation in the school's efforts demonstrated a conviction that schoolwide action research is a worthwhile, important part of what people in the school should be doing. Principals in successful schools also nurtured those teachers who were leaders in the school's action research efforts. These teacher leaders opened their classrooms to the process and demonstrated their belief that action research could benefit students. They also developed sufficient expertise so that they were able to join with, and in some schools replace, the administrator in leading the school's efforts.

**Finding 7.** The efforts of schools to conduct schoolwide action research benefited from integrated external and internal facilitation. As people in schools began conducting action research, questions and needs for support arose that couldn't be anticipated and answered in advance or couldn't be put on hold until a facilitator could be brought in. Schools needed internal facilitators who could help support the process as questions arose. The most successful internal facilitators also had the authority to provide such support through assigning substitutes, making minor changes in the schedule, and purchasing needed resources. These internal facilitators profited greatly from collaborating with an external facilitator. External facilitators were able to examine the school's efforts from a fresh perspective, help expand local knowledge of action research, assess where the school was in the process, and decide where it needed to go.

**Finding 8.** When schoolwide action research was pursued vigorously and fully implemented, positive changes took place in the learning environment. In schools that incorporated schoolwide action research into the life of the school, teachers reported that their participation in such research helped them focus their attention on teaching and learning issues that, in turn, directly affected students. These "high implementation" schools showed increases in student achievement that were attributed in part to the schoolwide action research efforts. Teachers deeply involved with the research reported an increase in their sense of efficacy and professional expertise. Schools reported that school boards appeared to take seriously the data generated by the schools' research efforts because requests that included data were more likely to be approved than requests that did not include data.

# IMPLICATIONS

Conducting schoolwide action research is an extremely difficult, complex pursuit that can provide schools with the clear focus and necessary information to succeed in bringing about schoolwide instructional improvement. However, the benefits of schoolwide action research will elude schools that are not prepared to invest the time and resources required.

Professional development. Professional development that reflects a deep understanding of action research and its many underlying issues is essential. Our findings indicate that the professional development supporting action research should have the following four characteristics.

- Substantial, ongoing opportunities for everyone involved to reflect together about the underpinnings of action research. Since most people will not bring prior experience of or knowledge about schoolwide action research to the process, they will need help in developing an appreciation for how it can benefit classrooms and students. This doesn't mean that schools should wait until everyone has a full understanding of action research before taking any action. Teachers in League schools, for example, found that the best way to learn about action research was to do it. School faculties need to recognize that much of the groundwork will need to be laid early and then built on as a common vision takes shape about what action research can accomplish and why it is worth the effort.

  *Teachers . . . found that the best way to learn about action research was to do it.*

- The content of professional development needs to focus, in part, on the actions that help change the culture of the school into a more supportive, nurturing community. How people feel about sharing their classroom practices with others is crucial to the success of any professional development effort. Fears of criticism or reprisals for making public what is happening in classrooms must be addressed if action research is to be focused on instruction. Before people will open up their classroom practices to the action research process, they need to be convinced that their professionalism will be respected. Action research that focuses on instruction flourishes in a culture that values collaborative learning and inquiry; it will not flourish in an atmosphere of evaluation and sanctions.

- Those who lead or facilitate schoolwide action research need to help organizers understand that it takes time to build a school's capacity. Schoolwide action research is not something that a school staff can focus on for a year and then leave to sustain itself. Each year the staff will need to build on what has been learned before so that an ongoing process of gathering information and taking action based on that information can become customary. For this to be accomplished, faculty members must create a self-sustaining process that provides a seamless flow of training, leadership, and internal facilitation.

- While schoolwide action research is intended to be schoolwide in its scope, facilitators and organizers need to recognize that the process must be relevant to the individual questions and classroom needs of teachers if they are expected to take part. Schoolwide action research means that all efforts are aimed at a common goal or question, such as improving the quality of students' writing. For example, teachers might collect and analyze student writing samples and look at the schoolwide picture, but not find the resulting information useful in designing their own classroom instruction. Facilitators need to help school teams collect data that can be used to guide actions at the individual, class, and school levels, and they need to demonstrate how to use the data in designing lessons.

School governance. Conducting schoolwide action research has implications for school governance. Action research cannot be viewed as an effort that is separate from a school's governance; rather, it is an integral part of that process. It is important that what is learned through action research be reflected in the school's practices. For example, it does a school little good to find out that there is a better way to teach social studies if the governance of the school won't respond to that finding.

Colleagueship beyond the school. Faculties that wish to engage in schoolwide action research should not work in isolation. The school teams that we worked with enjoyed working with teams from other schools. Without support from outside the school that extends the staff members' picture of what is possible and offers them encouragement and help in staying the course, many schools will abandon their efforts.

Continuous technical assistance and time for cooperative inquiry. We work with many valiant teachers and administrators who want instruction to be as powerful as it can be in each classroom in each school. However, despite their own and their schools' best efforts, they appear to need more assistance in learning to study teaching and learning, in studying what works for students, in establishing routines that support collective inquiry by all members of the faculty, and in broadening their capacity to generate and sustain substantive initiatives in student learning. Consequently, the final implication that we would like to examine has to do with the facilitation process.

The journey toward continuous, collective inquiry that is being undertaken by schools in the League and in Ames is the same long and difficult road that faces those who facilitate their efforts, whether these facilitators work in universities, school districts, regional education agencies, or state departments.

Facilitators are as bound by culture as school faculty members, and it is as difficult for us to change how we behave as it is for our school-based colleagues. Allocating time for collaborative inquiry and discourse, finding time for disciplined inquiry into the goals of the organization, providing staff development for ourselves as learners, and coupling continuing inquiry and exploration with personal knowledge to make decisions and take actions are difficult undertakings for us as well. Engaging in collective study and taking action to improve teaching and learning are hard work for any organization—even those responsible for helping others move forward. Time for collaborative work and the support of others are essential to successful schoolwide action research.

## NOTES

1. Kurt Lewin, "Group Decisions and Social Change," in Eleanor E. Maccoby, Theodore N. Newcomb, and Eugene L. Hartley, eds., Readings in Social Psychology, 3rd ed. (New York: Holt, Rinehart & Winston, 1958). pp. 197–211; idem. "Resolving Social Conflicts," in Selected Papers on Group Dynamics (New York: Harper & Row, 1948). pp. 201–20; and Stephen M. Corey, Action Research to Improve School Practices (New York: Teachers College Press, 1953).

2. John Elliott, Action Research for Educational Change (Bristol, Pa. Open University Press, 1991); Sharon N. Oja and Lisa Smulyan, Collaborative Action Research: A Developmental Approach (London: Falmer Press, 1989); Richard Sagor, How to Conduct Collaborative Action Research (Alexandria, Va: Association for Supervision and Curriculum Development, 1992); Carl D. Glickman, Renewing America's Schools: A Guide for School-Based Action (San Francisco: Jossey-Bass, 1993); and Emily F. Calhoun, How to Use Action Research in the Self-Renewing School (Alexandria, Va.: Association for Supervision and Curriculum Development, 1994).

3. Emily F. Calhoun, "A Wide-Angle Lens: How to Increase the Variety, Collection, and Use of Data for School Improvement," paper presented at the annual meeting of the American Educational Research Association, Chicago, 1991; idem, "A Status Report on Action Research in the League of Professional Schools," paper presented at the annual meeting of the American Educational Research Association, San Francisco, 1992; Emily F. Calhoun and Carl D. Glickman, "Issues and Dilemmas of Action Research in the League of Professional Schools," paper presented at the annual meeting of the American Educational Research Association, Atlanta, 1993; Emily F. Calhoun and Lew Allen, "Results of Schoolwide Action Research in the League of Professional Schools," paper presented at the annual meeting of the American Educational Research Association, New Orleans, 1994; Emily F. Calhoun et al., "Action Research on Action Research: A Quest for Understanding," paper presented at the annual meeting of the American Educational Research Association, San Francisco, 1995; Emily F. Calhoun et al., "Schoolwide Action Research: A Study of Facilitation," paper presented at the annual meeting of the American Educational Research Association, New York, 1996; and Emily F. Calhoun, Lew Allen, and Cal Halliburton, "A Report on the Implementation of and Results from Schoolwide Action Research," paper presented at the annual meeting of the American Educational Research Association, New York, 1996.

# 14

## Ecology and Ethics in Participatory Collaborative Action Research

### *An Argument for the Authentic Participation of Students in Educational Research*

Steve Collins

## ECOLOGY

Relationships and interconnections describe the ecology of the classroom community. What affects a single member affects the entire class. There is also a symbiotic exchange between the classroom and its environment. That environment includes the physical structure of the school, the administration, the atmosphere of the school community, parental involvement and the influence of the community at large. Individual students are interdependent with their classmates, while all are interdependent with their environment. There are levels of interdependent communities. These can be listed from the microscopic to the global: from the individual as a coherent organisation of body parts and cells, to the family at home, to the

SOURCE: "Ecology and Ethics in Participatory Collaborative Action Research: An Argument for the Authentic Participation of Students in Educational Research", by Steve Collins (2004) Educational Action Research, Volume 12 (3): pp. 347–362.Taylor & Francis Ltd., http://www.tandf.co.uk/journals. Reprinted with permission of the publisher.

classroom at school, to the school as a coherent organisation of classrooms, to the community around the school, to the city community and its politics, to provincial, national and global communities.

Fritjov Capra (1983) avoids the use of the word hierarchy to describe this leveled kind of organisation. He prefers the term stratified:

> To avoid confusion we may reserve the term 'hierarchy' for those rigid systems of domination and control in which orders are transmitted from the top down. The traditional symbol for these structures has been the pyramid ... That is why I have turned the pyramid around and transformed it into a tree, a more appropriate symbol for the ecological nature of stratification in living systems. As a real tree takes its nourishment through both its roots and its leaves, so the power in a systems tree flows in both directions, with neither end dominating the other and all levels interacting in the interdependent harmony to support the functioning of the whole. (Capra, 1983, p. 282)

In organic, adaptive systems, connections, links, or relationships among parts are the focus, rather than the parts alone. In a classroom that promotes authentic participation, interactions among students and relationships throughout a stratified school structure are important. Individual qualities lose their meaning when considered in isolation. Talents or skills are valued when they enhance the community. Individual problems and needs are a concern for everyone. Knowledge is shared, interactions are encouraged and the teacher, who is in a traditional position of authority, learns from students and actively seeks to share decision-making about various aspects of the classroom community.

For the purposes of the following discussion, the classroom and those immersed in classroom research, are considered to be a dynamic, adaptive, 'living' system in which ecological considerations are paramount.

## A DEFINITION OF ACTION RESEARCH

Action research is when people reflect on and improve their own work and their own situations by tightly linking their reflection with action and making their experience public, not only to the other participants, but also to other persons interested in the work and the situation (Altrichter et al, 1991). Data are collected by the participants themselves, they participate in the decision making, power is shared democratically, and members collaborate. Reflection is a key characteristic of action research. The practitioner-researchers self-reflect, self-evaluate, and self-manage the research autonomously and responsibly. More concisely, McClutcheon & Jung (1990) define action research as the inquiry teachers undertake to understand and improve their own practice.

Collaborative action research demands that research becomes practitioner-based, and that all theorising and practice takes place in the context of the classroom setting. 'Praxis is the notion that through action, theory is developed; that theory is in turn modified through further action' (Houser, 1990, p. 59). The understanding that results from this research is not necessarily concerned with global issues of education, but rather with particular learners and specific cases.

A perspective that seems suitable for classroom research is one of participatory, collaborative action research. It is ecological in the sense that it includes all the significant actors in a classroom research setting, including the children.

## ECOLOGICAL ETHICS IN RESEARCH

Ethics in research is problematic, particularly in the social sciences and especially in education where young children may be involved. It is impossible to create standards to address all potential research situations and the standards that we do create tend to be non-specific, sloganised ideals. Ethical responses to unanticipated events are difficult to rehearse. They are situation specific. A code of ethics, therefore, has limited value, Punch (1986) says 'A code can be useful as a moral pathfinder sensitising students, researchers, and supervisors to ethical elements in research prior to, during, and after a project' (p. 80), However, the range of unpredictable, complex and unique surprises in the field make the non-specific nature of codes of limited use in many cases, Furthermore, it is difficult to reach a consensus regarding ethical standards that resists varying interpretations. In action research, referring exclusively to a generalised code of ethics seems insufficient or perhaps dangerous. We have relegated moral discourse to the periphery of our discussions . . . while making scientific discourse . . . our primary concern' (Schwandt, 1989, cited in Flinders, 1992, p. 101). In collaborative action research, I suggest that moral discourse and moral reflection must be a central theme, and included in constant negotiations of authentic participation, power issues and language.

David J. Flinders (1992) traces varying orientations of ethical thought. For the purpose of this discussion, his commentary on utilitarian and ecological ethics provides a particularly useful contrast. Utilitarian ethics is the most familiar kind of ethics and is commonly the type used in university ethical review committees. This type of ethical thought is based on utility. 'An action or decision is considered moral if it produces the greatest good for the greatest number' (p. 102). Ecological ethics is a conception of the world, environments, or communities (including classrooms) as unified systems. 'A chief characteristic of all ecological systems is that no part is capable of exercising unilateral control over the entire system' (p. 109). Members of such a system are concerned with language, relationships and ideas in a holistic regard for their culture. Each member, whether a teacher, student or researcher, is an integral part of a co-evolving whole. As such, it is not enough to make discrete judgments of the morality of specific actions or decisions. Rather, there is an ongoing process of negotiating power structures to maximise the inclusion of all. An ecological approach to ethics fits well with the collaborative action research methodology to be described here. It is compatible with the participatory aspect of the research and setting, and the focus on ongoing interactions within the community.

Flinders analyses research ethics in three areas:

- recruitment;
- fieldwork; and
- reporting.

I summarise Flinders' (1992, p. 113) terminology in Table I.

**Table I**    Ethical frameworks

|  | *Utilitarian* | *Ecological* |
| --- | --- | --- |
| Recruitment | Informed consent | Cultural sensitivity |
| Fieldwork | Avoidance of harm | Attachment |
| Reporting | Confidentiality | Responsive communication |

In utilitarian ethics, informed consent is the basic right of self-determination. Participants should know what the research is about and agree to their involvement. Action research, of course, does not allow for a very high level of predictability. Therefore, it is difficult to be able to fully inform a prospective participant to gain their consent. Similarly, avoidance of harm is difficult to guarantee. Such subtle events as causing stress or risking a professional reputation may inadvertently occur even though this was not the intent of the researchers. There is no way to predict or avoid such accidental situations even if the participants have given consent. Although we may promise to avoid deliberate acts that are harmful, there is a range of potentially harmful events beyond our control, Promising avoidance of harm can be misleading, especially if we have an ethical concern regarding all consequences of research activities. Confidentiality is a very difficult thing to protect in qualitative research, which depends so much on rich descriptions: 'the better the research, the more readily others can recognise the participants' (Flinders, 1992, p. 104).

Flinders also examines recruitment, fieldwork, and reporting in an ecological framework. Ecology refers to a set of interdependent relationships. It is a view of the world in terms of unified systems. The classroom, then, is a holistic cultural environment organised by language, relationships, and ideas. Beyond just informed consent at the start of the research, cultural sensitivity must be an ongoing focus of reflection and discourse. More than avoidance of harm, ecological ethics demand that we recognise the individual as part of a larger system. Therefore, protection of the entire environment is necessary, including the attachment of every individual to the whole culture. To damage one part of an ecological system is to damage the whole and vice versa. Responsive communication in reporting, as contrasted to confidentiality, is necessary in ecological ethics. The language that is used must maintain the culture, rather than unilaterally controlling it through language that is outside of the growing relationship. The holistic nature of ecological ethics makes it a good match for participatory collaborative action research, which also embraces the authentic participation of all partners in creating a community of inquiry through discourse,

It is important to note that this framework was constructed to aid in conceptualising approaches to ethical thinking. In practice, there is much overlap. Flinders (1992), rather than pursuing one best system, seeks 'a frame of reference that is able to encompass multiple points of view' (p. 101). Many orientations of ethical thinking have value. For instance, we probably do not want to do away with university ethical review committees of research, even though they lie within the utilitarian concept of ethics that is, indeed, limited. That said, an ecological conception of ethics is relevant to this discussion. This model of research focuses as much on process and reflection as on solutions and standards, Those participating in this kind of research, rather than only promising to meet standards before beginning, continuously work towards creating a community of cultural sensitivity.

> all research is context-bound, and . . . the circumstances encountered in a given study will always interact with various ethical frameworks in unpredictable ways. Researchers must learn to 'read' ethical concerns as they emerge, anticipate relevant considerations, and recognize alternative points of view. In qualitative research, these skills are not marginal; they are at the heart of what we do. (Flinders, 1992, p, 114)

My own doctoral research was very nearly abandoned in favor of a conceptual dissertation because of my initial orientation in utilitarian ethics as embodied by the university ethical review committee. Within this perspective, I could see no true ethical approach to research involving children. I could not control the unpredictable events of a classroom so I could not be sure that I would never accidentally do harm. However, as a primary teacher, I realised that every day we take ethical risks with children. We make a constant renewal of our professional and moral promise to do our best in regard to the children and our colleagues. Flinders' work allowed me to understand and extend this appreciation of a teacher's daily interactions, which imply an ecological orientation, to ethical research.

In fact, my research was deeply immersed in an appreciation of classroom ecology. It examined the potentials and difficulties of democracy in a primary classroom. As such, my research partners included a dedicated and enthusiastic grade 1/2 teacher and 22 children aged between 6 and 9 years. This was an extremely diverse group in terms of ability, language and cultural background. The children's research role included being reflective about their learning activities and other classroom experiences.

The teacher's role was to provide her perspectives and feelings about the changing interactions in the classroom, and manage the implementation of new ideas and strategies. My role ranged from consultant to teacher to classroom assistant as the situation demanded. The main challenge of the research was to find ways to include everyone in our discussions and activities. I will draw on these experiences as a context in which the concepts described here were applied.

# RATIONALE FOR THE INCLUSION OF STUDENTS

The goal of educational research of any kind is to improve the learning situations of students. Students, regardless of age, are very much involved in any research on education whether they are given the status of participants or not. In fact, they are central players. If we believe in the principle of authentic participation in research, then we are obliged to recruit students as research partners. Indeed, we are ethically, logically, and professionally obliged to invite students to be part of participatory collaborative action research. If we value the research benefits that could result from reflections on learning by the students themselves, we must value their participation in research. If we believe in the learning benefits to students who have the opportunity to actively plan, implement and evaluate their own learning strategies, we will be enthusiastic about participating in such a learning community.

Clearly, there are other parties, such as parents, administrators and other school district staff, who have a vested interest in research in the classroom, at least at the level of informed consent. In practice, they are a significant part of the ecology of the research context. However, for clarity in this discussion, I focus only on the university-based researcher, the classroom teacher, and the students.

I will now discuss the ethical obligation to include students in their own research, the benefits to research that might result and our educational interests, namely gains in learning by all involved in the research. I shall then discuss in more detail how these obligations and opportunities relate to four major considerations of participatory collaborative action research.

## Ethical Obligation

Whether or not we invite students to be our research partners, they are involved in our research. It is ultimately about them that we are researching. In traditional research, we are minimally bound ethically by having to obtain informed consent. Often, consent for student involvement is given on their behalf. So, although they are central to the research, they are generally silent in influencing their own involvement in the research. If cultural sensitivity is sought, rather than mere consent, students must be recognised as part of the ecological whole of the research team. To avoid detachment, rather than merely protecting them from harm, *they* must be part of the ongoing discourse to make real contributions to the determination of research goals and plans.

If responsive communication is needed, rather than just confidentiality, this implies that students share the language of the research and contribute to the reporting. This does not mean that students will have an unreasonable burden of learning a difficult new language or have to report in a highly academic sense. Rather, it means that the language of children will gain acceptance in the research environment and that the variety of ways that children express ideas will be included as an aspect of reporting.

## Benefits to Research

The addition of the students' perspective in planning, implementing, reflecting and evaluating provides the potential for unique understanding in itself. To restrict the voices of students through non-inclusion is to erect a barrier to communication. We would then have to work to break down that barrier to gain access to the thinking of those we are studying. If, instead, we include student voices as part of the research discourse, the thoughts of these partners will be much more readily forthcoming. Additionally, the unique perspectives of students can provide valuable insights into classroom structures. What activities are motivating? Which result in what kinds of learning? What conditions promote the best engagement? Finally, students' involvement in reporting research, integrated into their ongoing learning activities can provide alternate ways of looking at outcomes and alternate means of reporting. Journals, stories, drawings, dance and metacognitive activities, can all be considered part of the reporting process, presenting data in its natural context. Clearly, reporting is more broadly conceived here than it is with standard research practice, but this widens the audience and engages the participants.

## Educational Interests

Action research can enhance teachers' professional identity by giving them some autonomy in the decisions regarding their own practice (Tripp, 1990). Similarly, increasing the autonomy of students in areas of research recognises their identity as research participants and may increase their ownership of learning:

> As teacher researchers, our primary responsibility is to our students, We need to balance the demands of our research with our other professional demands. This issue becomes far less troublesome when classroom inquiry becomes an intrinsic part of how we teach, and when students take an active role in our research—and their own. (Zeni, 1998, p. 16)

Zeni's statement challenges the dichotomy of teaching and learning, the assumption that one party teaches, while the other party learns. Rather, for this perspective, the activities of university workers, teachers and student partners are continuing as all parties teach each other and learn from each other simultaneously. Students, as well as teachers or university researchers, learn from their inquiries.

Including children in research does not compromise their role as students or coerce them into an adult agenda. Their role is still that of learners and much of their school routine would necessarily remain unchanged. However, the metacognitive activity of reflection and discussion may be increased for students, teachers and researchers alike.

This is an adjustment in attitude and self-perception in a community of inquiry. Students begin to gain more control and ownership of their learning and are self-reflexive, In reflecting and sharing their understandings, the understanding of the whole learning community is enhanced. This is participatory collaborative action research.

# CONSIDERATIONS FOR EFFECTIVE PARTICIPATORY COLLABORATIVE ACTION RESEARCH

Four prominent issues arise in the literature that provides challenges to effective action research. They are collaboration, authentic participation, power and language. An appreciation of the ecology of the research setting and practice is at the core of these concepts. Inclusion and interconnectedness permeate the discussion. These terms are defined and explored in the following description of an idealised conception of participatory collaborative action research between schools and universities. For action research to be truly participatory and collaborative, it demands that students also enter an organic collaboration, have authentic participation, work to resolve power differentials and share the language used by the community of inquiry of which they are a part.

## Collaboration

Betty Lou Whitford (Whitford et al, 1987) compares three kinds of collaboration: cooperative, symbiotic and organic, in order to frame the kind of arrangements that best lend themselves to the linking of reflection and action.

The cooperative arrangement is usually project orientated, with defined starting and ending dates. One party is the provider of service and the other is the receiver. An example is a university-sponsored summer institute for school staff. The symbiotic arrangement is characterised by reciprocity. One party helps the other in return for their help. For example, the researcher is allowed to use the school for research in return for designing a staff training day. The organic arrangement addresses ecology. It identifies issues that are jointly owned. Each party can independently provide parts of the solution to a goal. One party by itself is unable to achieve the goal. Whitford et al term this kind of collaboration, necessary for effective action research, 'boundary-spanning' since both parties have a vested interest in the outcome and require each other's assistance to achieve their goals. This interdependence recognises the ecology of collaborative research, which includes both the university-based researcher and school-based participants. Each draws on the assets of the other and each is affected by the other's actions. The ultimate shared goal of both university education programs and schools is improved education for students:

> universities and schools are interdependent agencies that could better serve the public by concentrating on a common agenda. Serving the common good rather than mutual self-interest should be the unifying theme around which collaborative efforts between universities and schools are organized. (Whitford et al, 1987, p. 155)

Working with other people, each with their unique perspectives and preferences can be challenging. Given these perspectives on collaboration and community, this kind of research is not likely to be comfortable. However, it is the sense of discomfort that drives the work of collaborative research. Sumara & Luce-Kapler (1993) state that it is in these times of disagreement and negotiation that we gain insights into ourselves, each other and the topic of investigation that draws us together (p. 394).

It seems that most topics of research in the classroom impact on students and, therefore, would be of interest to them at some level, even if that interest is self-defence. The discovery of boundary-spanning issues is dependent on finding a common language and in facilitating participation. Regardless of the choice of research topic, in an organic collaboration in which partners are ecologically dependent on each other, all partners achieve a consensus on roles that are both of personal interest and of mutual benefit (Whitford et al, 1987). It is not likely that, in the average elementary school, the first issue chosen for research that includes students will be of general school reform nor classroom-wide restructuring (Chisholm, 1992). Rather, important issues of limited scope and high familiarity may be an acceptable place to start.

For example, in my research project which examined classroom democracy, the first issue that was raised for democratic participation during a class meeting was a contentious and, therefore, authentic issue. Some of the older students were excluding and demeaning some of the younger students. The older students would not let the younger ones play soccer with them at recess and even 'made mean faces.' Since this issue was real to the students, they were all engaged in the conversation and a search for a solution.

The second activity in the research depends on the outcome of the reflection on this first step. As the spiral of inquiry emerges, these limited research endeavors could become very significant and sophisticated. Robin McTaggart (1991) recommends that research start small and build a basis for collaboration:

> It starts with small cycles of planning, acting, observing, and reflecting which can help define the issues, ideas, and assumptions

more clearly so that those involved can define more powerful questions for themselves as their work progresses, (p. 178)

## Authentic Participation

McTaggart (1991) differentiates between action research that is institutionally initiated with varying levels of involvement of school staff and participatory action research, which is necessary for effective collaboration. Participation is problematic in research situations where people have different power, status, influence or language facility. There is a difference between the meaning of the words 'involvement' and 'participation.' Involvement means merely to be included where participation means to share or take part. Authentic participation in research requires: '[1] people's role in setting the agenda of the inquiry, (2) people's participation in the data collection and the analysis, and (3) people's control over the use of outcomes and the whole process' (Tandon, 1988, p. 13; cited in McTaggart, 1991, p. 171).

This framing of participatory action research does not allow for the concept of people as subjects in research. That is, the traditional practice of the university researcher doing research on people in the field does not constitute participation. Although research participants in the classroom may have distinct roles, expertise and perspectives, they must have equitable status in initiating, conducting, analysing and reporting the research for there to be a claim of authentic participation.

As previously cited, McTaggart (1991) states that participation is problematic in research situations where people have different power, status, influence and language facility. Each of these concerns present a challenge to the authentic participation of students. As previously claimed, there are no global standards that can be applied as a solution to specific cases. Rather, a collaborative research team must address these concerns on an ongoing and specific basis. It is essential that students have an active role and an equal voice in this continuing discourse.

In the previous example of my research project, the use of class meetings that share governance served as the forum in which issues were pursued, together with reflection and planning for the research content. As a result of several meetings, the class developed a list of seven problem solving strategies to deal with future issues. These ideas were celebrated in many ways: through writing activities, art projects, acting and music. Clearly, various levels and means of participation in research are possible.

### Power

Any coming together of people involves politics. This leads to the necessity of addressing issues of power, since participatory collaboration recognises both the autonomy and the responsibility of all the actors involved in research. Whatever the source, power needs to be carefully examined. Even if it is not intended, when schools and universities come together, there may be pre-existing expectations of academic imperialism.

This is the result of traditional research in which university personnel often direct the interactions in a top-down approach. It may be that school staff wish for the university staff to take control of the project and direct, rather than they, themselves, engaging in the decision making required in participatory action research. It is challenging for researchers to exercise leadership without creating dependency (Somekh, 1994).

Clearly, in participatory collaborative action research, joint ownership of the research is necessary, despite differing roles among the participants. However, power differences are subtle and pervasive. Authors on the subject fall short of offering solutions. However, they do emphasise the continuing processes towards suspending power differentials. McTaggart (1991) points to the substantive knowledge that exists in the academy, which can help people to understand that their own subjectivity is likely to be gendered, colonialised, nationalised, westernised and capitalistic (p. 174). To address issues of power, group members must change their language, activities and social relationships. They do this collaboratively by deliberately setting aside time to reflect on these matters in an effort to make individual and group decisions. As part of the participatory aspect of their research, researchers must work toward improving their own practices. Regular checks are made to ensure that the least powerful have authentic input.

Rita Irwin (1997) struggled with the contradiction of leading a group of researchers, while also trying to share power through the democratic principles of shared understanding and shared decision making. Irwin rejected the idea that one should abandon their expertise, allowing others to stumble, in the name of sharing power:

> Rather, a delicate balance must be maintained so that empowerment of the collective is nurtured while the power of the individual is recognized . . . The only way to truly accept this dynamic is to develop a level of trust within the group that allows for reflection and action that constantly examines the effects of teaching and leadership. (Irwin, 1997, p. 10)

Part of her role as a leader was to teach leadership to the others. Consistent with the sense of reciprocity embedded in collaborative action research, she found that the others were capable of mentoring her in significant ways.

With these authors, the important aspect of addressing power issues was not in finding solutions, but in becoming involved in the process of continually reflecting and acting on the distribution of power in specific, contextualised ways. Reflection and action on power issues are an inseparable part of the process of participatory collaborative action research regardless of the overall research topic.

The issue of power is, indeed, problematic in proposing a partnership in research with students, particularly children. On one hand, there seems to be a logical and ethical argument for the inclusion of students, but on the other hand there are enormous methodological barriers due to the status of children in western society. Lynne Chisholm (1992) talks about the wide endorsement of symmetrical or democratic relations in research, especially for action research. Bridging the cultural distances of race, gender and class is being attempted optimistically and, at least in principle, seems possible. Bridging the gap between adult and child in research may seem too daunting for many to make the effort. However, some practitioners and researchers are providing excellent examples of including students of all ages as partners in their research.

Many authors (Carr & Kemmis, 1986; McTaggart, 1991) claim that action research should be a participatory and emancipatory process. Its purpose is to enact social change. Although I do not anticipate a classroom revolution where students dominate the teacher and control without reason, there is an opportunity in action research for students to assume some negotiated autonomy with regard to their own learning in the current research. There is also the potential for students to acquire an intimate knowledge of social activism and experience the possibilities for social change. This is a chance for students to learn about leadership. In action research, the focus is not only on an end product, but is also on the process and the discovery of new questions. If this proposed research community is committed to the continuing process of renewing participation, addressing power differentials and developing discourse, then the focus of this research will be as much on the power arrangements as on the subject of research.

In my research project, I first had to find a teacher with similar interests, and then negotiate the format and initial direction of the research. Then I had to obtain parental consent to satisfy the ethical review for the university and the school administration. Then I also had to ask for the consent of the children to assist me and their teacher. This required a lot of explanation of the terms and the intent. This topic was broad enough for all to find some value in participation. The children did very little differently than they would have normally, other than to reflect on their daily activities and have those reflections recorded. The children began to take on more and more responsibilities in the research. The following is an interaction that took place during that research, where 8-year-old Adam took an active role in collecting data. He was looking for a change in routine and decided he would use the tape recorder to interview his teacher, rather than his classmates, in regard to improving the class meeting format:

Adam: How would you like to change the class meetings?

Donna: Adam, I would like to change the class meetings by having more kids involved. Maybe if we could somehow figure out a way that people would talk to each other in partners more often to get more ideas. I'm thinking what is it we need to do to get everybody thinking?

Adam: To make it less boring, let's do some kind of activity with the agenda items instead of just talking? (Collins, 2002, p. 77)

This brief exchange illustrates how a child research partner was valued in his ability to elicit important data, to use equipment to record data and to make significant suggestions that affected the course of the research. Adult questioning may not have revealed the need for more activity during class meetings.

### Language

As McTaggart (1991) states, language and discourse are a central aspect of any culture (p. 173). Research cultures, in particular, are of interest. In collaborative research, each group brings with it unique patterns of language that are formed within the group to enhance communication, thereby constructing the culture of the group as well as individual identities. However, when school and university cultures come together, language can be an obstacle between the two groups.

Somekh (1994) describes the continual tension over discourse in their collaboration. Even the word 'research' itself seemed to alienate the teachers. Similarly, substituting non-specialist terms for academic terms changed their meanings, lowered the status of the project in the eyes of the academy and simply became patronising. Instead, both partners learned the language of the other and moved from one discourse to the other as the circumstances demanded. However, as with the issue of power, the continuous confrontation on discourse provided a challenge that strengthened their collaboration, Once again, reflection on the ongoing process of negotiation is as relevant as finding solutions.

Teachers and children generally participate in language development as a normal course of events. Collaborating in research, with an emphasis on discourse, will accentuate the challenge and the enjoyment of this process. Of particular interest is the language of reporting. Rather than relying on university journals as the primary source of publishing results, teachers may wish to publish papers for their peers and provide workshop presentations, and students can present their new understandings through a range of media, such as posters, stories, poetry, plays, multimedia or dance. These expressions could well be highlighted in the university journal report and the teachers' reports. If they are a central focus of reporting, perhaps a source of data, then there is a likelihood that students will understand some of the content and intent of the reports of the other research partners. Additionally, more interest could be generated in the research by expanding the audience beyond the university community to include other teachers, administrators, parents, classmates and other members of the community at large. The use of class web pages, internet postings or links with other classrooms, schools or districts are other possible outlets.

The example of 8-year-old Adam is salient here. In fact, a major finding of this study was that young children need to be active physically and verbally in order to fully participate in both decision making and learning. This led to the use of role play during meetings so that these children, whose verbal capacities had not yet fully developed, could participate in expressing their thoughts and feelings.

Adam made an authentic, valued contribution. This was not within the ability or inclination of all of the students in that class, but the research team was open to and searched for similar significant contributions by all participants.

## SUMMARY OF THE RESEARCH MODEL

This is a largely conceptual exploration of action research and much of it is speculative. Based on a wide range of perspectives, many of the more salient features of various authors' descriptions have been synthesised to construct an idealised model of participatory collaborative action research, which includes the participation of the students themselves, At the core of this model is a commitment to reflection and discourse, which continuously and dynamically renews the classroom-based research community. It recognises the ecology of the classroom in that all class members are interconnected. What affects one affects all. The model focuses not only on the research issue, which is mutually owned through organic collaboration, but also on ecological ethics and authentic participation. It seeks to address issues of language, roles and power differentials.

The proposal to include students as authentic participants may seem to some to be an insurmountable challenge (Chisholm, 1992). However, there are examples of action researchers who are engaged in a process of including students of all ages as partners in research.

At the university level, Owen van den Berg (Lee & van den Berg, 2003) describes instituting a Master's Program in action research in South Africa in 1987 to promote educational and political transformation at the time of the apartheid regime. Action research took place in the graduate students' classrooms and the story of the Class of 87 became part of van den Berg's doctoral research. Students were actively encouraged to evaluate the program at the end of the year and again in 1993. At the latter meeting, students validated van den Berg's draft chapter on the research and he also incorporated the students' feedback into a reworked chapter. He then had the students again validate that these additions were accurate and fair.

At the secondary level, Mariam Mohr (2001) describes her grade 10 students variously as co-workers, co-researchers and collaborators, and emphasises the need to share credit for classroom research with students. Her classroom action research was very transparent, with students drawing her attention to key events and making suggestions about log entries.

At the elementary level, my research partner still continues to work with children as young as kindergarten in a participatory way that respects the ecology of the classroom. Children are involved in classroom decision making where appropriate and, where possible are given explanations for what they are learning and why. Children's input allows her to modify her teaching according to student needs and styles, and helps her to adjust her practice in increasingly productive ways. The insights gained from these interactions with young students are shared at staff in-service days, conferences and university courses. Student work is shared with these adult audiences. Also recounted are those salient conversations with children that are significant in expanding the knowledge of professional teachers.

While these teachers provide examples of efforts to include students as research partners, some authors (Flinders, 1992; May, 1993; Davis et al, 2000) also suggest an ethical obligation, hope for improved research methods and anticipation of significantly enhanced opportunities for learning by all involved in the research.

Of particular significance is that the preceding discussion does not provide a solution for ethical, inclusive research. To the contrary, it is doubtful of solutions and, rather, focuses on the ongoing processes of negotiation and continual adjustment of the methodological framework. The change recommended is a subtle shift in attitude resulting in more challenging reflection. Granted, all participants enter the research agreement with their own agendas and there will be asymmetrical apportioning of power. The attitude shift is in recognising the importance of each person's significance to the setting, and in actively and authentically searching for ways to respect each person's contributions. All participants are regarded as ecologically essential to the whole.

## Correspondence

Dr. Steve Collins, Curriculum Studies, University of British Columbia, 4997 Mariner Place, Delta, British Columbia, Canada V4K 4V4 (steve.collins @ ubc.ca) .

## REFERENCES

Altrichter, H., Kemmis, S., McTaggart, R & Zuber-Skerritt, O. (1991) Defining, Confining, or Refining Action Research? in O. Zuber-Skerritt (Ed.) *Action Research for Change and Development.* Brookfield: Gower Publishing.

Capra, F. (1983) *The Turning Point: science, society and the rising culture.* New York: Bantam.

Carr, W. & Kemmis, S. (1986) *Becoming Critical: education, knowledge and action research.* London: Falmer Press.

Chisholm, L. (1992) Action Research: some methodological and political considerations, *British Educational Research Journal,* 16, pp. 249–257.

Collins, S. (2002) The Complexity of a Participatory Democracy in a Public Primary Classroom: the interplay of student autonomy and responsibility. Doctoral Dissertation, University of British Columbia.

Davis, B., Sumara, D. & Luce-Kapler, R. (2000) *Engaging Minds: learning and teaching in a complex world.* Mahwah: Lawrence Eribaum Associates.

Flinders, D.J. (1992) In Search of Ethic Guidance: constructing a basis for dialog, *Qualitative Studies In Education,* 5(2), pp. 101–115.

Houser, N.O. (1990) Teacher-Researcher: the synthesis of roles for teacher empowerment, *Action in Teacher Education*, 12(2), pp. 55–60.

Irwin, R., Crawford, N., Mastri, R., Neale, A., Robertson, H. & Stephenson, W. (1997) Collaborative Action Research: A journey of six women artist-pedagogues, *British Columbia Art Teachers' Association Journal for Art Teachers*, 37(2), pp. 8–17.

Lee, S.S. & Van den Berg, O. (2003) Ethical Obligations in Teacher Research, in A. Clarke & G. Erickson (Eds) *Teacher Inquiry: living the research in everyday practice*. London: Routledge Falmer.

May, W.T. (1993) 'Teachers as Researchers' or Action Research: what is it, and what good is it for Art Education? *Art Education*, 34(21), pp. 114–126.

McCutcheon, G. & Jung, B. (1990) Alternate Perspectives on Action Research, *Theory into Practice*, 29(3), pp. 144–151.

McTaggart, R. (1991) Principles for Participatory Action Research, *Adult Education Quarterly*, 41(3], pp. 168–187.

Mohr, M.M. {2001) Drafting Ethical Guidelines for Teacher Research in Schools, in J. Zeni (Ed.) *Ethical Issues in Practitioner Research*. New York: Teachers College Press.

Punch, M. (1986) *The Politics and Ethics of Fieldwork*. Beverly Hills: Sage.

Somekh, B. (1994) Inhabiting Each Other's Castles: towards knowledge and mutual growth through collaboration, *Educational Action Research*, 2(3), pp. 357–381.

Samara, D. & Luce-Kapler, R. (1993) Action Research as a Writerly Text: locating co-labouring in collaboration, *Educational Action Research*, 1, pp. 387–395.

Tripp, D. (1990) Socially Critical Action Research, *Theory into Practice*, 29(3), pp. 158–166.

Whitford, B.L., Schlechty, P.C. & Shelor, L.G. (1987) Sustaining Action Research through Collaboration: inquiries for invention, *Peabody Journal of Education*, 64(3), pp. 151–169.

Zeni, J. (1998) A Guide to Ethical Issues and Action Research, *Educational Action Research*, 6, pp. 9–19

# Subject Index

**CORWIN PRESS**

The Corwin Press logo—a raven striding across an open book—represents the union of courage and learning. Corwin Press is committed to improving education for all learners by publishing books and other professional development resources for those serving the field of PreK–12 education. By providing practical, hands-on materials, Corwin Press continues to carry out the promise of its motto: **"Helping Educators Do Their Work Better."**